PETER SCOTT

Collected
WRITINGS
1933–1989

PETER SCOTT

Collected
WRITINGS
1933–1989

Compiled by
Paul Walkden

Foreword by
HRH The Duke of Edinburgh

WWT

First published in 2016 by the
Wildfowl & Wetlands Trust (WWT)
Slimbridge, Gloucestershire, GL2 7BT
Registered charity in England & Wales,
no. 1030884 and Scotland, no. SC039410

www.wwt.org.uk

British Library Cataloguing-in-Publication Data
A CIP record for this book is available from the British Library.

ISBN: 978-0-900806-69-8 (hardback)
ISBN: 978-0-900806-70-4 (ebook)

*WWT would like to offer special thanks to Paul Walkden, who initiated
and did much early work to make this project a reality, as well as
Barbara Cooper and Paul G. Harding whose determination
and expertise have brought it to fruition.*

Designed and Produced by Compass Books Ltd. with Paul G. Harding

Printed and bound in the UK by CPI Antony Rowe

CONTENTS

FOREWORD

by HRH The Duke of Edinburgh

One of my earliest memories of Peter Scott is when he invited me to open the Wildfowl and Wetlands Trust on the Severn Estuary. After an extensive and intensive tour of the, at that stage, potential facilities, we repaired to lunch at the small cottage where he and Philippa were living at the time. Somewhat to my surprise, a roast duck was produced and, sensing that there was some hesitation about who was to carve it, I offered my services.

Peter Scott had achieved world fame by the time he became one of the founders of the World Wildlife Fund, and he recruited me as a Trustee. I attended as many meetings of the trustees as I could, and I always tried to sit next to Peter because he had a habit of doodling throughout the meeting on any bit of scrap paper available. Some of these masterpieces are now framed and on display at Sandringham.

I think that his most apparent characteristic was his utter dedication to the conservation of wildlife and wild places of all kinds. He endured the inevitable committee work, but his heart was always in the wilderness, and his passion was to ensure that it survived for future generations to admire and enjoy. This collection of his writings is ample proof of a lifetime spent in the single-minded pursuit of effective and adequate protection for the wildlife and wild places of this limited planet.

INTRODUCTION

by Martin Spray CBE, Chief Executive of WWT

Great and lasting achievements are usually brought about by individual vision matched with talent, and the drive and determination to achieve. Sir Peter Scott had all these attributes and in quantities beyond the comprehension of most of us.

He was an accomplished artist, a gifted communicator and writer, one of the first natural history broadcasters, a champion skater, a world-class glider pilot and an Olympic yachtsman. Above all Peter Scott was, without doubt, one of the most visionary and influential conservationists of his generation and the architect of modern conservation.

Peter, through his passionate interest in nature, and especially wildfowl, saw what was happening to the world and was determined to do something about it. But his vision went further. He recognised then, nearly seventy years ago, something that the modern conservation movement now puts at the centre of its action. Unless we inspire, interest and educate people about nature and its relevance and importance to our lives, it will not be valued and our attempts to conserve it for future generations will fail. He set out on this mission with drive and determination which surpassed even the extraordinary achievements of his parents, with a talent for communicating and engaging people, and with the vision necessary to make a huge difference.

Among his many gifts and achievements, Peter was a prolific and accomplished communicator. This selection of his various writings is extraordinary in the way each brings to life the story, the place and his feelings and thoughts so vividly and engagingly. Reading them, you can almost hear him speaking to you personally. Just one example for me is a portrayal of the sound of geese calling—'a music of indescribable beauty and wildness, a harmony with the flat marsh which is their home'. It was this gift of being able to convey serious science, combined

with passion and emotion, that I am sure enabled him to reach out to so many people and to achieve the considerable advances in conservation he achieved during his life.

These writings give a real insight into the development of Peter's thinking. His curiosity and endless thirst to know and understand more stand out, together with his personal connection with and love of the natural world. He was an internationalist, multi-talented, a man with a powerful mission. We are very fortunate, through this collection of his writings, to be able to experience the thoughts and passions of a man who loved life, lived it to the full, and made a real and lasting difference to the world we know today.

ABOUT THIS COMPILATION

by Paul Walkden

Peter Scott was one of the first leaders of the conservation movement and an outstanding communicator. This book arose from my interactions with him over an extended period, and more recently from discussions between myself, Barbara Cooper, who has edited this compilation, and Paul Harding, who has designed and produced it. It was felt that Peter Scott's legacy should continue to be shared with all those interested in conservation. During my research as Scott's bibliographer, I have found many of his less well known writings such as magazine articles, speeches, diary entries and broadcasts, and the ones chosen here reflect the many spheres in which he was involved.

I was very fortunate to have known Peter personally, an exceptionally kind man who encouraged and helped people in whatever way he could. To me he offered much help and time in putting together his bibliography. We met and discussed books on various occasions, his library an important source of information for me; he was always very generous in allowing me access. He had a real passion for whatever he was working on at the time and he loved sharing his thoughts and ideas. I was privileged to have sat and discussed the new Slimbridge centre project being planned shortly before he died, including his ideas for a Tower allowing all people, including the disabled, to be able to look out over the River Severn from the centre. I also enjoyed watching him paint at the easel or sketching whilst we talked. His artwork was always immediate and fresh, living and vibrant. His final exhibition was held at Ackermann's gallery in Bond Street London in March 1989 which was opened by HRH The Duke of Edinburgh and was a sell-out. At that time Peter wrote: 'I have been excited by wildfowl for most of my life and have been painting them and the wild areas they live in for more than sixty years. Wildness is the aspect that specially appeals to me. I believe Thoreau was right when he wrote, "In wildness is the preservation of the world". He was ahead of his time.'

THE AURA

From *Morning Flight* (Country Life, 1935)

There is a peculiar aura that surrounds in my mind anything and everything to do with wild geese. That I am not alone in this strange madness, I am sure: indeed, it is a catching complaint, and I hardly know any who have been able to resist its ravages, when once they have been exposed to infection. It is difficult to know just why this should be so. It is perhaps a matter both of quality and quantity.

I wish it were possible accurately to estimate numbers after they have reached the thousands.

I remember an afternoon at the end of September when a great gathering of geese were sitting on a big grass marsh. All day we had watched them straggling down in bunches of half a dozen to a dozen—tiny specks in the sky suddenly hurtling downwards to settle on the marsh. They had done it all the day before, and the day before that, too—arriving from Spitsbergen and Iceland and Greenland.

Some of them flew out and settled on the sand, and we tried to estimate their numbers. We counted and multiplied, counted and multiplied, starting first at one end and then at the other. Eight thousand was our estimate after half an hour of eye straining through a field glass.

And then suddenly behind us a roar broke out, and the whole surface of the marsh seemed to rise into the air. A black cloud of geese, which conveyed just the same oppressiveness as an approaching rainstorm, moved out over the sand where sat the ones we had been counting. They did not settle with them, however, but stretched away down the crest of the high sand until those that pitched farthest were only visible as they turned to head the wind; fully two miles of solid pink-footed geese.

It was idle to return to our futile estimates. We could only gasp and murmur that our 8,000 were but a quarter of them.

Is it possible that 20,000 geese made up that black line which stretched as far as the eye could reach along the high sand? Perhaps there were half of the pink-footed geese that exist in the world here before us. Nearly all of them winter in England and Scotland, except for the few flocks which go to Holland. They breed in Spitsbergen and Greenland and a few in Iceland, and although it is possible to see vast numbers together, yet in their world distribution of the pinkfeet are a tiny species of probably no more than 50,000 individuals, possibly much less.

When they first come south on migration, they collect on this particular marsh, but after about a fortnight they split up and go to other marshes and estuaries to spend the winter.

However many there may have been on that September afternoon, it was a sight and sound that must have thrilled the hardest heart. In this case perhaps it was their very numbers, or the volume of sound, or the mystery of their arrival from Arctic regions on the very date upon which they had arrived every year for who knows how long; perhaps it was the thought of so many great birds together, for pinkfeet are more than five feet from wing tip to wing tip; or the thought that, although the flocks are so big, yet the places they come to are so very few —or perhaps it was a combination of all these things.

But probably the chief reason why wild geese hold such a peculiar fascination is because of their wariness. They are so difficult to be near, that being near them itself is thrilling, whether one is painting them or shooting them or photographing them, or catching them alive in a net. If you have been within five yards of unsuspecting wild geese you have achieved something, and that achievement alone has its special thrill. It is the knowledge that you have outwitted, not one, but perhaps a thousand *very wily creatures*. And there is another thing that makes wild goose chasing so good. If you go after wild geese you will assuredly go into beautiful wild places at the most beautiful times of day—at dawn, or dusk, or moonrise—and, best of all, you will hear them call.

I have been many hundreds of times on a certain marsh in Norfolk, but I see it now as I have only seen it once or twice each season. And I hear the geese calling—a music of indescribable beauty and wildness, and fitness for the flat marsh which is their home. The moon has just risen, very large and orange over the sea, and the tide is high, half covering the salting, and filling the creeks right up to the seawall. There are a few wigeon calling as they fly along the shore, and away to the west a big pack of knots and dunlins twitter incessantly. Just an occasional call note reminds one that the geese are there waiting for enough light to come in and feed on the potato fields over the bank.

Suddenly there is a little burst of calling—the first ones are up—they're coming.

BOROUGH FEN

From *Morning Flight* (Country Life, 1935)

In the heart of fens is a little pond nestling in a wood. It is less than two acres in area, but in the winter it is the daily resting place sometimes of three thousand ducks, sometimes of more.

To a duck high above it, the pond must look something like a starfish, for it is a decoy pond, and from it radiate eight curved ditches, which are the 'pipes' of the decoy. Each ditch, twenty feet wide at its mouth, is spanned by hoops over which a net is stretched; and along each side are screens of reed, high enough to conceal the decoyman, and cunningly arranged in overlapping formation on one side, so that when the decoyman appears at the mouth of the pipe the ducks which are in it can see him and fly away from him round the bend and into the rapidly narrowing funnel, whilst the thousands which are outside are quite unaware of the presence of a human being within a few yards of them. These thousands and their predecessors have spent the winter days floating on the sheltered pool or sunning themselves on the 'landings' in the pipes for nearly three centuries.

From 1670 comes the first record of the decoy—a request for
permission from King Charles to pierce the newly built flood
bank of the River Welland, to supply water for the pond. In
those days, as today, the decoyman was a Mr. Williams, and
the same family have been decoymen there ever since. The
decoy has never been altered, but by constant replacement the
nets and hoops and screens have been renewed and now it is
one of the few which remain in working order in England.

Mallards and teal come to the decoy in the greatest numbers,
but in February there are sometimes a thousand wigeon,
especially if the river should be in flood. In the spring and
autumn there are shovelers in abundance. Once there were two
hundred there and on another day I counted eighty-one drake
pintails, each of which doubtless had a mate. One autumn,
thirty garganey teal came. There are undoubtedly some every
year, but being in their eclipse plumage at that season, they are
difficult to pick out from a thousand or more common teal.
Oddly enough, with the exception of an occasional pochard,
these are the only ducks which come. In vain I have looked for
the rarer diving ducks. It is too shallow for their tribe and the
gadwall never seem to stray to the decoy from their breeding
strongholds in Norfolk.

Near the edge of the pond we have built a little hut, reached
by a screened path, from which to watch the ducks at close
quarters. It has a horizontal slit across the front, no more than
half an inch wide, but it is enough to give a view of the pond,
and the ducks themselves cannot see through it because it is
dark inside. I have spent many hours watching from this hut,
the nearest ducks not fifteen yards away, and the whole host
within a hundred, for the pond is no more than that across.

At night the ducks flight out for food. They spread through
the surrounding fens, feeding in the drains and ditches and in
the potato fields, and at dawn they return, bringing perhaps
fresh ducks with them. After a drink and a wash, out in the
middle of the pond, many of them go ashore on the landings,
which form the banks of the pipes, for elsewhere the banks of
the pond are vertical and surmounted with a hedge, so that there

is no footing for a duck. These ducks, which are banked, are catchable, and should there be enough in the pipe to warrant a catch, the decoyman, who has peeped through a tiny slit in one of the reed screens, then creeps quietly to the mouth of the pipe, passing within three or four yards of the ducks as he does so. There he shows himself and up go the ducks and away from him, around the corner and into the *cul-de-sac*. As he follows they are driven farther and farther into the narrow end of the net, where there is a detachable tunnel net spread on two-foot-wide hoops. In this the ducks are trapped and their retreat cut off.

Taking ducks in the decoy is a skilled and subtle art. The wind plays an important part, as ducks must rise facing the wind like all birds and aeroplanes. The wind therefore which would be most favourable for the ducks to rise into the pipe would be one blowing directly out of it. But in that case the scent of the decoyman would be blown across the pond and in a moment every duck would be in the air. There is, however, just one angle for the wind which is ideal in both respects, and only the one pipe of the eight which the wind strikes at that angle cah be taken. The other pipes may be full of birds, but until the wind changes they cannot be caught. There are times when the ducks will not come to the landings of their own accord, and it is then that they are decoyed in the most astonishing way. Just as bullocks will follow a retreating dog across a field so long as it goes on retreating, so will ducks, in a spirit of bravado—or with the idea that they are driving it away—follow a small dog or cat. (At Borough Fen it is usually the latter.) It jumps over the low screens which connect each of the high overlapping ones, and, retreating from the ducks, rapidly disappears again, jumping out over the next low screen. It is a most extraordinary sight to see the ducks swimming in towards the pipe as soon as they have seen the cat. At once the pond becomes a network of bow waves as the ducks follow up the pipe. When they are well under the net the decoyman runs back and shows himself in the ordinary way. This decoying with dog or cat is excessively difficult, as the whole thing depends upon careful timing. To catch a few ducks is easy, but the art lies in getting the last dozen under the net without disturbing those that are often only two yards from the decoyman as he works his animal. If the leading bunch are teal, the job is even more subtle, for if they once become nervous they will flush out of the pipe, taking the rest of the ducks with them.

There was an afternoon in February when, as I had done every day for many weeks before, I accompanied Billy Williams round the decoy. The pond was full of ducks, and had been for a week, but they would not come to the pipes and we decided to try the cat.

I ran back to the house, which stands no more than 500 yards from the nearest pipe of the pond, but nowhere could I find the properly trained 'coy cat'. I found a kitten, however, and since it was getting late and the ducks would soon be thinking about flighting, I returned with that. There had been some snow and the ground was white; the cat showed up against it to perfection. The ducks came, it seemed, from all over the pond until the little bay outside the west pipe was crowded with them. In a great wave they came into the pipe until it was full. Under the net were, without doubt, two hundred ducks, and if all went well in two minutes they would be ours—the catch of a lifetime!

The kitten came out for the last time and I signalled to Billy, who was waiting to run in and show. But the snow was crisp and he had taken no more than two steps before it was clear that he could never reach the 'show place' in silence. I peeped and already the ducks had heard something: they were nervous. In a minute they would be up. There was just one chance that if Billy could run fast enough he might yet cut off their retreat. I signalled feverishly and he ran. But he was no more than halfway before, with a rush of wings, they flushed out. At once I showed them the cat again so as to give those outside a reason for the flushing. Again they started to swim in, and this time Billy was already at the show place and waiting. The ducks did not, of course, come nearly so well the second time. Many of them were nervous and, besides, the kitten was getting bored with her part in the proceedings. But in spite of that there were sixty or seventy ducks well under the net.

The kitten went over the last screen and sat down by the edge of the pond and started to wash herself. It is useless to try to drive ducks down a pipe past a cat or a dog. They always turn back and fly out again. Before I could signal to Billy I had to make that kitten come out of the pipe, and there she sat, curled up and blinking at me. I threw snowballs and prodded her with reeds, but the ducks were not five yards away now, and more I dared not do. Meanwhile Billy was waiting impatiently. Through a rabbit hole at the foot of one of the screens he had seen the ducks swimming past up the pipe, and he knew that there must be a goodly quantity well under the net. But nothing would move the kitten, and after five minutes the ducks grew nervous and again flushed out. We caught nothing that day.

In time of frost the decoy works on a different principle. The pipes, instead of providing the only landing places, then provide the only open water, if, as he should, the decoyman has been at work breaking ice in the early morning before the ducks come in. The ducks sit out in the middle of the pond in a great crowd on the ice. In parties they come to the pipe that has been opened to wash and drink and also to feed, for this is one of the few occasions when the pipes are 'fed'. It is usually the House Pipe which is opened; it is just right for the northeasterly wind, which usually accompanies frost. It is sometimes possible to catch a pipe twice or even three times in a day under these conditions, although in ordinary weather a careful catch will disturb a pipe for at least three days, whereas a bungled catch may upset the whole of that side of the pond for a week or more.

I have spent many early mornings crashing about among the ice in rubber boots, and sometimes after a long frost, when a fresh pipe must be opened, an axe is the only instrument that will do it. Just as the light breaks through the trees the first returning ducks come slipping in. Then all work must cease so that there shall be no disturbance when they start to stream in in their twos and threes and dozens and twenties from the fields and drains where they have been feeding.

At night the decoy is not empty. It is the roosting place in the winter of often more than a thousand wood pigeons, and sometimes as many rooks and jackdaws. Its nineteen acres of low trees are crowded with them, and the few high poplars appear to be in full leaf.

One day Billy told me there was a strange mallard in the House Pipe. I went to look and saw a bird with a long tail almost like a pintail's. He had a green head with a buff-coloured patch on the cheek, and a pale blue bill and orange legs. It was altogether a most handsome bird and clearly a hybrid. There were half a dozen mallards with it, and the wind was entirely wrong for the pipe.

'We must have this bird,' I said.

'You'll put the whole pond up if you do,' said Billy.

'Hang the pond!'

'All right, hang it—let's have the bird,' agreed Billy.

So we showed. We caught the hybrid and by great good luck hardly a bird on the pond was disturbed. We kept our prize alive and he still lives with the tame birds in the pen at the decoy.

For some time, owing to his tail, we supposed him to be a cross between mallard and pintail, but after consultations at the Natural History Museum I was inclined to think that him a mallard-wigeon hybrid. This he proved to us in most satisfactory fashion, for in the following autumn he went into eclipse plumage. In this dull red-brown dress, except for his orange legs and his size, he was quite indistinguishable from the wigeon drakes with which he always consorts in the pen.

Besides being a past-master in the art of duck catching, Billy Williams is a keen ornithologist and most delightful companion. Often he has been punting with me on the coast, and sometimes with considerable success. And I have spent many happy months at the Decoy Farm.

The Decoy itself is a beautiful quiet place. A little sinister perhaps, but abounding in human associations. On the post of one of the screens is carved 'John Williams 1833 Aged 21'. It was carved by Billy's grandfather and two years ago we held centenary celebrations.

A BROADCAST

From *Wild Chorus* (Country Life, 1938)

'*Angank, Angank*—That peculiar noise, which you may have mistaken for atmospherics, was me imitating a wild goose!'

Thus began a broadcast talk which occupied fifteen minutes of the Empire programme one August night in 1936, at what was midnight at home, but all sorts of different hours to the people who may have heard it in faraway parts of the world. I went on to tell of my home and the birds which live there.

'By trade I am a painter. Amongst other things, I paint birds, and the sort of birds that I paint most are wildfowl—ducks and geese and swans and the like. They are the wildest of all birds, and so they live in the wildest parts now left in England, which are the marshy estuaries of our coast. On the lonely wastes of mud and saltmarsh they collect in winter in enormous crowds, and so as to be near them I live, and do my painting, in a lighthouse on one of these estuaries on the east coast of England. Some lighthouses have raging seas all round them and some don't. Mine is one of those that don't. It stands on the end of the bank of a river just at its mouth. When the tide is in there is water on three sides, but when the tide is out you can walk for about four miles to seaward, first over saltmarsh, then over soft mud, and then over hard yellow sand. And *then* you would only come to a narrow channel of water and after that there would be more sand, some of it stretching out ten miles from the shore—but all covered when the tide comes rushing in as fast in some places as a man can run. In order to have some of the birds that I paint always near, more or less as models, I have enclosed about six acres of the salting round the lighthouse, and in this enclosure I keep lots of tame waterfowl. It is about these, and how they were caught and how I hope to catch more and different kinds, that I want to tell you.

'My birds are mostly pinioned, which means that they cannot fly, but then they do not have to fly to get their food, and they have no enemies to escape, so they really live a very contented life. They grow a little lazy perhaps, but they also grow very tame, and that is one of their greatest charms. In less than a week a goose caught wild will come up and feed with the others within five yards of what was its most-deadly enemy—a man. Of course they very soon distinguish between one man and another, and they may be a little shy of strangers, although they are perfectly tame with the person who feeds them. Besides their engaging tameness they are also very handsome. Some of them are brilliant in colour and pattern and others have quieter colours but are beautifully trim in shape.

'Most of my geese have been caught in nets at various times, either flight nets or clap nets; the clap nets are the most exciting. Some of the geese are those that have been wing-tipped when shooting. They recover in a day or two and get just as tame as the netted ones. Some of them breed in captivity: more particularly the ducks than the geese, and rearing the young ones is very difficult, but, of course, correspondingly fascinating. The most exciting part, however, is the actual catching of the geese. As many wildfowlers know, it is pretty difficult to outwit wild geese even with a gun, and when it is a matter of catching them alive it is five times as difficult and therefore five times as thrilling. If you are successful you have a bird that will give you infinite pleasure, perhaps for years and years. As you watch it feeding at your feet, or preening its feathers or chasing away some unfortunate young gander, you can say to yourself, or better tell to some friend, "Now the morning I caught that chap was awfully exciting," and then you can tell the story.

'I went out to Hungary this spring to see the geese which live on a great green plain called the Hortobarge, which is spelt *Hortobagy*. They come there in countless thousands on migration, and they only stay for about three weeks in the spring before going north to breed. In March there were, I believe, at least a hundred-thousand geese. They lived all over the plain in flocks of between five and ten thousand, so that when they rose they almost darkened the sky. They were mostly white-fronted geese with some of a smaller very beautiful bird, the lesser white-fronted goose, which has only once ever been recorded in England, although they probably come from time to time without being recognised.

'At the end of a week in Hungary I had fifteen live geese, which included one of the lesser whitefronts which had been wounded by a wildfowler out there. He had a badly broken wing, but we put it in splints made of two pieces of firewood, and bandaged it up and then wound the bandage twice right round his body, so as to keep the wing in close to his side. On the way home, we spent a night in Budapest and the geese were given a sort of pantry on the third floor of one of the biggest hotels, because I did not at all want to leave them cooped up in their crates all night. Next morning we went on board an aeroplane—geese and all—and the same evening we were in London. That night, the geese roosted in our garden in London, which has a little pond in it, and they cleaned themselves up after the journey and had a good meal of wheat, and then next day I took them to the lighthouse by car. They all arrived safely and within about four days they came up to feed with the others almost at my feet. The little lesser whitefront had preened himself up so that the bandages round his body were quite hidden in the feathers, and no one would have known that they were there. In Hungary they call lesser whitefronts 'kishlilliks'; *kish* being small, and *lillik* because that is the noise they make. I think it is rather a nice name.

'After about three weeks or so I caught up my *kishlillik* and cut off all the bandages and splints. The wing was completely mended. I could just feel where the break had been, and now you would never know that he had been wounded at all. He is almost the prettiest of all my geese, because although his chief colour is dark brownish grey, he is beautifully marked and he has smart black bars across his breast. His legs are brilliant orange and his beak is a delicate pink. His forehead is white, which of course is why he is called white-fronted, and he has bright yellow eyelids which make a little yellow ring round each eye. He really is the neatest, most perfect little goose, hardly bigger than a duck. In fact, he is at present the apple of my eye. But there is another even more beautiful kind of wild goose called the red-breasted goose. Its breast is the richest dark chestnut and the rest of it is black and white. The white traces beautiful patterns on its head and neck and sides, separating the red from the black. Red-breasted geese are very rare in England, indeed there are only about a dozen records of them ever having strayed so far west. Their real home in winter is the Caspian Sea, and they breed on marshes at the mouths of the rivers Obi and Yenesei which run into the Arctic Ocean in the very north of Siberia. A few redbreasts come as far west as Hungary in the winter, and when I was there I saw about thirty altogether. It was my first sight of them alive. One morning a big crowd of geese were passing over, just after sunrise—about six or seven hundred of them, and then suddenly l heard a different call note amongst them. Straight overhead were thirteen little geese flying in a bunch with quick wing beats. They were dark and had short necks and white sterns, and every now and then one would turn or twist and show a glint of red in the morning sun. I saw another lot of sixteen redbreasts that day and later I saw several odd ones and a bunch of four.

'But I couldn't catch any, chiefly because there weren't really enough there amongst the countless thousands of white-fronted geese.

'I am determined to get one, however, even if I have to go to the Caspian Sea for it. In fact I have a bet with a friend that within twelve months there will be a red-breasted goose in the pen at my lighthouse. First I shall try Hungary again, and failing that I shall work gradually eastward until I come to the Caspian. There—perhaps on the delta of the Volga, or perhaps in the South Caspian, which is in Persia—I may find a red-breasted goose.

'With any luck I might catch more than one. Three or four pairs I should like to bring back. They are terribly rare in captivity, so if one wants to have red-breasted geese walking about in one's garden, there is nothing for it but the Caspian Sea; unless, of course, one was lucky in Hungary, or the Danube delta or the Crimea; but on the whole it would be a pity to be done out of a visit to Astrakhan.

'One of the pink-footed geese in my pen was very lame and eventually his foot had to be amputated. So since he had not the use of his foot I decided to let him have the use of his wings, and this year I let him grow full wings.

'The moult is in July, and then the old flight feathers which had been cut off short were shed and the new perfect ones began to grow. By August they were nearly full length. I was away in Germany at the time, and when I came back, as I drove down the bank towards the lighthouse, I saw a single goose flying far out over the salting. It was Long John Silver in person, my old one-legged goose. He circled in towards home, flew once round the lighthouse, and then swept down and made a perfect landing in the pen.

'The geese will soon be here again, migrating southward from the land of the midnight sun. I shall go to Scotland, as I do most years, to meet them in September and watch them arriving, tired and hungry after their long journey, but still the wildest of all wild things, and I shall get as much of a thrill from the sight as I have always got. There will be about five thousand geese on this one special marsh when they have all arrived. Perhaps if it has been a good breeding year in Spitsbergen and Greenland there will be more, and when they rise from the marsh in the evening to fly out to the sand to roost, there will be a roar as of thunder. Skein after skein will pass across the sunset, calling in glorious chorus. Those are the moments that I try hard to capture in my paintings.

'If I have been able even to suggest how thrilling it can be, perhaps it will be some sort of explanation of that peculiar madness from which some of us suffer—a desperate longing to be out at dawn on the mudflats with the flood tide rustling past up the creek and the call of wild geese in our ears.'

BEWARE!

From *Wild Chorus* (Country Life, 1938)

It is exactly one hundred years since the last great bustard walked the plains of England, but the species holds its own in other parts of the world. Such a loss, though sad enough, does not compare with the extinction of a species the world over. The tribe of wildfowl are not altogether immune from such a fate, even in this age of scientific enlightenment. We may read indignantly of the great auk and passenger pigeon and say complacently that such a thing could never happen nowadays, but only by the narrowest margin is the trumpeter swan of North America, the largest of all waterfowl, still included in the avifauna of the world. After a remarkable recovery there are now a few hundred individuals again, and it seems that the crisis is passed owing to the vigorous protection which it is receiving in its breeding haunts in Canada and its winter haunts in the United States.

Like the passenger pigeon and the Esquimaux curlew, the trumpeter has near-allies which are still quite common.

The whistling swan, though much smaller, is otherwise almost the same, just as the Hudsonian curlew closely resembles the Esquimaux curlew and the Carolina dove is but a smaller edition of the passenger pigeon. To scientists the loss is none the less on that account, but I mourn more the extinction of the little Labrador duck who filled a genus of his own and is now gone for ever. He was a sea duck akin to those romantic birds the eiders and his plumage was gaily piebald. Sixty years ago they were to be seen occasionally hanging in the markets of New York. No one knows why they disappeared, for they were little-persecuted by mankind. We must beware that the rare spectacled eider does not share the fate of the Labrador duck.

The Hawaiian goose who lives in the Sandwich Islands is another species which has reached the danger mark. It is said that the introduction of the Mongoose onto the islands is partly responsible.

Whatever the cause, it would be a major tragedy in the ornithological world if such an interesting and striking bird, which stands in a genus by itself, were to disappear.

The nene or Hawaiian goose, *Nesochen sandvicensis*, is an island race which has evolved far from the original stock whose other descendants now live on the North American continent.

It is an extremely handsome bird with a black mask and crown and cream-coloured cheeks and neck, at the base of the neck the cream is bordered by a narrow black ring, and the neck feathers themselves are pleated even more sharply than are the necks of the grey geese. These pleatings, as well as some other anatomical features, show that the grey geese are distant relations, but the Hawaiian goose is most-closely related to the genus *Branta*, which includes the Canada goose, the barnacle and the various brents as well as the redbreast. The relationship, however, to the genus *Branta* is no closer, the scientists tell us, than the relationship of *Branta* to the genus *Chen*, which includes the snow geese.

So *Nesochen sandvicensis* stands alone, with only the most distant cousins, as an insular form which has become less aquatic and less aerial and correspondingly more terrestrial.

Its feet have grown less webbed, its wings have grown shorter, and its legs have grown stronger and it climbs and runs over the lava beds in Hawaii in, alas, ever decreasing numbers. Perhaps there are just enough left for its impending doom, like that of Europe, to be averted at the eleventh hour.

These are amongst the acute problems which ornithology must face, but there are many others which must never be allowed to become acute. America's waterfowl have just been saved. Conservationists expect a twenty per cent increase this year in the total duck and goose population of that continent. Europe's waterfowl are still decreasing, and no far-reaching action has yet been taken to arrest the decline.

A shooting season of six weeks; no shooting between four in the afternoon and seven in the morning; a bag limit of five geese and ten ducks per day; no feeding or 'baiting' as it is called over there—these are some of the limitations now in force in the USA. Many of the less common species enjoy absolute protection.

Such drastic measures will only be necessary in England if we leave it until too late. But who, amongst true wildfowlers, would not at once willingly forego a month of his shooting season to ensure that the music of the wild geese may be heard over the moonlit marshes far into the future?

ANABEL

From *Wild Chorus* (Country Life, 1938)

At my home, which is a lighthouse standing upon a seawall at the mouth of an East Coast river, live several hundred wild geese and ducks...

The lighthouse is surrounded on three sides by a salting (or saltwater marsh) in which there are tidal pools, and on and around these tidal pools the geese and ducks have their home. There are many different kinds from distant parts of the world, most of them pinioned (that is, with the first joint of the wing removed) so that they may not risk their lives by flying out into the world of the wildfowlers. Amongst them there are also some of the common kinds, whose wild relatives frequent the nearby marshes. Every year a number of these wild birds come into the lighthouse enclosure, where they find others of their kind living a sheltered life with plenty of food and no dangers. Some of them take for a time to this life, and become quite tame and unafraid. And this is the story of Anabel.

I suppose the return of Anabel on that October morning is one of the half dozen most-stirring events that I have ever experienced. The thrill was no less because it was half expected. I had never really doubted that she would come back, but when she did I was overwhelmed with joy and relief and wonder.

Anabel is a pink-footed goose. On 25 September 1936, she came first to the lighthouse... It was early in the season, and the winter flocks of geese that live on the nearby marshes had not yet arrived. Soon after sunrise, she came to the saltmarshes of the Wash. She heard some geese calling below her, and swung in towards them. There were twenty-nine of them, sitting on the marsh quite near a strange round building (my lighthouse), but they did not seem to be alarmed by it, so Anabel swept round low over them and called in answer—and immediately a great babel arose. Anabel was very pleased to find others of her kind, and she circled round again. She did not realise that they were tame pinkfeet which had lived several years at the lighthouse.

As she passed a little plantation, some rooks came out and mobbed her, but she was too tired to care, so she curled back with set wings and settled near the pinioned geese on the marsh. They didn't greet her in a very friendly way, considering she was one of their own kind. Some of the more pugnacious ganders chased and pecked her, but Anabel was too tired to run away, and so she just crouched down and waited until they had satisfied their anger. Then she stood up again, preened herself, flapped her wings, and walked after the other geese towards a freshwater pool which is just above high-tide mark on the side of the seawall.

On her way to the pool she walked past me as I stood watching from the top of the bank in my bright-blue dressing gown (for it was not yet breakfast time), and she showed no fear, although she passed no more than twenty yards from me, indeed, she gave me the most casual glance, although I was possibly the first human being she had ever seen. From her plumage I knew that she could only be at most three months old, and it was clear that, in her manner towards human beings, she thought it wise to follow the lead of her elders and betters. Since they showed no undue alarm, why should she?

A week later Anabel would come up to feed with the other geese within a few yards of me, and if in the course of the winter I managed to create some impression upon her, it was perhaps more the bucket of corn which I carried than my own personal charm that created it.

In February, the geese which had returned in their thousands to the neighbourhood started their northward migration, and by mid-March no pinkfeet remained at the lighthouse except the twenty-nine pinioned ones—and Anabel. She seemed to find the sea pool, the salting grass, the shelter of the bank and the lighthouse, the freshwater pond and, above all, a daily cropful of corn, exactly to her liking. From time to time she would fly round, but she did not seem particularly restless, and I had gradually come to think that she would probably stay right through the summer.

Then, on the morning of 16 May 1937, when I went out to feed the birds, there was no sign of Anabel. During the night she had slipped away, and set off northwards to catch up with the great flocks which must already have left Scotland for the far north.

Greenland, Spitsbergen and Iceland, the breeding grounds of all the pinkfeet in the world, are dangerous places for a single goose. There are Arctic foxes, and gyr falcons, and men, for all of whom a goose is just a very good meal. As October began, I became apprehensive. There were also the dangers of the early autumn to be overcome, when the geese are stubbling (that is, feeding among the stubble after harvest) in Scotland, and later in Yorkshire, a hundred possible fates might have overtaken Anabel. But none of them had, and at noon on 9 October 1937 I heard her shout high up in a dappled autumn sky. She was a tiny speck when I first saw her, almost straight above me, and with bowed wings she hurtled downwards. She came in confidently, without circling at all, and settled at the foot of the bank, twenty yards from where I stood with my bucket of corn. I called to her, and she walked straight up to me. Any doubt which I might have had that it was indeed Anabel was at once dispelled. There she stood, a plump little round person, with her queer angular forehead, her uncommonly pink bill pattern, and the few white feathers at its base. To me she was as recognisable as a stray sheep to a shepherd, or a stray hound to a huntsman.

So Anabel was back: she had been away for four months and twenty-four days. The very day she came, my friend Michael was broadcasting a talk about the geese and ducks on his marsh on the West Coast. I sent him a telegram, and at the end of his talk he read it and told listeners about Anabel. This was less than seven hours after her arrival. A week later I chanced to be broadcasting and was able to tell the story of her return more fully, so that Anabel became quite well known. She stayed again through the winter with the birds at the lighthouse. Several other wild pinkfeet came in to join the throng, sometimes singly, sometimes in pairs, and occasionally in small bunches. Anabel often flew round with them, but she knew that the lighthouse was her real home. When the others went off, as most of them did with the departure of the main mass of the pinkfeet in February, Anabel stayed behind and came up to feed when she was called, with the pinioned birds.

Although she led a sheltered life, safe from all enemies and with regular meals, hers was not a dull one. With her lived a hundred and fifty wild geese from all parts of the world, to say nothing of a crowd of ducks. Many of her neighbours were not at all easy to get on with: there were disagreements and quarrels, and occasionally (though, of course, only among the more ill-bred members of the community) there were even fights; but there were compensations too, for few pinkfeet, after all, have had the opportunity of hobnobbing with an Emperor goose, as Anabel did.

I was ready for Anabel's departure in the spring, and just as she had done the year before, again she slipped away during the night, and on the morning of 19 May her familiar dumpy figure was nowhere to be seen...

It is almost certain that geese do not normally breed until they are three years old, and Anabel is only two. If she survives this summer's dangers in the far north, and next summer's too, then in October (1939), perhaps, she will bring her first family with her to spend the winter in the lighthouse pen.

THE LIGHTHOUSE BIRDS

From *Wild Chorus* (Country Life, 1938)

I want to write a chapter about the waterfowl which live on the salting at the lighthouse, and so I have brought my pencil and paper and a bucket of corn and have sat myself down on the bank to write it in their presence, so that they wont be offended and think that I am doing anything behind their backs.

When I came out of the door I called to them, 'Come on,' and immediately they answered me from away out on the marsh. There was a great babel of voices, led by the greylags and the emperor geese, with the snow geese joining in, and then as I sat down there was an ugly rush and a great slapping of wings as the geese came tearing towards me. They slowed up as they got closer, and walked up to me with an air of dignity, as though they were not hungry at all but simply chancing to walk that way.

Not so the eiders, who came waddling up and stood waiting in a little semicircle, pecking occasionally at the sleeve of my jersey. The eiders get their crops filled from my hand by what is nothing more nor less than blackmail. 'Until we are full,' they say, 'we wont allow any other birds to come near you, so if you want the rest to come and feed out of your hand you must give us as much meal as we can eat first.' So the eiders are stuffed with meal, which they grab greedily from my fingers. Towards the end they become top heavy from the weight in their crops, and then they sit down and go on shovelling down what they are given. At last, replete, they wander off to drink, and to digest lying down, bulging under some tuft of grass. Then the more timid shelducks and the geese have a chance to come to my hand. In a collection of small ducks no one could describe shelducks as timid, but when they are amongst a crowd of geese their characters show up quite differently.

The birds at the lighthouse have two special ways of giving me pleasure. The first is that they are very tame, and the second is that they attract the wild birds to come and live in the enclosure with them.

As I write there is a crowd of more than two hundred birds all gathered around me. There are twenty-five different kinds of geese from all parts of the world, and a great many different kinds of ducks, too.

Two years ago it was impossible to see them at close quarters. Even a year ago they would go flapping away to the far side of the enclosure on impulse; but now with infinite patience we have at last made them tame. Many of them feed freely from the hands of strangers, and some of them will even follow me into the house.

In winter there are always wild wigeon in the tidal pools below the studio window. They come up to feed with the rest of the birds, keeping perhaps a little more to the outskirts of the throng; but to have a perfectly wild wigeon feeding within four or five yards is, to me, a thrilling event, and it is no less thrilling because it happens twice a day the whole winter through.

The wigeon have learned their tameness gradually. Only half a dozen come regularly to feed of the flock that fluctuates between twelve and forty. But a pintail drake, which came for two days in the spring, had no time to become gradually tame. It was most exciting and interesting to watch him.

At the foot of the bank below the lighthouse, not more than ten yards from the studio window, is a sea pool, and on the bank itself at the edge of the pool is some long grass. In this grass my two pairs of pinioned pintails were wont to sit sleeping through the day, occasionally pushing out on to the pool to wash and then going ashore again to preen and afterwards to sleep some more. The visiting drake joined them and slept apparently as soundly as they, but when I emerged from the door at the top of the bank and called up the birds at feeding time, he was bewildered. At first he swam off onto the pool and hung about on the far side about twenty yards away. But as he saw his fellow pintails come racing up the bank to be fed, he did not know what to do. Very much on the alert he swam back across the pool and walked ashore at the foot of the bank. Slowly and with many a doubtful pause he began to climb towards me, where I stood with a friend by the door. He came up to within about four yards of us, and then stood, not far from the other four pintails, who were by now part of a great crowd of birds hurrying hither and thither after each grain of corn. He might have been thinking, 'How stupid those four are to go so close to those two human beings. Now, my mother always told me to keep well clear of them, as they were dangerous. I suppose they can't have been properly brought up. However, I feel it my duty to warn them. And see how they are eating all that corn. There's something very fishy about all this, something highly suspicious. I'll keep very much on my guard. Nobody's going to take me in. Oh no! Not *this* pintail! '

So he stood there on his guard. He never ate a single grain of wheat, but waited faithfully beside the others of his kind. Sometimes a duck scurrying from the peck of a goose would run into him and he would jump to one side and stand again alert and graceful, his long white neck stretched up, surveying in bewilderment the whole strange scene.

Two days later he had flown off on his northward migration and four pintails only remained at the lighthouse.

Of the geese that are clustering around me at this moment, undoubtedly the most beautiful are the little red-breasted geese. Their black and white and chestnut pattern, sharply divided and intricately interwoven, catches the eye at once.

At first I had two of them, a present from the Duchess of Bedford just before her last tragic flight. The redbreasts at Woburn Abbey, the only ones ever to have bred in captivity, lived there for fifteen years before they consented to nest. Now their offspring, hand-reared, breed freely every year.

These two turned out to be females and later I was lucky enough to acquire two beautiful ganders from a friend in Belgium. These four birds have now paired up and I am hopeful that next spring may see my first clutch of red-breasted goose's eggs.

Though quick to tame, redbreasts have a nervous disposition. My Woburn birds will take corn from my hand, but only if my hand happens to be where they are passing. They will not come running for it as many of the other kinds will. They are good-tempered little birds and their high, clear, disjointed double call is a cheerful noise to hear.

Lately the little flock of redbreasts at the lighthouse has grown because of some more which have arrived from Russia. But although I need no longer go to the North Caspian or to Siberia in order to have redbreasts feeding on the marsh at my home, I still hanker after the sight of a thousand of them in the air at once, and some day maybe I shall renew my search for these mysterious and elusive little birds.

Another beautiful, rare and rather mysterious goose is the emperor goose from Alaska and the Aleutian Islands. There are not many of these birds in the world, and the flocks, it is said, only migrate a short distance, for the south side of the islands is warmed by an ocean current from Japan and in winter the geese need go no farther south to avoid the snow and ice which covers their breeding grounds on the north side. Whether this is the reason for the emperor goose's short wings and bulky shape I cannot tell, but that they are birds of delightful disposition— very tame and gentle, strikingly handsome in plumage and most attractive in voice—I do know, or so at least have found: but a minute or two ago the two pairs of emperors were feeding from my hand. Their merry chirruping call is always one of the first to greet me when I emerge at feeding time and they come to my hand eagerly for corn.

Fortunately there are few class distinctions amongst the lighthouse geese, though I have seen a certain amount of snobbery. The snow geese are usually to be found in company with the emperors, and on one occasion I heard a new arrival actually ask one of the lesser snows whether he would mind presenting him to the emperors. Of course, one can well understand that such a thing must make a great impression in the life of a wild pinkfoot—something to tell his grandchildren, but the matter has been a standing joke in court circles ever since.

My emperors, who were hand-reared, delighted in human companionship from their youth up and became much attached to the human voice. They travelled to the lighthouse in a hamper in the back of my car right across England, and they listened in silence to the music dispensed by the BBC through the medium of the wireless set in my car. But every time that the announcer's voice was heard, all four of them would call loudly in unison. Now that they are nearly three years old, when I hear their hum of conversation, like the soft baa-ing of lambs, close under the window, I lean out sometimes and call softly to them and I am sure of their clarion-clear reply, as they turn their white heads on one side to look up at me.

The most peculiar of all goose calls is made by that strange and slightly unbelievable bird, the Coreopsis goose of Tasmania. The cry of the female more closely resembles that of a pig than any bird call. It is a deep, croaking grunt.

The Coreopsis is a big bird and it stands high upon its legs which are pink, but it appears inadvertently to have stepped into some tar and to have emerged with its feet quite black. Its toes are less webbed than in most geese and the pads of its feet are more callous, which is said to be an adaptation for walking on hot lava in the volcanic regions it frequents. But alas, it has now become rare through over-shooting and lack of protection. Its plumage is grey with peculiar black spots and its bill is pale yellowish green as its name implies.

The ganders are rather quarrelsome and I keep only a single female at the lighthouse and she is full-winged. She often flies round the lighthouse on her great slow-beating, owl-like wings, but she never attains any great height and she has shown no tendency to wander away. No doubt she considers the flight to Australia rather too ambitious a project, even in these days of aerial progress.

The swan goose, sometimes at the lighthouse affectionately called the 'swoose', is a fine large bird which is rarely seen in captivity in Europe, though it is the wild form from which the farmyard Chinese goose was domesticated. It is a strange long bird with a very long black bill, a long fawn-coloured neck with a chocolate stripe running down the back of it, and orange legs. But unlike its domestic cousin it has no knob on its forehead and its tummy clears the ground more easily. Indeed, it is quite a graceful bird, for as the trim greylag is to the farmyard goose, so is the swoose to the Chinese goose.

My pair of 'sweese' are delightfully tame and the gander will bury his great long bill in my hand with the utmost confidence, at the same time making his strange, deprecating, wheezy call and wearing a most disdainful expression.

I have quite a large flock of white-fronted geese whose calls bring back spring days in Hungary. That is where most of them came from, but one is a young bird which with its mate frequented the lighthouse pen in the winter of 1936. They were stupidly shot near the pen one day and the goose was brought to me with a broken wing. She recovered and I have her still, but the gander was killed. Later in the same winter a single whitefront, also a young bird, with a badly broken leg came to the pen. The leg was dangling and she could not stand. She would feed lying down and then flap to a new patch of grass and start feeding there. I tried to catch her so that I could set the leg, but she was at first too wild. On the second day her mate arrived and from then on until the end of March they stayed at the lighthouse. By the time that they had grown really tame the broken leg had set itself and though, if taken in time, I could have made a better job of the mend, yet in a fortnight she was able to hobble about quite well, and before she left she was walking strongly,

if a little stiffly, on it with a pronounced limp. Whitefronts
are not common near the lighthouse, and I was surprised that
same spring when a family party of eight turned up. They only
stayed one day, however, and were clearly passing through on
migration. In the autumn of 1937 I looked in vain for the return
of the lame goose and her mate. They never came; but four other
whitefronts arrived in November: an old bird and three young
ones. Soon after their arrival they took to wandering away onto
the marsh, and one day when they were feeding just along the
sea wall, a wildfowler came over the top, and only two of the
four returned to the pen. They came straight from the scene of
the tragedy and settled close by the lighthouse door, and from
then until their departure in May they were wise enough never
to stray. Occasionally they flew rounds, but seldom, if ever, did
they settle outside the enclosure. They were two young birds,
both females, and one of them attracted a pinioned gander, who
was always with them. I do not expect them to return, for I
believe that there is no regular migration route of whitefronts
over the lighthouse. The ones that come are usually young ones
that have strayed and got lost. But there is, nevertheless, just a
chance that they might come back.

All these whitefronts have pinkish flesh-coloured bills,
and their plumage is lightish grey-brown. When David (Haig
Thomas) first returned from West Greenland he brought with
him a pair of whitefronts which had been hand-reared by the
Eskimos, and whose bills were orange. Their plumage was
much darker brown, almost chocolate-coloured. At first we
thought this was just a chance variation, but two years later he
returned to Greenland and sent home eight more whitefronts,
and every one was chocolate-coloured, and every one had an
orange-bill instead of the flesh-pink which is described in all
the textbooks. Four of these now live at the lighthouse, and the
difference between them and the Hungarian and English ones
seems more marked than ever.

Amongst the greylags on Brogden—the great goose marsh
in Westmorland—a single young whitefront was shot last
autumn. It was very dark, and it had an orange bill.

The questions which arise are: where, if anywhere, are these dark whitefronts with orange bills common? Where do the ones which breed in West Greenland spend the winter? Not, it seems, in Eastern North America, for in that continent the whitefront is only known from the middle and west. When I have seen, as I hope soon to do, the white-fronted geese in California, including the giant whitefront or tule goose, which is said to be as large as a Canada goose, I shall know more of the subject.

In the meantime it seems that there is a western race of whitefronts, possibly wintering in Ireland, which is darker than the typical race of Europe and Asia, and has an orange bill; and this is analogous to the races of greylag goose. Our English and Scottish greylag, which still breeds in small numbers in Scotland and the Outer Isles, has an orange bill, and by comparison with the pink-billed Eastern race, is a much darker bird. It is clearly a very different bird, yet Alphéràky, author of the great Russian monograph on the geese, refused to admit in that magnificent work that there was or ever had been such a thing as a live greylag with an orange bill. When he read of such in English bird books he explained it away by saying that the description was from a dead bird, in which the flesh-pink must have turned orange when it dried up!

There are two pairs of these eastern greylags at the lighthouse to compare with our own western and, according to Alphéràky, 'non-existent' orange-billed ones.

There are strange nocturnal magpie geese from Australia, and tiny maned geese and ashy-headed geese from the Falkland Islands, barheads from India, bean geese and barnacles and brents, Canadas and cackling geese. All these and many others help to make up a collection which gives great pleasure not only to me, but to hundreds of other people who come to look at them.

When I let the true collector's instinct take command, I think of the kinds which are not represented at the lighthouse and of the strange places I shall perhaps visit in search of them. Amongst the ducks there are many, but amongst the geese there are few, such as the rare Sandwich Island goose, which is too near to extinction to be exported, and the kelp goose of Southern Chile, which dwells by the seashore and cannot live without the particular green seaweed upon which it feeds. Perhaps, some day, the Sandwich Island goose will become numerous, perhaps a substitute will be found for the Chilean kelp weed, and in the meantime there is always Korea and the mysterious crested shelduck.

THE CHORUS OF THE GEESE

From *Wild Chorus* (Country Life, 1938)

In the crazy world of today, when the human race seems so little able to control its destiny, when crises and depressions follow each other in mad succession, the need for escape is more urgent and the call of wild places more insistent than ever.

In England, few of these wild places are left. For some there are forests and fells and moors, for others the ocean, but, for me, wildest of all are the saltings and mudflats of the coast. Here the sky is master of the scene; the grandeur of sunrise and sunset is reflected in the tidal pools and, dully, on the surface of the wet mud. The creeks wind sluggishly from the marshes towards the open sea, and at flood tide the sea itself comes wandering back. At spring tides it whispers through the grass and washes against the sea walls. In this world live the wildfowl, and in this same flat world I like to live, within sight of their winter hordes and within sound of their wild chorus.

They are mysterious birds coming from faraway northern lands, impelled by an unknown force and kept infallibly on their course by an unknown sense. They are wild and wary birds, a traditional quarry of man from immemorial times. Their flight is swift and their formations fill the sky, but I believe that their greatest appeal is to the ear. When the northeast wind blows at dawn, and the flood tide creeps in across the mud, it is the sudden call of geese, half heard above the roar of wind and waves, that brings the greatest thrill of all. When the full moon rises over the marsh at dusk, and the creeks are brimful, when eyes are strained to see which way the bubbles float, so that one may know if full-sea is past or yet to come, it is the call of geese which makes one's heart leap.

The wigeon whistle as they come swishing low along the edge of the marsh; the mallards chuckle to themselves as they go inland high up in the sunset sky; the curlews call as they flight from the incoming tide and the redshanks pipe in their creeks. These are the familiar sounds of the saltings in winter, but the music of the geese is the most stirring of all.

Whether they are pinkfeet in East Anglia, greylags in Westmorland, barnacles in Scotland, brents in Ireland, whitefronts in Hungary, lesser whitefronts in Persia, or snow geese in Canada, and widely different as the calls of the various species are, the music of the great skeins is always moving in its grandeur, always perfectly appropriate to the wild places in which it is heard.

The works of a composer may perhaps be judged by the musician after the first hearing, but for me the full enjoyment of a symphony does not come until I am familiar with it. So it is with the chorus of the geese. The familiar high note of the pinkfoot remains my favourite wild goose call: the note that I have heard across the moonlit potato fields, across the saltings of my home, and out over the bare mudflats in the dawn.

BARNACLE BILL

From *Wild Chorus* (Country Life, 1938)

There was already a glow in the eastern sky when we got to the punt on that fifth morning. She lay on the sand at the edge of the channel where we had left her the day before. We got her afloat after a struggle, and then packed in the gear and folded up the anchor and cleared everything for action, with as little noise as possible, because the barnacle geese were not far away and we might come upon them almost as soon as we set off. When the big gun had been loaded and all was ready, we started to drift down noiselessly with the stream. So started the story of a strange coincidence. At this state of the tide the channel was more like a little trout stream than a tidal estuary, and we were constantly running aground. There was no great hurry because we were waiting for the coming of a small and still decreasing tide, which would, we thought, just reach us; it would slow up the flow of the stream and hang almost slack for half an hour before starting to ebb out again.

In the growing light the world was full of gulls. Thousands of them roost where the channel bends westward. But the barnacles had not woken up yet. We had heard no sound from the high sand whence we hoped they would come to the channel to wash before going to the saltings for the day. For four mornings we had waited, and each time they had gone elsewhere, settling sometimes behind us up the channel after the tide had left it too shallow to float the punt, sometimes in some inaccessible lead or runnel, sometimes away from the river in some splash far out on the sand. This, our fifth morning, was our last; the last when the tide would be possible, and the last before our return to London and civilisation.

For the twentieth time we ran aground and stepped out half-crouching into the shallow water to swing the punt into the deeper channel, where perhaps the water was seven inches deep instead of less than two. Above the squawking of gulls we suddenly heard the geese, and they were up. In a moment the punt was afloat, we lying flat in it whilst the chorus grew louder. All at once they came into view flying low over the sand in a close pack, three hundred together and barking their short, sharp, high-pitched call. They came to the channel below us and flew up it as if to settle just in front of us, and then they came on and swept past us very close, beating their long pointed wings much faster than grey geese. In a moment they had swung away from the channel, out over the sand and back whence they had come. Presently we heard their calling die away and we knew that they had settled far up the big lead, much further up it than this small neap tide would ever float our punt.

We lay under a little cliff of sand, only a few feet high, yet enough to hide us well should the geese fly round again, and we waited as the day dawned. Beyond the gulls which covered the sand and filled the air with a shimmer of half-seen wings, we could see a darker line. Through the glasses we made out a little party of thirty barnacles sitting at the head of a little bay. To get to them we must pass broadside on within one hundred and fifty yards, go far below them round the point, and back towards them up the bay. The tide had already slowed the current down and would float us nicely in to the birds.

But we had hardly started before these barnacles also rose and flew down channel. They crossed the sand and curled back to join the main bunch, whose calls came faintly across a mile of sand. Perhaps they had seen us as we tried to slip past them, or perhaps the tide had woken them, but whatever the cause, it seemed that our last chance had gone. For four mornings we had waited in vain for the barnacles to fly round and perchance to settle within reach of the navigable water, and now on the fifth we were waiting again. Twice our hopes had been raised, and both times dashed, and still we lay waiting under the little sand cliff.

By now it was quite light and the atmosphere was very clear. The hills looked terribly close and blue-black, and the sky leaden and grey. To the east was a rift in the sharp-edged clouds and at first came a golden lining. Then suddenly the sun rose and cast an orange light upon the sand and upon some whitish specks at the far end of the bay. They were swimming at the edge of the tide, and they were barnacle geese, eighteen of them that we had somehow overlooked.

We pushed out and set off towards them. The sun was behind us, but below it the sand cliff was a dark background, and for once we were almost unnoticed as we pushed across the bay at top speed with the shortest setting pole. At first success was a faraway thing, and then with glorious rapidity it became a possibility, a probability, almost a certainty, and—*woomf*—an accomplished fact.

As the smoke cleared away I sat up and pushed the boat in to the shore without delay. It had been a good shot: but one goose was making off across the sand and I jumped out and gave chase. Only the tip of his wing was broken, the tip of his right wing. As I ran I felt sure, from the trailing primaries, that this would be a splendid bird to keep alive. Throughout the chase, the pace was killing and when I eventually caught up with him nearly half a mile from the punt, I sat down exhausted and panting on the sand with Bill exhausted and panting in my lap. The capture of Bill might well be the end of this story, but actually it is the beginning, at any rate of that part of it which is strange and extraordinary.

Bill had the very tip joint of his right wing badly broken, and it was only a small operation to remove it altogether. On it grew the first four of the ten flight feathers or primaries. To stop a goose from flying, all its primaries must be cut, so with a pair of scissors I clipped the remaining six.

Now Michael, who lives in Cheshire, wanted to add a barnacle to his collection of geese, so at once I sent Bill off by train, with a warning to Michael that a year later when the cut feathers were moulted out, he would be able to fly. In the meantime it would be wise to pinion him properly so that the remaining six primaries would not grow again.

Somehow the summer came round and Bill had not been pinioned. In July he moulted, and new wing feathers grew— all but the four at the very tip of his right wing. Even without these four he could fly fairly well, and during August he often made short flights around the enclosure. Then one September day he was gone. For a week Michael expected him to turn up again. Bill had probably, he thought been blown away by the westerly equinoctial gales. A farmer would ring up to say he had caught a strange-looking duck on his farm, which was now in a bag in his barn, and would Michael kindly come and fetch it. But no such message came, and Bill was lost.

It was about five weeks later that, running my eye over the little flock of pinioned barnacle geese which live amongst the many other kinds on the saltmarsh at the lighthouse, I noticed that there were ten instead of nine. When we walked out to look at them close to, we expected the newcomer to be a wild one, and to fly off, but we walked close to them and none flew. Indeed, we could not pick out the new arrival because they all seemed to be pinioned. When eventually they flapped away one was just able to lift, and fly across the creek, though he was rather lop-sided.

We herded them all into a corner and caught the stranger with a hand net. From his right wing the first four primaries were missing. The primary coverts on the underside of the wing, the smaller feathers which overlap the bases of the flight feathers themselves, had not been moulted and bore the marks where they had been cut with scissors, showing that the other six primaries must have been clipped sometime during the year before the July moult.

The lighthouse is about a hundred and fifty miles from Michael's home in Cheshire, in a southeasterly direction. During that September and October there were westerly gales, and it was the season of the year when the instinct of a barnacle goose would lead it southward with the approach of winter.

Was this newcomer our old friend Bill? I am inclined to believe that he was, because barnacle geese are rare enough in captivity for the coincidence to be even greater, should one assume that during those five weeks there were two barnacle geese at large without the first four primaries of their right wings.

Ours is pinioned now, and we call him Bill anyway.

THE WILDFOWL PROBLEM: A NEW RESEARCH STATION IN GLOUCESTERSHIRE

Country Sportsman (April 1948)

The Severn Wildfowl Trust has been formed for three reasons: first, because still very little is known about wildfowl, especially wild geese; and one of its objects is therefore to learn as much as possible about these elusive and wary birds. This object is purely scientific—to add to knowledge.

The second reason is that ducks and geese are decreasing in the world rather rapidly—and it would be a great pity if they were allowed to disappear altogether or even to become extremely rare. To prevent that happening some sort of action is required—but what? Another of the Trust's objects is to find out where and when and how to take such action.

And the third reason is to interest people in wildfowl, partly because to deal with a problem like this—a problem of declining numbers—public opinion must be roused to a sense of responsibility about it; and partly because there is a wide field of interest and delight to be had from the study of birds—birds of all kinds, but wildfowl in particular—and education, in my view, still has easily the most important long term influence on the future of our civilisation.

The Trust has established a bird observatory on some marshes known as the New Grounds on the south side of the Severn Estuary just above Sharpness Bridge. These marshy fields got their name because they were reclaimed from the high tides, but the first reclamation was in 1360, so the name 'New' is relative. Outside the sea wall there are about 200 acres of saltmarsh and the area is the main winter feeding ground of the geese which roost at night on the mudflats of the estuary. At various points along the seawall the Trust has built little huts which peep over it. Sometimes the geese are feeding only a few yards from these huts and, with the sun behind one, it is an amazing and beautiful sight. There they are, perhaps 2,000 or more geese living their lives—feeding, preening, squabbling—all unaware of one's presence only a few yards away. Probably nowhere else in the world is there such an opportunity for watching these proverbially wary birds.

Just behind the sea wall is a little wood containing a duck decoy. It is called the New Decoy, but like the New Grounds, the adjective is relative, as the decoy was built in 1843 and called 'New' to distinguish it from another old one about a mile and a half away. A duck decoy is a special pond built for catching ducks. Leading from the pond there are, in this case, three curved ditches covered by netting. The ducks are enticed by a little dog to swim into these ditches; they follow the dog to mob it, as cows sometimes do, or as small birds sometimes mob a hawk or an owl. When the ducks are in the ditch, or 'pipe' as it is called, the decoyman, who has been hidden behind some special reed screens, shows himself at the mouth of the pipe, cutting off the retreat of the ducks. They jump and fly away from him, on up the pipe, thinking no doubt to escape around the comer. But the end is closed and they are caught.

There used to be 200 decoys in this country, used for catching ducks for market, but there are now only nine still working. The ducks caught in the Trust's decoy are marked with a little aluminium ring on the leg which has a number on it and an address, and then the bird is released. If the bird is shot, or recovered in another decoy, the finder sends in the number, and part of the migration route taken by that particular bird becomes known. The wild geese have also been caught on the saltings with special rocket nets and have been ringed in the same way as the ducks.

In the marshy fields around the decoy wood, paddocks enclosed by fox-proof fencing have been built, and in them a collection of tame ducks, geese and swans—tame wild ones, as it were—has been established. It is now almost certainly the most representative of its kind in the world. The birds are most engagingly tame. They feed from one's hand and crowd round one's feet so that one has to be careful not to tread on them. They come from Canada, Siberia, China, South America, Australia, New Zealand—indeed, from all over the world. Some have been sent from their native lands, but the majority are from breeding stocks in this country which survived the war.

Altogether, there are about 400 tame waterfowl at the New Grounds, among them sixty-five different kinds. There are thirty different kinds of geese, and only three more are required to represent all the species in the world.

Such are the Trust's activities, and already considerable interest has been aroused in its work. More than 2,500 people have visited the New Grounds during the past year.

Some of the studies, especially those connected with the ringing, are being undertaken in conjunction with the International Wildfowl Inquiry Committee whose British section is doing such valuable research work on the causes of the decrease in wildfowl. That ducks and geese are, in general, decreasing is now, alas firmly established, although there are signs of an increase as far as certain species are concerned. The pink-footed goose, for example, seems to be increasing; but the bean goose has almost vanished in winter in Britain:

only a few hundred now visit this country, where there used to
be thousands. Gadwall, garganey, pintail, shoveler—formerly
rare ducks—have been increasing, but there has been a far
greater decrease in the numbers of mallard, teal and wigeon.
The reason seems chiefly to be that the world in general, and
Western Europe in particular, isn't such a healthy place for a
wild goose or duck as it used to be. The main enemy is man,
but they have other enemies too. The geese, for example, breed
mainly in the Far North. There Arctic foxes and Gyr falcons
prey on them, in some areas the geese have been forced by the
foxes to breed on inaccessible cliffs from which only a small
percentage of the goslings survive the inevitable fall to the
feeding grounds below. In the North, too, eggs are taken on
a large scale by sealers and by special egg expeditions, for food
and also for albumen for use in photographic films. Then, when
the geese are moulting in July and unable to fly, vast numbers
are herded together and killed by the natives—Samoyeds and
the like. For instance, in one drive on Kolguev, an island in the
Arctic Ocean north of Russia, 6,000 were clubbed to death.
They were cured and used for food for the rest of the year.
This is nothing new. It has gone on for hundreds, probably
for thousands of years, but it becomes more significant,
representing a bigger proportion, as the numbers decline.

In this country, the chief contributory cause of the decline
seems to be the enormous reduction in suitable winter quarters
for wildfowl—the drainage of marshes, the disturbance of wild
areas due to increased population, and to the invention of the
internal combustion engine.

Shooting—the incomparable sport of wildfowling—
appears at the moment to be only a secondary danger to the
wildfowl stocks, although, of course, when their numbers are
decreasing it does not help the situation to shoot them. On
the other hand, in this world you cannot persuade people to
take concerted action unless they are interested in a thing; and
the chief people interested in wildfowl are the wildfowlers.
They are likely to mind more than most if ducks and geese are
wiped out, and most of them have the foresight to help to see

that steps are taken in time to prevent this happening. In that respect, wildfowling and wildfowlers may prove a safeguard to the ducks and the geese.

All the same, with the greatly increased numbers of wildfowlers since the war, I think some contribution towards the problem will have to be made by those interested in the sport. It may be necessary for them to accept a slightly shorter shooting season. At the moment it runs from 12 August to 1 February inland and 21 February on the coast in some counties, 15 February on the coast in others. I think that it would be simpler, and better for the birds too, to make it run from 1 September to 1 February everywhere. It is very muddling for wildfowlers at present, and also for the police to enforce.

An equally valuable step would be the establishment of wildfowl reserves in various parts of the country. The Severn Wildfowl Trust's research station is in some respects a pilot scheme for the National Nature reserves which are being planned in conjunction with the National Parks. Several of the proposed reserves will be devoted to the protection of wildfowl and the experience gained at the New Grounds may be found to be especially useful.

This international problem of our declining European wildfowl is urgent. It is still possible to avert catastrophe, but there is no time to be lost, and we in this country must give a strong lead and show that we are awake to our responsibility to future generations not to allow these beautiful and romantic birds to disappear from the face of the earth.

WILD GEESE AND THEIR MUSIC

Boy's Own Paper
(Volume 7, Number 3, December 1948)

You may wonder why, for so many people, wild geese hold a unique position among birds. Why should people think them especially romantic? Why should those who have once seen and heard them over the wild marshes and tidal estuaries be cast under a kind of spell?

I can only tell you the reasons why geese have affected me so strongly; what I have found beautiful and stirring about them; why their wild cry, half heard through a windy dusk, sends prickles down my spine with a feeling of pure delight and exhilaration; and why I have been led on by that delight to a specialised study of these great, strange birds.

Wild geese are proverbially wild, which means that they are difficult to approach and to study; they are large—five feet across the wings—and they are mysterious, for they migrate thousands of miles each year to and from their far Arctic breeding grounds; they often fly in great flocks and often in tidy 'V' formations, and the roar of their wings and voices as they rise in a cloud and fly out across the sunset cannot fail to stir the imagination.

Above all, I am sure that the principal fascination of wild geese is that they are *wild*. If you are a wildfowler seeking a Christmas dinner from the saltmarshes, or a naturalist trying to watch and to study and also perhaps to draw or photograph them, you will know well enough the meaning of the phrase 'wild goose chase'; you will develop a great respect for the object of your pursuit. You will have to crawl and stalk, to make use of every scrap of available cover in order to get near them, and, if you are to be successful, you must develop a good knowledge of their habits and movements. All that is, in itself, exciting, and you will find that success in the endeavour is intensely satisfying.

I have had many adventures when trying to stalk wild geese with a gun. But, recently, I have found it even more exciting and even more difficult, and a great deal more satisfying, to stalk them and to lie in wait for them in order to watch them. Then I can draw them, photograph them, and even catch them alive. We have been catching them alive to ring them and release them again, and in that way we are learning about their migration routes. It is exciting at times but, to be successful, you must know your geese, and you must have infinite patience; and all the time you are at work the cries of the geese ring in your ears. After a while you find that these cries begin to mean different things to you. You will find that you are learning the language of the geese. Of course it is not very complicated like human language, but certain calls mean certain things; when you hear them you know that the geese will react in certain ways.

Of the thirteen different kinds of geese which have been recorded in Britain, I suppose I know best the white-fronted goose, and next to that, probably, the pinkfoot. In the case of the whitefront I can distinguish about

twenty different calls, which have such meanings as:
'there is plenty of good food here—this is splendid.'
'There isn't much food here—let's go and see if we can find a
better place.'

'Look! There are some of our friends down there, let's join
them.'

'Leave me alone, you great bully.'

'I don't think this is a very safe place.'

'I'm pretty sure it's not, I saw something move in that ditch.'

'Look out! There's the arch-enemy—a man!'

Birds do not think like human beings, and it is a great
mistake to expect them to have human reactions. I have
expressed them this way so as to explain the kind of differences
which I can detect in the various call notes of the white-fronted
goose. But although it is all wrong to humanise the mental
processes of animals, it is also quite possible, in my view, to
underestimate the powers of consecutive thought which some
of them have developed. Many, including the goose, are not
such fools as they look.

The call of the white-fronted goose is a particularly musical
liquid cry. The bird is known in some parts of the world as
the 'laughing goose'; but the Eskimos call it 'lulluk', and the
Hungarians call it 'lillik', and both those names must be derived
from the birds voice. I have heard it for hours upon end in the
great plains of the Hortobagy in Hungary where more than a
hundred thousand whitefronts pass through each spring and
autumn on migration; I have heard it on the Danube Delta,
and in the lagoons of the Caspian Sea; I have heard it, mixed
with the cries of snow geese and the high bark of the cackling
geese, in the valleys of Northern California, and I have heard it
in the red bogs of Western Ireland. Lately I have heard it most
of all from the three thousand white-fronted geese which come
in winter to the estuary of the Severn, where we have been
concentrating our study.

Although the whitefront has perhaps the most universal
call (this species is the most numerous of the geese and has

by far the widest distribution in the world), yet I think the
ringing cry of the pinkfoot is still my favourite goose music.
It is more metallic and sharp than the call of the whitefront,
and it brings back to me the bitter winds of the East Anglian
coast, blowing over flat potato fields, and the rustle of the
creeping tide among the crab grass of the salting, and a white
cold moon in a dappled sky. Among the geese the pinkfoot was
my first friend and I cannot entirely desert him for the gayer
orange-legged whitefront with the black stripes on his belly
and the smart white blaze on his forehead.

The five species of grey geese which come to Britain are
not easy to tell apart. If you see them in flight they are most
easily identified by their call, once you know it. The soft, high-
pitched 'lulluk' of the whitefront is easy to distinguish from the
'angank' of the pinkfoot. The greylag, a few of which still hold
on as breeding birds in the very north of Scotland and in the
Hebrides, makes a noise like an ordinary farmyard goose; but of
course it is much more impressive when you hear it coming from
skein after skein of Iceland- or Scandinavia-bred birds, sweeping
out over the marshes of the Solway Firth on a winter's afternoon.

The bean goose makes a deep call rather like the baa-ing of
a sheep, and the very rare little lesser whitefront makes (in the
case of the gander) an incredibly thin, high-pitched call, which
in its general tone is not unlike that of its bigger cousin.

The snow goose (for greater and lesser snows, both natives of
North America, have been recorded in Britain) have a strangely
dull call when it is made individually—a single, simple bark.
When the great flocks are on the wing when the greaters are
coming in to feed on the marshes of the St. Lawrence River
in the Canadian fall, with the flaming-red maple forests of
Cap Tourmente in the background, or the lessers are rising
in shimmering clouds from the cornfields of the Sacramento
Valley in California, there is wild music in the air.

The two black geese which come to our British shores each
winter have easily distinguishable calls. The barnacle has a
monosyllabic barking call, muted and a little nasal, but very
beautiful. When you hear a great flock you might mistake it,

over the dark sea, for a flock of pinkfeet, but the individual call is single instead of double. Barnacles are getting much less numerous in their chosen haunts in the islands of West Scotland and Western Ireland. They badly need protection if they are not to be wiped out altogether.

The call of the brent goose is a rolling 'cronk', from which the name 'brent' and the Latin 'Branta' was surely derived. To me, the call is less wild and more friendly than the calls of the other geese. This is perhaps appropriate for, strangely enough, this beautiful little goose which so very seldom crosses the high-tide mark, which lives on the sea grass or *Zostera* growing far out on the mudflats of the estuary, and which is the only goose never to have bred in captivity, is, nevertheless, the most tame and confiding bird when captured alive, and one of the quickest of all waterfowl to learn that its captor means it well.

The thirteenth of the British geese is the rare and brilliant little red-breasted goose with a sharp staccato double call 'kikwik'. I once heard ten of them flying together over the plains of Hungary. I went to the Caspian to hear them in their thousands and I failed in my quest, for I found none at all.

Their home is in Russia and I may never hear them in a mass, flighting from the arid grasslands of Trans-Caspia or along the shores of the Aral Sea.

In September I listen for the call of the pinkfeet, newly arrived from the Arctic, and a week or two later I shall hear the laughing call of the first whitefronts as they come down on to the sandbanks of the Severn. As ever, the prickles will go down my spine at the sound!

They will come again to their winter haunts in Britain as they have done for thousands of years; it would be a tragedy if greed, stupidity or thoughtlessness ever broke the long tradition.

THE MIGRATION
OF WILD GEESE

From *The New Naturalist* (Collins, 1948)

Of the migratory birds which come to Britain in winter, few are more impressive than wild geese, for the great skeins in which they fly and the wild music of their call must catch the attention and imagination of those who normally show little interest in birds. It is surprising, therefore, that so much should remain unknown about them, and particularly about the methods and even the routes of their migration. One of the greatest additions to the study of migration was the development of the marking scheme by which an individual bird may be traced by affixing a numbered aluminium ring to its leg. This has been done with many species, including wild ducks which have been caught in various duck decoys in this country and in Holland; but until now it has not been attempted on a large scale with wild geese. The problem of catching the geese in bulk has hitherto appeared to be insuperable. It was to this problem that the newly-formed Severn Wildfowl Trust turned its attention in 1947. It was thought that no better locality could be found for such an attempt than the wildfowl observation station at the New Grounds on the Severn Estuary, which had recently been established by the Trust and which was largely devoted to the study of the great flocks of white-fronted geese which frequent this area in winter. Special nets were made and experiments were carried out in throwing them by means of rockets. Early in 1948 the system was put into operation for the first time in the field and 31 geese—30 of them whitefronts and one pinkfoot—were caught at the first attempt.

The net has to be set out in the hurrying darkness before dawn. For 25 yards across the marsh it is laid in a straight line, and concealed as well as may be in a groove cut in the turf. At each end a rocket is attached and from each leads a length of wire flex towards the hide which conceals the netters. It takes at least five people to set the net, working feverishly by the light of a hurricane lamp. The team must make a very early start and by the time the preparations are complete the first geese have usually appeared and caused a headlong rush for cover. It is always a hectic introduction to a long and exciting wait.

The net has so far been placed in such a way that the geese first settle well out in front of it and then walk in towards the 'catching area'—the square of 25 yards or so immediately downwind of the net itself. As the geese feed into this area quite slowly and as the numbers gradually increase, the suspense becomes terrific. For several hours—sometimes for a whole day—the watching netters are subjected to alternating paroxysms of optimism and disappointment.

A phlegmatic disposition is essential for the successful goose netter, for at any moment a false move, a cough or a sneeze from the hide, a passing farm worker, or a passing aeroplane, may put up the geese and ruin the day's chances to which the team has been devoting its energies since 4.30 a.m. But if all goes well, the 'pressure' of geese mounts in the catching area and only the leading birds have shown S.O.R., or 'Strange Object Reaction'. About four yards from the net they have suddenly noticed something which they do not like. How will they react? Will they go no closer, but continue to feed, or will they turn and walk out of the catching area? Upon this depends the pressure of geese behind them pushing forward into the C.A. And who shall say when there are enough in the C.A. to warrant a 'pull'? The loud noise made by the rockets suggests that the apparatus should be used as little as possible. Should we ever pull for fewer birds than were caught at the first attempt? We thought not and since that time, we have had 28 geese in the C.A. and at another time 20, and at yet another 14. In each case we waited in vain for more, and then in due course the geese set off on their northward migration.

But the triumph of the successful first attempt remains. Early observations have already been made of the birds which were ringed on that day and since then they have been watched frequently moving about among the remainder of the flock. Unfortunately on this first occasion we omitted to take certain details of the birds caught which would greatly have added to the interest of the subsequent observations. It is a curious fact that the black bars on the breasts and bellies of adult white-fronted geese vary from one bird to another. The extent of this individual variation appears to be infinite, so that the pattern can be used, like fingerprints, to identify an individual bird. This identification appears to be absolute over the winter season, but minor alterations in the black patterns on the breast and belly take place during the summer moult. At present, however, it appears that these changes are only in degree and not in fundamental pattern, and there seems every likelihood that birds can in future be identified from season to season by this means. Had we recorded the breast patterns of these adult white-fronted geese which were ringed at the first attempt with the rocket net, we should subsequently have been able to identify the ring numbers in the field from the drawings of their breast patterns. Meanwhile the single pink-footed goose which was ringed on the same day is, of course, recognisable. He remained at the New Grounds until 15 March when he was in company with nineteen whitefronts and one other pinkfoot, the last party to leave for the

North on the spring migration. The bird was constantly present from the date of ringing, which already provides some useful information upon its movements.

The main flocks of geese which winter annually on the New Grounds on the Severn Estuary are white-fronted, although every species and subspecies of goose on the British List has been observed there at one time or another. These particular white-fronted geese belong to the typical race *Anser albifrons albifrons* which breeds in Northern Europe east of the White Sea, in Asia and in North America. Those which come to England in winter are from North Russia (so far as is at present known). Their migration line appears to follow the south side of the Baltic to Holland where they remain until frost drives them across the Channel to England. As is always the case with geese, a few pioneer flocks (usually those with the highest proportion of young birds) strike onwards to the end of the migration line—to the terminus, as it might be called—early in the season. In the case of the New Grounds these flocks are only a few hundred strong. Just before Christmas they are augmented by flocks several thousands strong and the dates correspond very fairly with the departure of white-fronted geese from the big marshes in the south of Holland.

On their return migration, however, the geese, which have arrived in autumn from an easterly and sometimes from a southeasterly direction, usually depart flying due north. There is some evidence that they may visit the Mersey for a short stop on the return migration. Thereafter all trace of them is lost, but it would not be surprising to find that they return northward by a different route from that which they took in the autumn. This is often the case with wildfowl; it has been observed with Canada geese passing through Jack Miner's big ringing station at Kingsville, Ontario, and also with teal ringed in Western Europe.

The northward migration from the New Grounds begins with the utmost regularity within two or three days of 10 March. Only in an exceptional spring, such as that of 1947 when snow-covered fields lay to the northward, was the migration delayed.

On the other hand, however springlike and warm the weather may be, there is no premature departure. The available evidence supports the theory that the amount of daylight rather than the seasonal temperature change is the stimulus which calls upon the flock to set out on its migratory flight.

Large flocks of white-fronted geese breed in Northwest Greenland and until recently they were supposed to be indistinguishable from those breeding in Europe and Asia and North America. Recently however, it has been shown that these birds which winter principally in Ireland are easily distinguishable from the typical white-fronted geese by their much darker plumage with a tendency to heavier barring on the belly; by their slightly larger bright orange-yellow instead of pink bills; and by the narrower white edging to the feathers of the tail. These birds have recently been described by the author and a colleague, C. T. Dalgety, as a new subspecies *Anser albifrons flavirostris*. Numbers of them have been ringed in Greenland by Doctor Finn Salomonsen of the Zoological Museum at Copenhagen, and recoveries have been made in Ireland, a few in West Scotland and in Wales and one on the eastern coast of Canada. The migration of these birds differs from that of the typical race in that the birds arrive all together in Ireland at the end of September or in the early days of October, and depart all together late in April. They cannot come south, neither can they return north, by easy stages, for they have long sea passages to make. In spring they must fly direct from Ireland across the sea to Iceland and thence across the Denmark Strait and the Greenland Ice Cap to their breeding ground. Observations have been made at the breeding ground indicating that the majority of the geese arrive and depart over the Ice Cap rather than round the coast by way of Cape Farewell.

Thus white-fronted geese of two races converge upon the British Isles in winter. In addition another form of white-fronted goose which is held by science to warrant the status of a full species—the lesser white-fronted goose, *Anser erythropus*—is also recorded as a visitor to the British Isles. It was first identified in 1886, when an immature specimen was shot at Fenham Slakes in Northumberland by Alfred Chapman, the brother of the distinguished sportsman-naturalist, Abel Chapman. Several subsequent records exist, but under the critical scrutiny of the late H. F. Wetherby at the time of the publication of his *Handbook* none of them was considered to be 'above reproach'. Thus at the beginning of the war the lesser whitefront was the rarest of British birds—for you cannot have a rarer bird than one which has only been recorded once. It shared this distinction with some 25 other single-record species.

The lesser whitefront is only slightly smaller than the common whitefront. Its plumage is a little darker and its general shape is slightly different; but its bill is little more than half the length and round its eye is a slightly swollen brilliant golden-yellow eyelid. The lesser whitefront breed in Lapland very considerably closer to Great Britain than the common whitefronts of the Russian Arctic east of the White Sea, and these birds from Norway and Sweden and Finland migrate regularly southward through Hungary to the coasts of Dalmatia and Greece. It had always seemed to me strange that lesser whitefronts did not come to this country more frequently and, indeed, I began to wonder whether perhaps they did not often pass unnoticed for there were few enough among ornithologists, as I believed, who would readily recognise this beautiful little goose among a large flock of its near relations. My theory was to some extent upheld by a record of a single lesser whitefront which, in 1942, visited the enclosures of a farmer friend, Mr. William Tinsley, in Lincolnshire, where he kept a pair of tame lesser whitefronts which I had given him at the beginning of the war. There was no room for doubt in this identification, for he was one of the few people in this country who was really familiar with the species, having kept it in captivity for several years, and it constituted the second authentic record of the lesser whitefront in Britain. Were the occurrence of this bird to prove regular, the most likely place in which to find it would, I thought, be amongst the largest flocks in this country of the white-fronted geese from North Russia, and these flocks were to be found at the New Grounds.

It was this theory which first led me to the Severn Marshes in the Winter of 1945, and, among 2,000 wild geese (which included seven different kinds), we found two lesser whitefronts—the third and fourth records for the British Isles. In the following winter three of these birds were present among 4,000 white-fronted geese, so that the evidence seemed to indicate that lesser whitefronts might come regularly to the British Isles in the approximate proportion of one per 1,000 common whitefronts or a little more. This theory has unfortunately not been upheld, since among nearly 3,000 whitefronts on the New Grounds during the past winter no lesser whitefront made its appearance.

It is of interest that whereas the Northumberland lesser whitefront of 1886 was an immature bird the six subsequent records have all been adults. Unfortunately no record was made of the belly markings of the 1945–1946 birds (these markings are as variable and individual in this species as they are in the common whitefront). It was not possible, therefore, to say whether any of the three which were present in 1946–1947 were those which we had observed in the previous year, and the complete absence of lesser whitefronts during the present winter has prevented us from using the careful drawings made the year before. Each of these individual birds was independent of the other, and by means of their special markings they were quite easily distinguished one from another. Certainly two and possibly all three were males. On the rare occasions when they met while wandering through the flocks they did not appear to recognise each other. They might, in fact, be said to have cut each other dead.

The presence of odd single birds of other species among a flock of wild geese is sufficiently common to warrant some special explanation. It seems probable that in winter the gregarious instinct is more powerful than that which links one member of a species to another. Thus a goose which has gone astray would rather take up with a flock of some other species of goose than remain alone. After a while the odd bird becomes so accustomed to seeing the other members of its flock around that it comes to regard itself as belonging to the species of the flock. In the majority of cases these single birds are young ones of the year. It would seem that young birds go astray from their own flock more frequently than adults. The significance of the fact that the lesser whitefronts were in all cases adults is not yet explained, if indeed any significance exists.

It seems possible that at a given time in the spring the instinct for rejoining its own species often reasserts itself; but this does not always happen. Two of the three lesser whitefronts of 1946–1947 were well-mated with common white-fronted females and there is considerable evidence that wild hybrids regularly occur among various species of geese. As an example, during the same winter a male bean goose and a female whitefront were present at the New Grounds for several weeks in company with a juvenile bird which was quite clearly a hybrid between them. Two other juveniles were present which exhibited hybrid characteristics. Several years previously two hybrids between the barnacle goose and the whitefront appeared at the New Grounds, in company with two pure barnacle geese, one of which may be supposed to have been one of the parents of the hybrids.

In the winter of 1945–1946, two and possibly three blue snow geese made their appearance on the Wexford Slob in the southeast of Ireland. It has never been possible to establish for certain whether these birds were of wild origin or whether they were 'escapees' from captivity, but they kept company with the white-fronted geese wintering in that area which belong, of course, to the Greenland subspecies. In the winter of 1946–1947 one of the blue snow geese was present again on the Slob in company with an immature bird which left little doubt that it was a hybrid *blue snow X white-fronted*. This leads to a fascinating field for conjecture; did the blue goose travel to Greenland in company with the whitefronts and if so does this fact increase the likelihood of its wild origin in Northern Canada? Or did the whitefront parent of the hybrid stay behind to mate somewhere in Ireland with a more-sedentary escaped blue goose which could have come from Whipsnade or from Mr. Bengt Berg's collection in Sweden?

However, ample evidence exists of hybridisation in the wild state and we may wonder what compensating force prevents the coalescence of these nearly related species. It may be that hybrid eggs are less likely to hatch, that hybrid young are less likely to survive or that, if they do survive, their fertility is likely to be less high. In any event the possibility of hybridisation between the common and lesser white-fronted goose as a result of these aberrant migrations cannot be discounted and a doubtful bird sent from the New Grounds, where it was shot in 1936 by Captain R. G. Berkeley, to the British Museum of Natural History, may well be such a hybrid. It was sent because of its noticeable yellow eye ring, but by its measurements it was placed in a drawer among common whitefronts. When we found it there last year we had no doubt, until we came to measure it, that it was a typical lesser whitefront, for so it seemed in every characteristic, and yet the measurements are all outside the range of *Anser erythropus*.

It remains to be seen whether any lesser whitefronts will return with the winter flocks to the New Grounds in December of 1948 and whether, if they do, we shall be able to recognise them as our friends of previous winters. It also remains to be seen whether any of the ringed common whitefronts or the single pinkfoot are recovered from foreign lands or whether they in their turn will come back to their traditional winter home. Meanwhile we shall be getting ready with our rocket nets to catch many of them next winter and to send them away with their identifying rings so that we may learn more about the migrations and the movements and the length of life of the most fascinating and romantic of all our winter birds.

THE SEVERN
WILDFOWL TRUST

First booklet (1948)

In nearly all parts of the world, wildfowl—ducks and geese—are declining in numbers. The kind of wild country which they need is being steadily whittled away by the progress of civilisation. If they are to survive, certain steps will have to be taken, and in order to make sure that these steps are the most helpful ones, much research is still needed into the birds habits, life histories and migration routes. For this kind of research, the area known as the New Grounds, on the Severn Estuary, is almost ideally suited, and *The Severn Wildfowl Trust* was therefore formed in November 1946, with the following objectives:

To promote the study of wildfowl and to undertake any activity which, in the opinion of the Council, is calculated to promote knowledge of and interest in wildfowl and in particular to establish and maintain a wildfowl research observatory at the New Grounds on the estuary of the River Severn which will provide facilities for:

1. *A close study of the winter flocks of wild geese and other birds.*

2. *The ringing of wild ducks in the decoy pools and of wild geese on the marshes for the further study of migration.*

3. *The study of a comparative collection of live waterfowl.*

The New Grounds—first so named in 1470—consist of an area of flat alluvial fields reclaimed from the Severn, some four miles long and a mile wide, lying to the south of the river, between it and the Berkeley–Gloucester canal.

These fields are protected from the high spring tides by a seawall, outside of which lies an area of salting known as the Dumbles, which is the principal winter feeding ground for between two and five thousand wild geese.

Along the seawall, four pillboxes were built during the invasion danger of 1940, and these are so situated that they can be entered without disturbing the geese feeding on the Dumbles. In between these pillboxes a number of thatched Observation Huts have been built overlooking the salting, so that wherever the geese may be feeding it is possible to watch them at fairly close range, sometimes at less than ten yards. The thrill of watching wild geese at such close quarters is most easily appreciated by those who have previous experience of their proverbial wariness, but even those who have never seen geese before cannot fail to be stirred by such an intimate view of these magnificent birds. They are mostly white-fronted geese, but a few pinkfeet arrive early in the season, and every species of goose on the British List has been seen at one time or another on this marsh. During the winter of 1946–1947, ten of the thirteen British subspecies of geese were recorded, and on one memorable day in December 1945, no fewer than seven subspecies were seen together, including two specimens of the very rare lesser white-fronted goose—only definitely identified twice previously in this country. Since then others have been recorded there during most winters.

It is possible for numbers of people to observe the wild geese at close range, but it is important that the geese themselves should be totally unaware of them. They have selected these marshes and kept to them chiefly because they have been carefully preserved from disturbance by the owners of Berkeley Castle for centuries past. This is because the Tidal Waters as well as the New Grounds have been, and still are, owned by the Berkeley family. We feel that our increased interest in the geese must on no account be allowed to discourage them from visiting this traditional winter home.

Beyond the Dumbles lies the mile-wide expanse of estuary sand and mud on which the geese and countless other birds roost. Some thousands of ducks spend the winter here and large numbers of waders pass through on migration. This broad estuary lying in the heart of Gloucestershire provides a sort of oasis for cross-country migrants; and a number of interesting birds, such as spoonbill, night heron, Bewick's swan, American wigeon, scoter, goosander, blacktailed godwit, curlew sandpiper, little stint, great and Arctic skua, black tern, Iceland gull, southern cormorant, snowy owl, peregrine and hobby, have been seen there in recent years.

The seawall passes within 300 yards of a group of three cottages, one of which forms the headquarters of the Trust and another houses one of the Wardens.

Between the cottages and the salting is a small spinney containing a decoy pool of about an acre. This decoy, originally completed in 1843, had fallen into disrepair, but it has been put into full working order again, and the annual catch is increasing. Each year more ducks are caught, ringed and released again for the study of their migration routes. A hut on stilts at the edge of the wood giving a view of the pool is available to members and the public.

Parts of some rushy fields adjoining the decoy have been enclosed with a fox-proof fence, and special ponds have been dug to make a home for a collection of live waterfowl. Some 500 swans and geese and ducks, of about 120 species, have been assembled and make up what is probably the most extensive collection in the world. It is of great value both ornithologically as an opportunity for the observation of breeding habits and also educationally as an introduction to the study of waterfowl.

Many of them breed and some of their offspring have been exported to hard currency countries. The birds in the enclosures become astonishingly tame, and it is especially delightful to have a crowd of these beautiful creatures around one's feet, and feeding from one's hand.

Such is the basis of the project. In order to administer it successfully, the Trust needs members and associates, and their subscription—to build and maintain the observation huts, to keep the decoy in working order, to keep up the collection of waterfowl and for many other improvements to the amenities of the New Grounds, including the establishment and maintenance of a Hostel for visiting students.

Membership costs one guinea a year for which there are certain privileges at the New Grounds, and for which you will receive the report of the Trust, copiously illustrated and giving details of the results of experiments, of birds ringed and of birds seen, and details also of birds bred in the collection.

Alternatively for 5 shillings you can be an Associate, which entitles you to visit the New Grounds.

If you agree to pay your subscription or indeed any sum, no matter how large or small, by Deed of Covenant annually for seven years, the Trust is able to reclaim the Income Tax on that sum. For example, a guinea from your taxed income was £1 18s. 2d. before Income Tax at 9 shillings in the pound was deducted. The Trust can recover that 17s. 2d. from the Inland Revenue, thereby nearly doubling the guinea you give. This arrangement is of great benefit to the Trust and we most strongly urge all Members to use it.

You will find forms for the Covenant and for Membership and Associateship and also a Bankers Order Form, at the end of this pamphlet. These should be sent to: *The Manager, The Westminster Bank Ltd., Park Lane Branch, London, W.1.* You will also find a form of Bequest in case you care to benefit the Trust by your Will—a method of assuring the continuity of the Trust for future generations of naturalists and ornithologists.

The Trust has gained a firm place in the sphere of scientific research, field study and education, but the initial expenditure has been heavy and further subscriptions, donations and legacies will be most welcome. We need your active interest and your financial support. We hope you think our project is worthwhile, and we hope you will help us.

For the Council, The Severn Wildfowl Trust

CATCHING WILD GEESE

Country Life (2 April 1948)

The world's stock of migratory waterfowl is decreasing at a rate which is in some cases alarming. Steps are urgently needed to help ducks and geese in their struggle for existence against the spread of civilisation. But the problem is to know where and when and how to give this help. To do this one must know more about the birds, and one of the ways of learning about them (of discovering their average length of life, their migration routes and the details of their local movements) is by ringing.

The marking of birds by means of a small aluminium ring, with a number on it and an address to which the finder is asked to send details of its recovery, has already produced very interesting results, but more information is still required, particularly about those birds which have not been ringed in any great quantity.

The Severn Wildfowl Trust, in cooperation with the International Wildfowl Inquiry Committee, has for two seasons been ringing ducks caught in its own decoy pool beside the Severn Estuary. It has recently turned its attention to the ringing of the winter flocks of migratory wild geese, a task which has never before been successfully undertaken in this country. The attempts, apart from the scientific interest of their object, have proved a most entertaining and exciting, if expensive, sporting venture, for the wild geese must be caught in nets, and the development of these engines calls for a high degree of invention and ingenuity.

We have never been able to settle who thought of it first. We had tried with only moderate success to catch geese with a net propelled by springs. An account of it appeared in *Country Life* of 4 February and 27 May 1933. But we had found that the springs did not propel the net far enough. We thought that rockets would propel it farther. And so, on a sunny summer day we carried out our first tests and found that a net could be thrown to cover an area 25 yards square. We believed that if the net were carefully furled in a suitable place frequented by the geese, and if the rockets were fired electrically with a line of flex leading to a hide, we should have some chance of success.

The first opportunity to try the net in practice came many months later, when the winter flocks of white-fronted geese were assembled on the Severn Estuary. At the beginning of 1948 the flocks were rather smaller than usual; and when the attempt came to be made, only about 1,300 geese were feeding in the area, most of them in the wheat fields lying to the east and the northeast of the saltings (known as the Dumbles) which are their more usual feeding ground.

On the morning before the attempt, we sat on top of a straw stack and watched the flight of the geese in from the estuary. They went in to a group of fields of not more than fifteen acres each, and we felt that there was a good chance for the net if it were set in one of these. During the afternoon this net, which had repeatedly been dyed in order to get it the right colour to match a field of young wheat, was thrown a couple of times experimentally. On each occasion a very indifferent throw resulted, as the meshes were caught by the stalks and stems of the coarse grass in which we had set it. Whereas in the summer, the little one-pound rockets had pulled it over the full 25 yards, on neither of these throws was more than ten yards of the centre of the net carried over, and only half the area was covered.

Later in the afternoon I made a reconnaissance of the feeding grounds with Keith Shackleton, the bird painter. The geese were no longer to be found in the three small fields into which they had flown at dawn. We came upon them at last around the edges of a 100-acre field about a mile farther on. Here, however, the wheat in the centre of the field had been grazed almost bare, and the geese had congregated in a thick swathe along two edges of the field. One of these edges was formed by a barbed wire fence and the other by a shallow flash of water, no more than a few yards wide. Along the top of the slope leading up from the flash, the geese were sitting most thickly, indeed, neither of us could remember having seen whitefronts more tightly packed.

We flushed them gently from the field, and walked over to examine the area and select the most suitable spot on which to set the net in the darkness before the morrow's dawn. In view of the northeast wind, we thought that it should lie along the drills of the wheat at the edge of the field where the shoots were longer because the geese had not grazed there so much. Then we explored the nearest available cover for concealing the netters. This seemed to be an old disused sea wall some hundred yards away across the flash and along the barbed wire fence. All this decided, we returned in the dusk feeling that our chances were reasonable good.

That night, great preparations were made. Mr. Schermuly, who makes the rockets we were using and who had come to help us at our first attempt, overhauled his wiring; Mr. Harris, a *Country Life* staff photographer, checked a telephoto lens; and the rest of us made lists of the objects which must, on no account, be forgotten on the morrow: the net, the rockets, the cartridges, the battery, a pressure hurricane lamp and torches for setting the net in the dark, rings for ringing the geese, sacks for setting up on sticks in the small fields in which we did not want the geese to alight, the portable hide (big enough to conceal half a dozen of us on the old seawall), pliers for crimping on the rings, a pencil and notebook for writing down their numbers, spare string, sandwiches and a spade.

We rose at four and set off in two parties, one by car with the heavy gear to go round to a bridge which was less than half a mile from the selected spot. The other party was to walk the mile and a half, planting the scare geese in the small fields on the way. I was not very familiar with the exact route from the bridge to our part of the 100-acre field, so with our various hurricane lamps and torches we started on the right bearing by the stars. This led us across a number of awkward ditches, but they were successfully negotiated and soon after 5.15 a.m., we joined the other party on the old seawall, and went out together, all seven of us, like a party of smugglers or bodysnatchers, across the flash at its lowest crossable point, and down the edge of the wheat to the corner of the fence. There we laid out all the equipment we had brought in a small heap so that nothing should be overlooked and left to frighten the geese when daylight came.

The patch we had chosen for the net was about ten yards from the fence, and, like the rest of the field, it was covered with small lumps of clay which were frozen solid. We found as we laid the new net that the meshes caught frequently on these little lumps and were held firm and immovable. The chances that the net could fly out freely, however carefully we folded it, seemed very small. But having got up at four and being on the spot, we felt that the best we could do was to lay it carefully and hope for the best. So we laid it carefully, seven of us in a row, with the hurricane lamp hanging on the handle of the nice little ferreting spade.

As soon as the net had been furled the party divided: some went off to fetch the portable hide which had been left beside the car, some stayed behind to set out the rockets and lay the firing wires. It was getting late. Already the eastern sky was bright and we knew that we had a bare twenty minutes until the arrival of the geese. We stretched out the wire and then our rocket expert decided that he must fire a couple of cartridges in order to make sure that the wiring was correct. The powder was removed from the cartridges and they were set up in the pistols. Then we set off with the battery, round the flash, to the end of the remote control. We were in a hurry and we turned to cross the water too soon. I had high waders and could cross anywhere, but my companion stumbled and filled one boot. We hustled to the end of the flex and found that it would not go into the terminal on the battery unless the insulation were pared away, and in trying to do this Schermuly cut the ball of his thumb badly.

But eventually the job was done, the contact was made, and two little sparks of light flashed at each end of the net. The circuit was correct, all that remained was to set up the rockets in place of the trial cartridges. Back we rushed round the end of the flash. The rockets were slid into their pistols, the head string of the net was attached. Grass was strewn over the heads of the rockets, and plucked wheat shoots were strewn over the grass. Twenty yards ahead of the net, five yards less than the net should, in theory, be able to throw. I made two tiny cairns of lumps of frozen clay, one opposite each end of the net. These were to be the markers, to show when the geese were within the catching area. With a last glance at the net, which looked painfully visible even in that early morning light, we collected together the spare equipment and started back once more round the head of the flash. As we walked along it we could hear the first geese coming and I extinguished the hurricane lamp. The geese were heading for the small fields and it was still almost too dark for them to see the sacks on their sticks. When we reached the old seawall we found that the rest of the party had erected the portable hide. The flex, however, had not been laid the full distance and a roll of it still lay twenty yards down a bank along the barbed wire fence. At this critical stage a large skein of geese came up to the field and looked as if they would settle. But fortunately they swept back, to circle yet again over the small fields, and while they did so I rushed out and collected the coil of flex, spreading it as I returned. It reached the portable hide with exactly two feet to spare and was laid under one corner to the battery. Meanwhile we tried to break the top-line of the hide with tufts of grass.

Two minutes later about 300 geese came straight for the 100-acre field, and settled in the middle of it. This was excellent, we thought for they were directly downwind of our net and seemed likely in a few hours to feed up to it. Meanwhile more skeins came slipping in over the belt of trees in the background. They came with great confidence, flying low and setting their wings as soon as they reached the edge of the field. They came in an almost unbroken stream. By the time that the sun rose, oval and orange red, behind us, there were over a thousand geese feeding in a tight pack in front. Then came a startling development. A family party of geese rose from the great crowd and flew low towards the corner of the field—our corner. They settled about twenty yards in front of the net. Soon they were followed by others, until a regular flight began. Bunch after bunch swept in and pitched among the ever thickening crowd in front of our net. So far everything had gone unbelievably right. For the next hour we lay patiently in the hide as the phalanx of geese advanced into the catching area. They were ten yards from the little clay cairns—five yards—two yards—passing between them, and then the cairns were swallowed up in the milling crowd of geese which advanced still closer to the net. Was all in readiness? The wireless battery, the leads—*the leads, where were they?* They were nowhere to be seen. Two feet of the end of the flex had been pulled under the edge of the hide in that hurried last minute, but they were not there now. We peered out through the observation slit in the front of the hide. The black shiny flex led towards us, but just outside the hide it turned off at right angles. While we had been camouflaging the hide someone had kicked away the end of the lead, it was outside the hide, on the same side of it as the geese. What were we to do? Slowly and dexterously we lifted a corner of the hide and reached out towards the lead. My fingers closed over grass stems, over a bramble, but not over the missing flex. The others squinted down through the observation slit. 'Another four inches and you'll do it.' With an effort I reached the flex and pulled it into the hide—and the geese had not seen me. The crisis was over, and the birds were another five yards closer to the net.

In the forefront of their advance, I noticed a pinkfoot, no doubt one of the three young birds which we had observed scattered among the whitefronts all through the winter.

Now was the critical time. At what distance would the geese first see and keep away from the net? Would they turn about and walk quickly away from it once they had detected its presence? We watched anxiously. The flock had been advancing in the usual manner of wild geese. The front line had been feeding steadily forward and bulging suddenly where an odd bird or a family party had been chased forward by a quarrelsome gander in the rear. At length there came a time when the fugitive birds would no longer run forward. If pursued they turned and threaded their way back through the flock. They would come no nearer to the net than about four yards. The crowd in the catching area could not get any thicker. It had reached saturation point. Now was the critical moment. Harris got ready with his camera and Schermuly with the ends of his flex.

'All right, let her go!' The circuit was made and the rockets fired, and simultaneously the whole flock of 1,300 geese rose into the air with a combined roar of wings and of voices. We all jumped up to watch. As the cloud of birds rose we could see that a small patch of flapping geese remained on the wheat field. We had made a catch. We climbed through the barbed wire fence and set off to run towards the net. I think the geese were more alarmed by the sudden appearance of seven people careering across the field in scattered formation than they were by the discharge of the rockets themselves (and indeed on any future occasion we have planned to remain hidden until the uncaught birds are well clear).

As soon as I came to the net, I made a quick count—32 geese. We had succeeded. We had made the first great catch of geese for ringing. It was a satisfying moment. Then began the laborious task of extricating the birds from the net. Almost before we had started, however, one bird extricated itself and flew off. But we lost no more. The plan was to ring the birds first and then extricate them afterwards. About the third bird at my end of the net turned out to be the pinkfoot which we had seen advancing into the catching area. So the total was twenty whitefronts and one pinkfoot. Some of the geese were released one by one, but more often they were released in couples, which we thought to be the better way, as the two then flew off together. Fairly soon it became apparent that many of them could not be extricated without cutting some of the meshes of the net, and this we proceeded to do. It was astonishing to what extent the birds had become ravelled in so short a time. It was also astonishing how docile and resigned they seemed to be, and how little they struggled while being disentangled. One old gander was full of fight and continuously pecked my knee while I was extricating his neighbour and finally him. We ringed several young birds, including a family of five with their parents, but we made an error in not recording the belly markings of the adult birds we ringed. In this way it would have been possible to know the ring numbers had we seen the birds later, and to identify each without the necessity of recapturing it, for the whitefronts' black bars are of different pattern in each individual adult.

We had pulled the net at 8.40 a.m., and it was after half past nine by the time we had finished. As soon as the work was completed we made a careful survey of the way in which the net had thrown. As on the previous evening, the rocket corner had gone over much farther than the centre. In the middle, however, more than half of its 25-yard stretch still remained neatly furled as we had laid it before dawn. Fourteen yards of net still lay in a heap and only eleven yards had gone forward to catch our geese. Had the throw been perfect at least twice that number would surely have been caught. But another snag had appeared. All the geese appeared to have been caught in the first few yards of the net, and those in the centre seemed to have pushed the net back. It seems that however free one may become of grass stems, thistles, and lumps of frozen clay, the throw may yet be spoiled by one or more of the quarry.

As we walked back to the hide some of the geese were returning to the fields, and one skein circled low over the hundred acre. They did not settle, but it was evident that they had not been disastrously frightened by the rockets.

We returned home greatly elated with our success which, in spite of the net's bad throw, was much greater than any of us, in our heart of hearts, had been expecting. At about one o'clock the geese were feeding on the Dumbles, and we went to look them over. A new game had been discovered—hunting the rings—and already at the first glance we were able to pick up, among the flocks, four of the birds we had had in our hands only a few hours before. One of the ganders was still pecking at his ring, which had not yet become familiar to him. Since that day it has been possible on occasions to find one or two of those ringed, with the numbered and addressed aluminium ring on their right leg shining brightly in the sun.

On one occasion the geese were so close to one of the Trust's observation huts, that by focusing the binoculars as near as possible I was able to read numbers on the ring quite clearly. 12804...and then a lump of snow adhering to the ring obscured the last and most important of the six figures.

That is the story of our first attempt with the rocket net. Good luck was largely the cause of its success—the sort of good luck which we have come to understand and appreciate after three recent days of complete failure, in which the geese have shown themselves, as usual, complete masters of the situation.

THE SEVERN WILDFOWL TRUST

RSPB Members' Magazine (Winter 1947–1948)

The waterfowl population of Europe is declining at a slow but constant rate for various reasons, but chiefly because our civilisation is advancing into all the wild places in which they live. If we are to stop this decline and save the waterfowl we must do two things: we must obtain more and more information about their habits and migration routes, so as to know where and when they need protection most, and we must secure some places free from disturbance for them.

Many people have long realised this and the International Wildfowl Enquiry Committee was set up some years before the war to study these problems.

Since the war, a Research Station has been established which works in cooperation with the International Committee, and which is called the Severn Wildfowl Trust. It was formed in December 1946, with three aims: scientific, educational and conservational. It was called the *Severn Wildfowl Trust* because it has established its headquarters at Slimbridge, in Gloucestershire, on the Severn Estuary.

There, a wood with a decoy pool and some twenty acres of land around it have been rented from the Berkeley Estate, together with various rights and keepering duties over some 1,500 acres of flat fields and saltmarshes where for centuries great flocks of geese have wintered.

The saltmarshes are bounded by a seawall and, as ancient manorial rights over the foreshore are vested in the Berkeley family, the privacy of the geese is well secured. At one time or another all the species of geese on the British list have been observed on this marsh, including the lesser white-fronted goose, which occasionally deviates on to the migration route of the common whitefronts, whose three or four thousand make up the principal winter flocks. The seawall provides ideal cover from behind which to observe these flocks, and the Trust has built small huts along it, specially designed to make scientific observation as convenient as possible and as unobtrusive. The geese often come within four or five yards of the huts.

But at the New Grounds (as this area has been called since the first reclamations in the 15th century) are not only excellent conditions for watching wild geese. There is also an old duck decoy pool, one of those ancient devices by which wild ducks are lured into a curved net-covered pipe or ditch by a small dog, which they follow out of bravado and curiosity. These carefully constructed ponds were originally invented in 16th-century Holland. One of the first to be established in England was built in St. James's Park by Charles II, and at one time there were more than 200 of them in England. Only nine are now in working order here, although there are still 120 working in Holland. These decoys are taking a larger toll of ducks each year than the stocks can support. Many of them catch more than 5,000 in a season, and the Dutch total is estimated at an annual 400,000.

Although, for market purposes, decoys are a grave danger to the wildfowl populations, the intriguing art of decoying can usefully be preserved for more constructive ends. The study of migration routes depends on the ringing of large numbers of birds, and this can be undertaken very successfully in a duck decoy. Such is the purpose of the Trust's decoy at the New Grounds. It is less than an acre in size, and it is well placed to attract some of the thousands of ducks which pass along the Severn Estuary on migration. It was constructed in 1843 and had fallen into disuse so that of the original four pipes, only two were in working condition even after some renovations in 1937. The Trust has repaired the two old pipes and constructed a new one, introduced decoy ducks, and built observation huts. Good catches were made in the 19th century, and already this season the Trust has caught six species of ducks: mallard, wigeon, teal, pintail, shoveler and garganey—as well as an occasional moorhen and one wood pigeon. These are ringed as part of the scheme organised by the Wildfowl Enquiry Committee and freed again. Frequently they go straight back to the decoy pond, quite undisturbed by their adventures in the tunnel net, and may be seen from the observation huts unconcernedly preening and even examining their newly acquired ring.

Around the decoy spinney are low-lying marshy fields, with small streams (locally called 'rhines') running through them. The Trust has had ponds and ditches dug in these fields and has enclosed them with fox-proof—and duck-proof— netting. Here has been established what is probably the finest comparative collection of waterfowl in the world. Sixty-five species of swans, geese and ducks are now represented, and only three of the world's species of wild geese are still lacking.

This season, although all the birds were newly established, young of more than a dozen species were reared, and next year, when the birds are more settled, we hope to do far better. Commissariat problems are, of course, considerable: three baby mergansers ate 600 sticklebacks daily as soon as they were hatched, and others needed elvers and maggots and puppy biscuits.

These birds, most of them completely tame, have attracted many visitors this summer, and we think that by interesting the

public in individual birds we shall also help to bring the whole
problem of bird preservation to its notice. These educational
intentions are also reflected in the special membership terms
for schools and training colleges. Eventually, when building
is again possible, we hope to provide some kind of hostel for
ornithologists and students to stay in; at present we can only
offer camping sites and cold water.

All this has, of course, cost a great deal of money, and
alongside the developments at the New Grounds, the Trust has
conducted a campaign for securing members. A booklet was
designed and sent out to people likely to be interested in the
scheme, and their response has been good, but, of course, we
need more funds, and the Council is appealing for £5,000. We
feel we have a great deal to offer beyond the mere virtue of our
aims. The facilities for watching wild geese are unique and,
to people knowing the usual wildness of these birds, it seems
almost uncanny to be able to sit in a comfortable little hut and
watch them feeding and living their lives only a few yards away.

There is also great excitement to be had in trying to lure a
party of wigeon or a spring of teal into one of the decoy pipes,
and a great sense of triumph when they are finally secured and
ringed and released.

To many people the tame collection is more immediately
attractive. These birds, some of them incredibly beautiful,
flying across a rushy field to feed at one's feet, and out of one's
hand, is a great delight—and a revelation.

This is a brief review of the history of the Trust in its first
year. It needs support, and the Secretary, whose address is
8 Edwardes Square, London, W.8., will be delighted to send
further information.

THE MYSTERY OF MIGRATION

From *Uncle Mac's Children's Hour Book*
(Sampson Low, Marston & Co, 1949)

I wonder if you have ever seen and heard a flock of wild geese?
In most parts of the world you will occasionally see them if you
keep a look out, and they fly in a sort of V formation, which
is called a 'skein'. They are not the only birds to fly in this
way; gulls often do, and ducks and also cormorants. In parts of
the world where they exist, pelicans sometimes do—and very
strange they look doing it. But if you have seen and heard the
geese passing over on their migration flights, or on their daily
flights to and from their feeding grounds, I do not suppose
you will easily forget it. They look so fine and they sound so
very wild and romantic. They fly in V formation because its
the most logical way of flying in order to avoid collisions. If the
birds followed directly behind one another they would fly in
disturbed air. If they flew in line abreast—wing-tip to wing-
tip—if one altered course very slightly, it would hit the next.
'Arrowhead' is a compact and tidy formation which avoids

these difficulties, and the birds use it for just the same reasons as airmen do.

The wild geese come to this country in winter from the Arctic where they breed. Every spring they fly back again to the bare tundras of the far north, and every autumn they return with their families to the same marshes which they have frequented for generations. They make these journeys with extraordinary regularity within two or three days of the same date each year. What makes them do it? Well, the scientists have been trying to discover for some time and they *think* they have just found the answer.

The main *reason*, indeed the main reason behind migration in nearly all birds and animals, is food. The birds which eat insects here in summer, swallows and martins, warblers and so on, have to go south to the Mediterranean in winter, otherwise they would starve. Insects are hard to find in our countryside in cold weather. The tundras of the Arctic, with their berries and grass and rushes are covered with snow in winter, and so the geese would starve if they did not come down to warmer places. But how do they know to come on the very same days? Why is it that the pink-footed geese, for example, arrive in the fourth week of September so regularly? The scientists believe that the length of the daylight is what tells the birds when to start. As the days get shorter an urge develops in the birds to fly south. They just cannot help it. They just must fly south. And in the spring when the days grow longer the birds just must fly north. The scientists proved this by catching some crows in America in the autumn when they were flying south. They then illuminated the cage with electric light and kept the light on a little longer each day, and after a short while they released the crow, who immediately started to fly north supposing it to be spring, although it was really still November and getting colder all the time! Of course, when they came to the snowline and realised that it wasn't spring at all, they had to turn back south again. That was how the scientists showed that it was *light* and not *temperature* which actually persuaded the birds to set off so regularly for their migration flight.

In order to learn what routes the birds take on these long flights, a scheme has been worked out for 'ringing'. If a bird can be caught alive a little aluminium ring is put on its leg. This ring, which is extremely light and not a bit harmful, has a number and an address on it. After if has been ringed, the bird is released and continues on its natural way. If, in due course, it is recovered, whoever finds it sends a postcard or letter to the address on the ring, giving the number on the ring and the date it was recovered. In Britain all the ringing is organised through a scheme promoted by the British Trust for Ornithology, and the address on all rings is the British Museum of Natural History, London. Other countries use their own organisation's addresses, so if you find one, or hear of one being found, make sure that the details are sent either to the address on it, or, if in doubt, to the British Museum of Natural History: or even, if you like, to me.

There are various ways in which the rings may be recovered. The commonest is the sad one that the bird has been shot or killed, but quite a number are found at other ringing stations, where the number on the ring is recorded, and a fresh one is put on if the old one is worn, and then the bird is released and sent on its way again. These records are of particular use as they may show three or more points on the migration route of one individual bird, which is obviously much more instructive than only two, the first where it was ringed originally, and the last where it was killed. Incidentally the rings also establish the ages of individual birds.

So we want more and more people to establish these ringing stations in various parts of the country. The more there are, the more interesting and frequent will be the results obtained by those already in existence. Down on the estuary of the Severn, for example, the Severn Wildfowl Trust is using an ancient duck decoy for ringing wild ducks. I am actively concerned in this new Trust. Duck decoys are specially made ponds in which ducks are persuaded to follow a small dog up a curved net-covered ditch called a 'pipe'. The birds follow the dog in order to mob it, but suddenly the decoy man shows himself behind them, cutting off their retreat to the pond. The ducks have no choice but to go forward towards the closed end of the pipe where they are caught. Decoys were invented in Holland before 1600, and the idea was brought to this country soon after that date. They were, and still are, used for catching ducks for market, but more and more are being taken over and turned into ringing stations. Of the nine still working in England, four are being used for ringing.

That is the way the scientists are learning where the migratory birds go. But they still do not know *how* they find their way. How, for example, the swallows can come back to the very same barn where they nested the year before. How the petrels and shearwaters and auks, birds of the open ocean, find their way back to the small islands on which they nest. How the wild geese return to the same meadows each winter. The great shearwater can be seen in large numbers in the North Atlantic through the summer. The only known breeding place of these birds is on the tiny island of Tristan da Cunha, thousands of miles away in the South Atlantic. Yet in some way or another the shearwaters find their way back to this island to nest, in the southern summer, which, of course, is our winter. Another kind of shearwater, the Manx shearwater, breeds on certain islands on the west coast of Britain. One was taken from its nest in Wales and sent by air to Italy where it was set free in the Adriatic Sea. Ten days later it was back at the nest on Skokholm Island off the coast of Pembrokeshire! Both male and female shearwaters incubate their single egg and in this case the male sat all the time that his mate was away. Still no one knows how that shearwater found her way back, nor yet for certain by what route. Did she come overland, over the Alps and across Europe, or did she travel round by the Straits of Gibraltar ? Shearwaters do not normally fly overland, but Mr. Ronald Lockley, who made the experiment, thinks that she probably flew over the Italian mountains, along the coast of the Gulf of Lyons and then across the neck of the Spanish peninsula to the Bay of Biscay and so home. Take a look at an atlas and see what this means.

There seems no doubt that her method of finding her way is the same as that used by homing pigeons. Of course, much more is known about pigeons in this respect than about other birds, because racing-pigeon owners have studied it very carefully: but in spite of that they don't know how it is done. It is possible to examine some of the more significant facts; and go on searching for the explanation. We know that pigeons need training, and that trial flights, especially in the same direction from home, increase the chances of a successful long flight. We know that pigeons find it more difficult in fog, but we also know that little auks find their way back to breeding islands off the coast of Labrador which are almost continually shrouded in fog during much of the breeding season. So it cannot be done *entirely* by the sense of sight.

A curious thing about the arrival of homing pigeons is that sometimes, even in clear weather, they fly over their loft and on, almost out of sight, then turn round and come back again. It makes it seem almost as if some other mechanism existed which was less acute than their sight, only felt by the bird after the homing point had been passed.

It is said that pigeons are troubled by wireless transmissions, and that they take longer to orientate themselves when released in the near neighbourhood of a high-powered transmitter. This might indicate that some special, as yet undiscovered waves were involved in the direction finding. But the scientists do not accept this possibility because they say that the whole range of wavelengths has now been explored, and that there are no 'new' rays or waves to find.

There has long been a school of thought which believes that the birds may be sensitive to the earth's magnetic field. But pigeons with little magnets on their backs have found their way home as quickly as those without, and such magnets so close to the pigeon would completely swamp the earth's magnetism.

It really all is still a mystery, and we can call it a homing 'instinct', which is just another way of saying that we do not know how it works. Birds almost certainly use the homing mechanism when they are migrating, but the instinct occurs in birds, and in mammals too, which do not normally migrate. There are many authentic stories of dogs and cats which have been taken long journeys by train and returned home on foot. One dog covered over 2,000 miles, right across North America. There is even a record of a hare which returned six hundred miles across Europe after it had been moved from Southern Hungary to a point near Berlin. So the homing instinct is not confined only to birds. The remains of it may even exist in human beings, and may account for the people who have what we call a 'bump of locality'.

Whatever the instinct is, it sometimes fails. Odd birds often get lost and settle on ships at sea for a rest. Sometimes whole flocks of land birds get lost in this way and fall exhausted into the waves and are drowned. But the majority find their way safely across the thousands of miles which they travel each year. The swallows come back in the spring to their own barns, the swifts to their church towers, the martins to their mud nests under the eaves, the chiffchaffs and the willow wrens to their own grassy bank, the reed warblers to their own patch of reeds.

Yes, the birds find their way home, but the mystery of how they do it remains unsolved: one of the most exciting problems of Natural History. I think about it especially when I see the little skeins of wild geese arriving on their chosen marshes in the autumn, and when I watch them set off again in the spring towards the barren tundras of the North.

PETER SCOTT TELLS
HIS OWN STORY

Ladies' Journal (September 1950)

I have always been in favour of balloons—full-sized proper balloons, preferably the kind in which you make an ascent. I have never been up in a balloon, but even captive ones have always been satisfying to me, perhaps because one of my earliest memories concerns one. I can remember being driven into London, with my mother holding on to the seat of my pants while I leant over the back of the motor car to gaze at one of the great sausages riding above the treetops.

My lifelong enjoyment of natural history had its origins in these early days, I think, because I can't remember a time when I wasn't interested in it. I was sent away from London's Zeppelin raids to a little coastguard cottage at Sandwich, and there I caught lizards and newts and frogs and watched birds, mostly waders. But one fateful day I saw a flock of wild geese and they have held an especial fascination for me from that day to this. I drew them all too.

It had been my father's wish that I should be brought up with an interest in natural history: and as luck would have it I was quite keen on the idea myself. My schools were helpful about it, too. Looking back, it seems to me that I spent most of my school days hunting for birds, catching rabbits, finding caterpillars and fishing—setting out with a fishing rod stock down my trouser leg and the limp which was supposed to have got me off playing games.

In the holidays I learned to sail on the Norfolk Broads—and the sailing and the place have both remained my friends ever since. The sailing I learned was precision sailing in small boats, and that to me is still the most exciting kind of sailing—in boats that plane, that get up on top of the water and scud along like speed boats—the sort of boats where the helmsman's touch on the tiller is the deciding factor in a race.

At Cambridge I was part-scientist, part-painter, for I changed sides at half time, and there were other new things like roof-climbing and the pursuit of wildfowl down on the mudflats of the Wash, which involved an escape over the college walls in the early hours, in order to be hidden in the creeks by dawn. This was my first acquaintance with the Wash, where, much later on, I lived in an old lighthouse. The best thing about Cambridge for me was to spend three years living in the middle of the supremely beautiful architecture of Trinity College.

After Cambridge came study at the Academy School of Art in Munich, and a Wagner period—with opera nearly every night at a shilling a time on a special student card, and weekends in the Bavarian Alps fishing for trout and eating wild strawberries—a combination of activities which led me back to Bavaria for many years after I had said goodbye to the Academy. Some say it is a waste of time to send a boy to a foreign university unless he means to specialise in languages. I don't agree about this, for travelling, especially in formative years, turns all of us into internationalists. And internationalists are a good thing in a world too full of nationalist prejudices.

From Munich I came home to work at the Royal Academy School in London; but time still had to be made for watching birds as well as learning how to paint. The two things seemed to go happily hand in hand, and they still do. Very often I think of the sheer good luck of it—of being able to make my job the thing which I most enjoy doing. At the moment this involves combining about four different jobs which have to be sandwiched in between my various wanderings to the Canadian Arctic, or to Lapland, or just to the wilder parts of Britain. Bread and butter comes to the table from pictures of birds and portraits of people and from books and broadcasts.

The war, of course, made for me, as for most people, a complete break when it began. I was in the RNVR. I remember that I was in a fever of anxiety lest hostilities should be over before I could get to sea, but there was plenty of war left when I joined the destroyer HMS *Broke*, and served in her in the North Atlantic for two years. Later, I was given command of a flotilla of steam gunboats which were mainly occupied in night fighting against heavily-escorted supply ships in the English Channel. By the time the invasion of Normandy came along I had turned into a different kind of animal—a staff officer ashore, but still with the Coastal Forces, better known as the Little Ships, of which my steam gunboat flotilla formed a part.

I did not go back to my lighthouse after the war. I was looking for a place to create a research station for the study of wildfowl, and the lighthouse didn't fill all the requirements. But in 1947 I found the perfect place—at Slimbridge, beside the Severn saltings, where great flocks of wild geese come every winter. The remains of a farm cottage (now converted to my permanent home), an ancient duck decoy just behind the sea wall, and some marshy fields and ditches which could be enclosed to make a home for a collection of live waterfowl—these were the things which convinced me that I had found my new home. Today, as the Severn Wildfowl Trust, we have built on our twenty acres a unique collection consisting of 119 different kinds of ducks and geese and swans from all over the world, as well as a model outfit of pens, ponds and observation posts for watching the wild geese. During last year, more than 10,000 people came to see the place, the birds and the work we are doing there. If only one per cent of those visitors went away with their interest kindled, I feel that we are offering something worthwhile to the community.

'And what,' people sometimes ask, 'is the real attraction of birdwatching? Why does it collect so many followers?' Well, for me its charm is that it's difficult, it's out of doors, it requires patience and an enquiring mind, and the objects of the study are not only interesting but beautiful. Having found something which commends itself to me for so many reasons, I'm afraid I follow it with what most of my friends regard as a disproportionate singleness of purpose, and those less charitable call a one track mind.

But I believe strongly that the pursuit of truth is a worthy aim: that it is worth finding things out for the sake of it. In short, I think that *pure* science is more important than *applied* science. It seems to me that human progress is only possible if the first consideration of the scientist is the advancement of knowledge. The application of that knowledge to the material requirements of man is by comparison a pedestrian affair, and much worse than that when more than half of it is devoted to destruction.

At Cambridge I had spent half my scholastic time being trained as a scientist and the other half as an artist. And still today I am half the one and half the other and, no doubt for that reason, not very good at either. But the life suits me well enough, and living in the country, in the atmosphere of the marshes and the birds, is surprisingly exciting and adventurous—if that is how one looks at life. As a result of lecturing and broadcasting, a good many letters come my way from boys and girls who seem to regard me as an authority on how to live an adventurous life. I can only say that my life has seemed adventurous to me because that's the way I like it. I try to exploit the contrasts in life, I look for things to be exciting and fun and interesting, and then I find that they are. It's an attitude of mind and you don't need to hit the headlines or go to Timbuktu in order to have an adventurous life.

A few weeks ago we found adventure on canals and rivers of the Midlands in a converted narrow boat. The object was a water-borne lecture tour, combined with an opportunity to write without telephone interruption or the guilty stultification of long-unanswered correspondence. The result was a month of exciting travel in which we covered 450 miles—from Gloucestershire up as far as Southport and Liverpool and back again. We went through 273 locks (working them ourselves), crossed the Mersey estuary, a fifteen-mile passage among the washes of steamers and tugs (the first converted narrow boat to make the crossing) and got stuck in the famous Harecastle Tunnel in the Potteries. The tunnel is nearly two miles long and our boat became wedged about the middle rather like a cork in a bottleneck. We couldn't decide whether to push it in or pull it out. After more than six hours of struggle, loading bricks from the towpath, pushing, pulling, jerking, we finally got her through, and emerged, completely black, in a snowstorm.

I believe there are great possibilities on our inland waterways for holidays afloat—possibilities which have so far scarcely been contemplated; for there are 2,000 miles of navigable canals and rivers leading from the centres of population right into the heart of some of our loveliest country.

Many people ask me what are the possibilities for themselves or their children in the field of Natural History—what openings and opportunities for a career. The answer is that there are sadly few. A good many of these enquiries come from people who cannot fit into other spheres of life, and in many cases would fit no better as naturalists; it must not be supposed that there is a future in Natural History for those who come to it as a last resort when all else has failed. But I could wish that the prospects were better than they are for those with ability and a special flair for Natural History—those who are ready to work hard for a degree in the subject and want to follow it above all others as their career. The prospects are better than they were, with the recent establishment of the Nature Conservancy and the greatly increased interest in wildlife, but they could be better still. I would like to improve those prospects; to create more opportunities for work in this field. I would like more people to be able to get as much pleasure from the study of Nature as I have and to enjoy their lives as much as I am enjoying mine.

THE MYSTERIOUS
SENSE OF DIRECTION

The London Mystery Magazine
(Volume 1, Number 1, 1950)

A pigeon is put into a basket and sent away by train. A hundred
miles from its home loft it is released, and three hours later
it is home again. A swallow is caught at its nest and a tiny
aluminium ring attached to its leg; in the autumn it flies
southward to Africa and returns in the Spring to the very same
nest in the very same barn, and is recognised by the number on
the ring. A Manx shearwater taken from its nesting burrow on
the Welsh island of Skokholm and released at Venice is back
in its burrow in ten days. A dog or a cat taken by train to the
seaside disappears, but is found again on the doorstep at home
when the holiday is over.

How can these creatures find their way? How do they know
in which direction to set off? How did Anabel return so surely
to the lighthouse? Anabel was a young wild pink-footed goose

who spent a winter in those far-off days between the wars, staying voluntarily with some tame pink-footed geese which lived in the enclosure round my lighthouse home on the Wash. It was in May that the migratory instinct finally overcame the instinct which directed her to stay with the little flock of tame pinioned ones, and she disappeared. Greenland, Spitsbergen, and Iceland are the breeding grounds of the pinkfeet, and Anabel's summer must have been spent in one or other of these northern countries.

I shall not easily forget the thrill on that October morning four months and twenty-four days later when I heard her voice high in the sky, and watched her circle and settle and come up to my feet to be fed. I marvelled then, as I have marvelled many times since, at the strange power which brought Anabel back so unerringly to the home which she had found a year before.

In the history of scientific discovery, certain mysteries and unexplained happenings have always made a special appeal to the imagination of mankind. In the field of Natural History, orientation is perhaps the most fascinating mystery still unsolved. So far, in spite of a recent and at first sight attractive theory, science has not been able to produce a satisfactory explanation of the phenomena. Scientists do not yet know *how it is done*.

Each year millions of creatures—birds, mammals, fishes— migrate hundreds, even thousands, of miles, many of them finding their way with considerable, if not perfect, accuracy. And apart from migration many animals seem to possess a well-developed sense of direction for independent and individual movements—such as those of the homing pigeon; of the shearwater from Skokholm; of the dog reported to have crossed the North American continent from west to east in order to get home; of the hare which returned more than 600 miles to its home farm in Hungary, including a crossing of the Danube; of the salmon which find their way back into the rivers in which they were born. Even among human beings we speak of a good or bad sense of direction. This may only spring from good or bad powers of detailed observation, but alternatively it may prove to be a subconscious remnant of an unexplained capacity still more or less highly developed among all these animals.

Is it safe to assume that the mechanism which finds the answer for them in their individual movements is, at least in principle, the same as the mechanism which takes the swallows on their migratory flight to Africa and back? I think that it is. I believe that the methods of orientation used by animals for homing will prove to be the same as those used for migration.

The most striking examples of this strange capacity are to be found in the bird world, and it is therefore among ornithologists that the most extensive work on the problem has been done, and although the mystery is not solved, its solution seems at the moment to be gaining ground.

How far have the scientists got and how do the different theories stand? The schools of thought can be fairly sharply divided into two—those who believe that the powers of orientation will be shown ultimately to be derived from the known senses and those who believe that some special sense or senses as yet unrecognised will provide the answer. Most of the recent theories have come from the second category; and those who back the known senses (and principal among them, the sense of sight) have for the most part been cast in the role of 'debunkers'.

Their argument goes on these lines. A bird may be born with an instinct to fly towards the midday sun as the days get shorter in the autumn. This is no more remarkable than many of the accepted instincts which are known to be inherited, as, for example, that a young grebe should, within a quarter of an hour of hatching, go to its mothers tail, where it can then climb on to her back and be protected by the feathers of her wings, or that the newly-hatched cuckoo should undertake the extremely difficult and arduous task of ejecting the eggs or young of its foster parents from the nest.

In the northern hemisphere the sun is in the southern half of the sky and therefore gives an indication of the direction in which to fly. The position of the moon, and even of certain groups of stars, might continue to give direction at night. An accurate sense of position might be obtained by a correct estimate of the height of the sun correlated with a sense of time, which birds are known to possess, and which is shown by the extraordinary regularity of their time of starting to sing in the morning. This time-sense is recognised in man and may explain the capacity, which many people claim, to wake at a given time without the assistance of an alarm clock. Bees and ants are now known to use the position of the sun and its relation to various landmarks as a means of finding their way back to the hive or nest.

Into this theory of a general migration line on a particular bearing and orientated by heavenly bodies can be fitted the experiments of the German ornithologist Rüppell, who found that young hooded crows, which migrate on a line northeast and southwest along the southern shore of the Baltic, continued to use a parallel line if captured and displaced several hundred miles north or south.

The phenomena of migration alone could perhaps be explained by such a comparatively simple theory connected with the sense of sight; but what of homing? The argument here begins with an area of familiar territory around the birds home from any part of which it could quickly return to the nest (or loft, in the case of pigeons). If a number of birds were released at some distance away and radiated evenly in all directions from the point of release, a proportion would hit this area of familiar territory. The percentage would depend on the angle subtended by the familiar territory at the point of release. But if the birds, instead of radiating, were to perform an even spiral outwards from the point of release, they would all in due course hit the familiar territory. It is not suggested that either of these things happens in this regular manner, but it is pointed out that a modified form is possible in view of the fact that birds are not infallible and that not by any means a hundred per cent of homing birds actually get home. In 1948, two Canadian scientists, Griffin and Hock, published an account of some experiments in which they released some gannets which had been taken from an island in the Gulf of St. Lawrence to a point about 100 miles inland. The gannets were then followed, at a respectful distance, by the ornithologists in a helicopter. About 60 per cent of the birds eventually got home to their island, but the initial directions which they took were apparently at random, and the tracks followed by the birds did not suggest any innate sense of direction.

Not only is the percentage of released birds which reach home very significant, but also the length of time which they take to do it. The gannets averaged about 190 miles per day; and Griffin has shown that in this and a number of other homing experiments the percentage of recoveries and the average speeds on the journey are not inconsistent with what he calls 'spiral exploration'.

Many other suggestions have been put forward in order to support the theory that the sense of sight is the key to the power of orientation. Professor V. C. Wynne-Edwards of Aberdeen University has suggested that the accurate time-sense of birds might detect the differences between the times of sunrise and sunset, which change rapidly if you travel east or west. For every hundred miles in these latitudes the difference is about ten minutes. James Fisher has ingeniously suggested the comparison between a bird trying to find its way and a man in a maze. If, he says, you accept the principle of always turning in one direction, it will probably bring you to the middle or to the beginning of the maze, but if it brings you back to a place at which you have previously been, you should take a new turn and then continue as before. You can do this in a maze because mazes have walls. For a bird, so Fisher's suggestion goes, the principal landmarks of geography—coasts, rivers, mountain ranges—take the place of the walls of the maze. And anyway, as Fisher points out, a great many birds do in fact get lost.

But although these explanations may cover a large number of the recorded phenomena of homing, they do not, as their adherents would be the first to admit, explain everything. For instance, it is well known that birds immediately after release, circle around gaining height, and that in a large proportion of cases they set off, after three or four circles, in the correct direction for home, irrespective of the topography of the neighbourhood and often without a sight of sun, moon, or stars. Furthermore, many of them can find their way in a fog and at night as well as they can by day, although this is not the case with pigeons, which are by no means the best homers among birds. On the other hand, pigeons are moderate homers which are easy to keep and to tame and which breed freely in artificial conditions. It is for this reason that they are used for carrying messages and for racing. Since they are descended from the rock pigeon, which is a non-migratory species, it is perhaps curious that their homing faculties are as good as they are.

If the stimuli of the known senses do not provide an adequate explanation of the homing performance of birds, what are the theories which postulate the possession of an extra sense or senses? Most of them are based upon a sensitivity to the earth's magnetic field, and in this different observers have obtained different results on two very important pieces of evidence about which further experiments should be performed. First of all, some scientists have stated that powerful wireless transmissions have upset the orientation of pigeons, while others have been unable to find any confirmation of this; and secondly, a number of experiments have been carried out in which birds have been released carrying magnets of sufficient strength to 'drown' the effects of the earth's magnetic field. In some of these experiments results indicate that the magnets may have had some adverse effects on the homing capacities of the birds, but it appears that in all such cases the results were not really conclusive, as insufficient control experiments were carried out at the same time. Other observers have tried in vain to show any significant difference between the performance of a bird carrying a magnet and one carrying a small piece of non-magnetic metal of equal size and weight.

In any event, an appreciation of the earth's magnetic field—a built-in compass, as it were—would not be enough to fix a birds position on the earth's surface, for a compass is no good to a man if he has not a map, a chronometer, and a sextant. He must know where he is before he can tell what course to steer to reach his objective.

It was at this point that Ising's theory of orientation by an appreciation of the Coriolis forces of relative momentum was put forward in 1945. Professor Ising's work was entirely theoretical, and it was taken a stage further by Professor H. L. Yeagley of the Department of Physics of Pennsylvania State College, who, in conjunction with the U.S. Army Signal Corps, put the theory to the test. Yeagley's hypothesis was a combination of previous theories of magnetic reception with the new suggestion that birds might detect the Coriolis force due to the rotation of the earth. What is Coriolis force? If you throw a cricket ball out of the window of a moving train and at right angles to the line, it does not follow a path at right angles to the line, but rather a diagonal path due to the momentum imparted by the movement of the train. If, instead of being in a train, you imagine yourself standing at the Equator and facing northward, you will be travelling at the speed of the rotation of the earth. Since the earth's circumference is 25,000 miles and it makes one revolution in twenty-four hours, the speed is a little more than 1,000 miles per hour. North or south from the Equator, your speed will be reduced until, as you reach the poles, it is nothing at all. If, as you stand at the Equator, you fire a rifle bullet, instead of throwing a cricket ball, in a due northerly direction, it goes from a part of the earth's surface travelling at 1,000 miles per hour to one which is only travelling at, say, 999.99 miles per hour, and it finishes up, as it were, a little farther ahead than the parallel of longitude along which it was fired; the rifle bullet drifts to the right. This is the effect of Coriolis force due to the earth's rotation. High-speed aircraft find it necessary to make corrections on the courses steered on northerly or southerly bearings, in order to compensate for this effect.

Ising's theory was that the semi-circular canals of the inner ear—the balancing mechanism of the bird—might be sufficiently sensitive to detect the Coriolis force.

Yeagley superimposed a magnetic sense upon the Coriolis factor and pointed out that a kind of grid could be built up based upon the two possible stimuli. Since the lines of latitude and longitude are related to the earth's rotational axis, the lines of latitude will also represent lines of equal intensity of the Coriolis force. On the other hand, the lines of equal intensity of magnetic field will be centred upon the magnetic rather than the true North and South poles, and might be termed 'magnetic parallels' as opposed to parallels of latitude. If these magnetic parallels are superimposed upon the parallels of latitude, the result is a grid of two systems of concentric rings which cross each other and which give an exact position on the earth's surface. If the bird could detect these two stimuli together, it could fix its position precisely. But any particular magnetic parallel crosses a parallel of latitude twice, although the points may be many hundreds of miles apart. Such points are found on either side of the line of longitude on which the magnetic pole lies, and this passes more or less down the centre of the North American continent. On one side of this line the pattern of both magnetic and Coriolis intensity is, as it were, the mirror image of the intensities on the other side, and any point will have on the opposite side what Yeagley has called a 'conjugate point' at which the magnetic and Coriolis intensities are identical with those at the original point. When Yeagley decided to put his theory to the test with homing pigeons, he found that the conjugate point to the Pennsylvania State College, where his pigeons lived, was 1,100 miles away at the town of Kearney in Nebraska. If the pigeons were trained to return to a special loft at Pennsylvania State College, and if the loft and pigeons were then transported to Nebraska and the pigeons released at normal distances from the loft (between twenty-five and seventy-five miles), they should, if the theory was correct, return to the loft at Kearney instead of attempting the long journey across the continent to Pennsylvania.

Between 1942 and 1945 the theory was tested, and the results, published in 1947, seemed at first sight to show that the birds were trying to return to the conjugate point instead of to their original home. For a while the mystery of orientation seemed to have been solved. But then, as scientists from all parts of the world began to study the details of the Kearney experiments, doubt crept back into their minds.

These doubts were crystallised at a most important meeting held a the Linnean Society of London on 13 May 1948. At this meeting the principal speakers were two scientists from Cambridge University—Dr. W. H. Thorpe, the distinguished zoologist, and Dr. D. H. Wilkinson, a brilliant young physicist from the Cavendish Laboratory. Thorpe and Wilkinson attacked Yeagley's theory from two entirely different quarters and virtually demolished it.

Thorpe pointed out that the experiments were not conducted in a conclusive manner. The mobile lofts, each painted bright yellow and surmounted by a captive balloon 150 feet above it, were taken to Kearney and the birds were apparently allowed to remain in the lofts for one day in order to rest and acclimatise themselves to their surroundings before being sent out in various directions for release. In spite of this 'rest day' and the captive balloons, only three pigeons out of 500 actually returned to the lofts. The results, therefore, were chiefly based on a number of recoveries in the surrounding country, which were judged to have indicated that the birds were *trying* to get back. These results were obtained by a method of plotting which Yeagley called the 'combined flight vector'. The fallacy of this form of measurement can be shown as follows: if six pigeons are released at ten miles from the loft and one of them flies directly towards home, but proceeds past it and continues for ten times the distance, and if the other five then fly in the opposite direction for less than ten miles, the combined flight vector will indicate that all six flew in the right direction for approximately the right distance. Finally, no bright yellow lofts with their captive balloons were taken to some quite different place which was not a conjugate point in order to ascertain whether the pigeons at Kearney, Nebraska, were doing something different from any pigeons released at random from any mobile loft anywhere.

Wilkinson attacked Yeagley's theory from the point of view of the physicist. Could the effects of magnetism or Coriolis possibly be large enough to be detected by any sensory mechanism in birds? He was almost certain that they could not, and his arguments convinced a gathering of Britain's most distinguished ornithologists. He considered first the magnetic effects and ruled out the possibility that a bird could respond directly to the magnetic forces which come into play when non-magnetic matter is placed in a field. This would require an organ sensitive enough to detect a change of less than 0.005 gauss, and pigeons have been subjected to magnetic fields of about 1,000 gauss without any visible reaction. It seems likely that any such sensitive mechanism would cause a visible reaction on the part of the bird when subjected to the shock of an application some 200,000 times greater than that which the mechanism was normally called upon to detect.

But there are two other ways in which a bird might be sensitive to a magnetic field, and Yeagley had put forward one of them as the basis of his theory. He had suggested that the bird might, in effect, be a conductor, and that if moved in the earth's magnetic field, a potential difference would be induced between the two ends of the conductor which could be detected by the bird. No current, however, is created, and Wilkinson showed that a bird accelerating from rest to 40 miles per hour would have to make an electrostatic measurement of the order of one-millionth of a volt. Since the most accurate man-made instrument for making such measurements—the cathode ray oscilloscope—cannot detect differences of less than about 0.1 volts, and since any such minute measurements would be hopelessly upset by the ordinary effects of atmospheric electricity, whose background intensity could not possibly be gauged by the bird, Wilkinson concluded that the 'induction effect as conceived by Yeagley is not operative'.

Yet another possible means of detecting the magnetic field might be available to the bird, however, if its anatomy contained a conducting loop which oscillated in the field. This would create an alternating current, and the measurement of that current might be easier for the bird than a purely electrostatic measurement. But Wilkinson showed that this current must be measured to an accuracy of 10^{-10} amps and that in view of the much bigger currents of physiological origin which are present in living matter, it was, to say the least, extremely improbable that birds could make the desired measurement of the earth's magnetic field.

Finally, Wilkinson turned to the computation of Coriolis forces. The effect of the Coriolis forces due to the earth's rotation could only be felt as a minute deflection of the downward pull of gravity. Its strength, in these latitudes, is less than 1/6,000 of the gravitational force itself and the angle of the deflection would be less than one minute. In addition, the effect would be masked by the irregular influence upon the vertical component of the force of gravity of land masses such as mountain ranges and also of the centrifugal component. But this is not all, since the Coriolis forces due to the rotation of the earth could only be detected if the birds course and speed were almost impossibly true. Any slight alteration, of course, would introduce Coriolis forces not related to the earth's rotation but to the change of course. Thus a bird would have to fly to an accuracy of 1/50 of an inch in 100 feet.

Ising's conception of the mechanism involved in measuring Coriolis forces included a more complicated principle—that the forces caused a swirling in the fluid of the semicircular canals of a bird of which the bird could become conscious. It has the additional significance that the method could be used when the bird is at rest; but once again the effect can be shown to be so minute as to make it an extremely improbable method by which a bird could determine latitude.

Both the magnetic and Coriolis effects vary directly as the speed of flight. Thus a change from 40 miles per hour to 39 miles per hour would be equal to a geographical displacement of 150 miles. Thorpe and Wilkinson have shown conclusively that it is at least very improbable that the Yeagley theory is the answer to the problem, more particularly since the normal perceptions of animals—as, for example, in changes of intensity in light or sound—do not register such minute changes as would be necessary to make use of the Coriolis forces and the earth's magnetic field. But they have not shown that such sensitivity is impossible, and it may well develop ultimately that some part or parts of the theories of Ising and Yeagley will be found to hold good.

Meanwhile, what other hypotheses are available? Wilkinson is thrown back to a visual explanation again. If random search or spiral exploration will not cover all the known facts, he suggests, might not these principles be materially assisted by an appreciation of latitude derived by a glimpse of the sun correlated with the time-sense which has been accepted? If the height of the sun could be estimated to within one diameter of the sun itself, then the necessary accuracy could be achieved.

In my view, this is not enough. But there are other theories, and we must consider in detail the most interesting experiments with swallows which have been carried out by two Polish scientists, Professors Wojtusiak and Wodzicki. Here are the important things which they discovered, the clues, as it were, from which they set forth once more to solve the mystery.

Swallows were taken from their nesting sites and released at various distances and in various directions from home. When released, they circled once or twice and then set off. In two-thirds of the cases the birds set off in the right direction. Some of the others began by following a railway line in the wrong direction. The birds returned as easily from any point of the compass. They returned almost as quickly through rain, thunderstorm, and fog, and their speed was reduced by only half at night, although swallows are not normally nocturnal. The farther the birds were taken away, the higher the speed of return up to a distance of about seventy-five miles, from which they returned at an average of twenty-two miles per hour. At greater distances the speed was much reduced, but remained more or less constant at about seven miles per hour. Four swallows were tried over the same course a second time. One took a fraction longer on the second run, one did it in half the time, and the other two took about a quarter of the time. (This was particularly interesting in view of the training which is normally given to racing pigeons over shorter courses on the same bearing before a long-distance flight.) Finally, experiments were carried out with house sparrows, and it was found that they could not home over greater distances than about six miles.

The two Polish scientists clung to the fact that the swallows could so often set off correctly both by day and by night, in fair weather or in fog. Here was evidently something outside the range of the conscious perceptions of the senses of man. Professor Wojtusiak put forward the suggestion that birds might have a visual perception of electromagnetic radiation, for it must be something invisible to man, but existing in darkness and capable of passing through fog. Infrared rays have those properties. In support of this theory, he called attention to some curious orange or red fat globules found in the retina of birds eyes and also in those of terrapins and tortoises. If this should enable them to detect infrared radiations, then by the power of sight they could distinguish between warm masses and cold, between land and water, between the brightness of the south and the darkness of the north. The professor began his experiments at once, and soon showed that tortoises gave preference to areas illuminated with infrared rays, which may well explain the extraordinary manner in which water-tortoises are able to find their way to the nearest water even if it is out of sight. The experiments extended to birds, and pigeons could apparently be shown to choose to feed from a dish lit by infrared in preference to one lit by an equal intensity of visible light, even though the positions of the dishes and the lights were frequently reversed.

But set against these results are some researches by Hecht and Pirenne into the sight of owls. These two scientists failed to find any evidence that the eyes of the long-eared owl were sensitive to infrared radiation. Although owls are for the most part non-migratory, yet the possession of a sense which would react to rays which are present at night would quite obviously be of the greatest advantage to a nocturnal bird. If such a mechanism were present in any birds, it is strange that it has not been developed in the highly specialised eyes of owls. Indeed, the researches of Hecht and Pirenne have put what seem to be almost insuperable difficulties in the way of the infrared theory.

All these experiments continue, however, and the evidence mounts up, but the answer is not found. To me it seems that the anatomists might now make a useful contribution. Birds which are known to be the most outstanding homers should be studied afresh and compared with those which are bad homers, in order to see if any part of the brain, nervous system, or sense organs can be shown to have become more highly developed in those birds with the best sense of direction.

I am convinced that the birds cannot keep their secret much longer. Soon an irrefutable theory must emerge. Soon we shall know definitely how the swallows find their barns, how the great shearwaters scattered over the Atlantic Ocean find the tiny island of Tristan da Cunha—their only breeding place, how Anabel found her way back to the lighthouse. Until then, the mystery remains unsolved.

SUMMER IN THE
CANADIAN ARCTIC

From *Uncle Mac's Children's Hour Story Book*
(Sampson Low, Marston & Co, 1951)

In the summer of 1949 I went with two Americans to the very
far north of Canada to search for Ross's snow geese, to learn
about their nesting habits, migratory movements, and to carry
out some general scientific research.

As many of you know, I broadcast four talks in Children's
Hour about my adventures, and now Uncle Mac has asked me
to set down some of them in this book. Well—for those who
did not hear the programmes, I had first better tell you where
we went and why.

The three of us—the two Americans, Paul Queneau and
Harold Hanson, and I—went to the Perry River, which runs
into Queen Maud Gulf in the middle of the very north shore
of the mainland of Canada—between the Mackenzie Delta
and Hudson's Bay. If you want to look it up in an atlas, it's at
longitude 102° west.

. We went there to see and to study the breeding colonies of this little white goose, with black tips to its wings. These birds were first found breeding on some inland lakes there eleven years before, but no white man had been to this very remote place since the original discoverer, a trader called Angus Gavin, working for the Hudson's Bay Company. A few travellers have been along the coast there, past the Perry River post, but they never go inland much. Of course the Eskimos do, and there is a tribe of them living in the area. They're only a small tribe— about thirty-seven of them—called the Kogmuit tribe. But there was no way of finding out the things we wanted to know about the Ross's geese except by going there and journeying inland to see for ourselves. So we went.

We went by air—in an Anson plane which we chartered to take us. We started at the end of May, and after one or two delays, and a rather sticky flight down a gorge in a snowstorm, we arrived at our destination—a barren-looking expanse of snow—on 6 June. There the plane left us, and we camped on the ridge of a hill about fifteen miles inland from the Arctic Sea. That camp was our headquarters, our home-base for the next two months.

It was a very late Spring, about a fortnight later than usual, so for the first weeks it was cold and raw, and most of our surroundings were snow covered. It's fairly desolate-looking country at that time of the year, no trees at all—just a flat expanse of snow, broken by little rocky hillocks and ridges, and the Perry River winding down across the plain, with fairly steep, sloping banks. On these banks, and on some of the ridges, the snow had been blown away—the wind blows up there nearly all the time, a cold, cheerless wind—very strong at times. Underneath the snow was boggy moorland, known as tundra, but we didn't see much of that during those early weeks.

What we did see, though, was a wonderful profusion of birds—exciting birds, a good many of them new to me, because they were the American migratory birds.

There were waders such as pectoral sandpipers, ruddy turnstones, American golden plovers and those brilliant and confiding little creatures, the pharalopes. And then there were cranes, and ptarmigan, and Buffon's skuas, and rough-legged buzzards, and the handsome little Lapland buntings. But the most exciting were the ducks and the geese, at any rate to me, because they're my special interest—the gorgeous king eider drakes, with bright pink breasts and orange knobs on their bills—the little long-tailed ducks with their delightful summer call, 'ah-adlow'—that is the sound which most quickly brings back the whole scene to me—somehow the long-tailed duck seems to be the very spirit of the Arctic Summer. And then the geese—not only the little Ross's geese we had come to study, but lesser Canada geese, tule geese, lesser snows and blue geese, and the little black Pacific brents.

I wonder if you can imagine how exciting it was to see these birds for the first time on their breeding grounds—in their true home? I'd thought about them so much before that I had a sort of picture in my mind. And when we got to the place, I suppose it wasn't so very different, but it just seemed three times as good as I'd expected.

All the same, we did have shocking bad weather. Snowstorms and wind and fog, and there were times when we couldn't do much except stay in our sleeping bags in our tents. That's where we were when the first Eskimos came to our camp. They must have seen the masts of our wireless aerial on the top of the hill behind our camp, and of course they'd probably seen our plane land. We had some difficulty talking to these Eskimos as they couldn't speak English, and we couldn't talk much Eskimo at that time. But we drew things, and used signs, and after a while we found we could make ourselves understood.

About a week afterwards, two families of Eskimos came up the river in a canoe, and camped about a mile away from us on the opposite side of the river—I think they thought it was a nice, good-mannered distance—after all, you didn't want to crowd anyone. Anyway, these Eskimos became our friends and helpers for the rest of the time we were there—Topelakon and his sixteen-year-old son Taanoo, and Taipan.

The Eskimos are very small people, with brown skins and straight black hair usually cut in a fringe across their foreheads. They are very merry, always laughing and smiling. These were dressed in the usual caribou-hide 'parka', as its called, a sort of tunic with a hood. The hood is trimmed with fur—usually wolverine fur—because that is the only kind of fur which doesn't mat up and freeze when you breathe on it. But sometimes it's Arctic fox, or barren ground wolf fur.

Topelakon was the leader of the party, and the most intelligent and helpful of all the Kogmuit Eskimos we met. He had a white-man name as well—he was called Patsy. Most of the Eskimos had been given Christian names, and many of them had been baptised when the missionaries visited the Perry River Post some time before. They liked us to use their 'Kabloona' name. (*Kabloona* is their word for white-man.) They felt that if you didn't use the name there must be something wrong with it. Taipan's Kabloona name was Jimmy.

There was a mystery about Patsy's son, Taanoo. We discovered that he was also called Korwik, and that Taanoo was supposed to be his Kabloona name. The clue came later when another Eskimo said the name was *Daanoo*, and we finally agreed that his name was probably Donald—the Eskimos had heard it pronounced by Canadians—Donald—and *Taanoo* was the nearest they could get to it. So Taanoo he remained, and a very charming boy he was—always with a wonderful smile, and with that eagerness to help which is one of the nicest characteristics of the Kogmuit Eskimos.

We found after a while that with drawings and signs, and with a vocabulary which we made for ourselves, we could talk fairly easily with them. We learned that the name for Ross's goose was *Kangowan*, and that the word for a nest was *Cooblui*—*Cooblui Kangowan*—a Ross's nest. 'Where?' The Eskimo word was *Humelto*. '*Humelto Cooblui Kangowan?*' The Eskimos pointed to the southwest. '*Avanni Congaheito*'—over there, far away. '*Kowak ikaong*'—across the river. '*Man-a-lokok Khang-agon*'—over the hill. 'How long would it take to get there?'

The Eskimos have no measure of distance, only of time—of days, or rather nights. So they said it was one sleep away. Actually it was much more, it took us three days to go there and back, but I think the Eskimos that if they told us more than one night we might not go, and obviously it was in our interests to go, so they were really being as helpful as they could. The other thing, of course, was that we couldn't get across that tundra, and over those stony ridges, at anything like the speed that the Eskimos could, so it took longer than they would have done alone.

It was Patsy and Jimmy who led us to the largest breeding colony of Ross's geese they knew—perhaps the largest breeding colony in the world: two hundred and sixty nests on five little islands in a lake. We went there twice, once when the birds were sitting, and the second time when the downy young were just hatched. Incidentally, these silvery downy goslings are the most perfect little creatures you can imagine.

In between the two trips to Lake Arlone, as we called it, we made several other trips with the Eskimos as helpers. We were still having trouble talking to them because of the language difficulty, but we devised rather a good scheme.

We had brought a radio set with us, and we had rigged it up on the top of the hill behind our camp. We called it Radio Hill. We could send out messages by cranking a couple of handles, rather like bicycle pedals. With this set we were in communication three times a week with the Hudson's Bay Company's Post Manager at Cambridge Bay, about a hundred and fifty miles to the west. It was very nice to feel we had this contact with the outside world should anything go wrong. And it was especially useful on this occasion as you shall see—not that anything had gone wrong, but we used it to get over the language problem.

D'Arcy Munro was the name of the Post Manager, and he spoke a certain amount of Eskimo himself, but also he had taught a young Eskimo boy at Cambridge Bay to speak English. So one evening we did a piece of long distance interpreting. We said over the radio to D'Arcy: 'Will you ask Patsy how far it is to the second lake where the Ross's geese breed?' There was a pause while D'Arcy told his boy—then back came the question to Patsy in Eskimo. Then while I cranked the transmitter, Patsy answered into the microphone. There was another pause while it was translated to D'Arcy, and then back came the answer to us: 'Not as far as the lake you went to the other day—does that make sense?' Well, of course, it did. In the same way we asked Patsy lots more questions, the sort that were too complicated to put over in sign language, or drawings, or through the few Eskimo words that we'd managed to pick up.

Actually the trip to this second Ross's geese lake was a flop, at least as far as the Ross's geese were concerned. There were none breeding there last summer, although we found old nests of previous years. That was the lake on which they had been found for the first time years before, so we called it Discovery Lake. You see, none of these lakes was marked on any map at all, so we had to invent our own names for them—otherwise we should have had to say: 'You remember the lake we went to the day before yesterday—the one to the east of our camp where we found the lesser Canadas nesting and saw that Arctic fox? It was much easier just to call it Discovery Lake—and also, it made a link with my father's old ship—the *Discovery*, which belongs now to the Scouts, and lies alongside the Thames Embankment in London.

Incidentally, new maps are now being made of that area, and so probably a good many of our names will be used for the lakes and rivers and hills we found.

Two of us, Harold Hanson and I, set out on the second trip to Lake Arlone—to the big colony of Ross's geese. By this time all the snow had gone from the tundra, and it was beginning to look green and gay with tremendous numbers of flowers— bright-coloured heathers, and cinquefoils, and lupins, and a tiny dwarf rhododendron. But another thing—not so nice. The mosquitoes were coming out—millions and millions of them. We managed to keep them off with the latest kind of anti-insect oil smeared on our faces and hands.

On the way up a little river in our canoe we came upon a lot of ducks and geese that were moulting. During the moult they become flightless for about a week, and it was a good opportunity to catch them, in order to put rings on their legs. These rings—tiny light aluminium things with an address and number on them—help us to find out the migration routes of the birds. Well, these birds were moulting earlier than we expected and we hadn't brought the rings with us.

Now here's a bit from my diary about that day:

Round the next corner were fifteen lesser Canadas of which ten were flightless. The sight of all these flightless birds at an earlier date than we had anticipated, made us regret that we had not brought the rings with us. We had a consultation, and came to the conclusion that we should feel continually frustrated if we went on without them. We were six miles from Radio Hill, and Harold had bruised one of the small bones in his left foot, which gave him great pain.

As it was 8.30 in the evening, we decided that I should set off back to fetch the rings, while Harold made camp and fixed up his museum specimens, I had a meal and then, at nine o'clock, I set off on the walk home. I had only one stop on the way, for about five minutes, and covered the six miles of boggy tundra in three hours, cheering myself along by reciting 'The Hunting of the Snark'. I saw surprisingly few birds, but we have repeatedly noticed that the birds sleep during the night hours in spite of the bright midnight sun. As I came to the river I hailed the Eskimo camp of old Matoombia.

'Matoombia!' I shouted. 'Kyak—Kowak ikaong!'—a boat to cross the river. Almost at once I saw young Marki start down to the boats. At the same time I could see Paul—that was Paul Queneau, the third member of our party—standing on the top of Radio Hill in the now familiar pose, holding a red spotted handkerchief by its corner to test the direction of the wind.

Marki rowed the boat over stern first, standing up and pushing on the oars. As he neared the shore I said, 'Hulloo Marki!' He grinned. (You always say 'Hulloo!' to Eskimos when you meet them.) I climbed in and pushed off again. He took a couple of strokes, then stopped and said solemnly: 'Hulloo, Peter!'

I think that his mind works slowly but he is a gentle creature. As we walked across the tundra to the camp, he found a Lapland bunting's nest with five young in a tussock. His delight in looking at the young birds was no less than mine.

Back at camp Paul was taking his weather readings. He looked up as I came in.

"Forget something?" he asked.

'Yes, the rings!' I said. Then I told him our news, ate a can of stewed fruit and turned in at about 1.00 a.m.

I set off again at 8.30, however, with the rings and the nets for trapping the geese, and I was back with Harold three and a half hours later. It was a hot day. We organised a great drive of all the waterfowl on a stretch of about three miles of river. I thought we were going to get seventy geese and about a hundred and twenty ducks (all pintails) but everything went wrong and we caught precisely one pintail. After all this, Harold's foot was much worse, and we debated whether to go on upstream or to turn back. I was pretty tired, having covered twenty-two miles of soft bogs during the last twenty-four hours.

Well, so much for the extract from my diary. We did go on, Harold's foot got better, and we had a tremendously exciting time among the young geese. Later we caught some moulting geese to bring back alive—Ross's geese and a pair of tule geese. We brought them, and they're now down in Gloucestershire, among the seven hundred live waterfowl which live at the Headquarters of the Severn Wildfowl Trust. We brought them back in the float plane—a Fairchild Husky—which flew in to fetch us. It landed on a lake, for the lakes were mostly free of ice by this time—the beginning of August.

Leaving our camp at Radio Hill was one of the saddest things. I was the last to go, because my two colleagues went with the plane to refuel at Cambridge Bay—and incidentally to meet our radio friend D'Arcy Munro. Meanwhile, I brought the gear down the Perry River by canoe, with Patsy and Taanoo. I was to meet the plane on Flagstaff Island, about four miles off the mouth of the river. On the fourteen-mile trip to

the coast we called at two of the Eskimo Camps on the way.
Here is another extract from my diary:

> *I was very cold, for I had got up without my winter woollies on,
> which was right for the early part of the day, but for a rainy
> midnight with a cold north wind it was all wrong! Just as
> heavier rain came on we came to Kiriakpak's Camp. Here was
> his wife with her very attractive, dimpled little daughter of
> seven or eight, and Haunga's wife, Ninayo. The old tattooed
> Matriarch, mother of Haunga was also there. She must have
> been a great beauty in her day, and is still in appearance the
> most striking woman in the whole tribe.*
>
> *We drank tea sitting on caribou skins, while the rain
> pattered down on the tent. I was still cold, and by now
> pretty tired after a long day. Patsy found an Eskimo drum of
> Kiriakpak's and began to play it and to sing. It was the song
> he had sung on the way back from Discovery Lake. 'Eeya-yaa-
> ya, Eey-ayaang-a, Eeya-yeya!' It seemed that Ninayo could
> perform in some way, but was shy. Kiriakpak's wife was trying
> to persuade her, and at last sent the little girl off to the other
> tent to get something. In a while she came back with a type
> of Jew's harp. Ninayo was too shy to start. Patsy tried it, but
> didn't play it very well.*
>
> *'In the end, Ninayo decided she could do it if she could
> keep her face behind the stove pipe from me. She even said this
> to the others. Then she began to play. It was a simple droning
> noise, but with a definite rhythm, and quite evidently she had
> practised it because there was a certain style in her playing.
> The playing would end suddenly without any closing phrase.
> She began a new rhythm and finally a third rhythm with a
> double beat. It was appropriate, simple music. Kiriakpak's
> wife was delighted with Ninayo's skill. 'Tuk-ke!' she kept
> saying—'Excellent!'*
>
> *'At last the rain stopped. We said a hasty farewell, and ran
> out and down to the canoe. It was pretty dark, and very cold
> with an east wind which was freshening. We went down the
> estuary. There was a little sea which slopped into the canoe.*

It was evident that once clear of the shelter of Rainy Island it would be rougher. Patsy was game to try to get out to Flagstaff Island—our rendezvous with the plane. 'Can we make it?' I asked. 'Nowra!' he replied: 'I don't know!' 'All right!' I said.

'We'd better shelter at Kingarullik's camp.'
   Patsy was vastly relieved. The rain had set in again. We came ashore finally beside the two tents and went up for tea. Kingarullik and his handsome, tattooed wife Pikooyak were pleasantly welcoming. Patsy and I were doing a good deal of yawning, and I was still chilled, but the stories of the last few days had to be retold—how Taanoo had been up in the plane, how Patsy had seen the big herd of caribou—even down to how Kaota had singed his hair on the Primus stove.
   Finally came the offer of shelter for the night, and an opportunity to climb into a sleeping bag and get warm again. We went out and unloaded the canoe in the rain.

I wish I had more space to tell you about the beautiful toys the Eskimos make for their children—little sleds and canoes, harpoons, and even a model of our Fairchild Husky plane. Oh! And lots more nice things about them. It wasn't until we had to say goodbye to these charming, gentle people, that I realised how very fond of them I had become. So I was really sad to leave, and I hope maybe that one day I shall be able to go up and see them all again—my delightful Kogmuit Eskimo friends of the Perry River.

TO SAVE THE HAWAIIAN GOOSE: AN EXPERIMENT IN ENGLAND

The Times (2 June 1952)

The nene or Hawaiian goose is probably the second or third rarest bird in the world. Fewer than half a dozen ivory-billed woodpeckers are believed to remain in the forests of Florida and Louisiana. Only 32 adult Hawaiian geese are known to exist at the present moment, although there may be as many as seventeen more on the slopes of the volcano Mauna Loa. Of the whooping crane of North America it appears that only 37 individuals survive.

A century ago it was estimated that 25,000 nenes lived on the island of Hawaii—the only place in the world where the species was found. But the introduction and release of pigs, cats, and dogs, which now run wild over most of the island, spelled disaster for all Hawaiian ground-nesting birds, and the work of extermination was almost completed by the mongoose, brought in to control the previously (and accidentally) introduced rats. At the end of the Second World War drastic steps were needed if this beautiful and interesting goose was to escape extinction; and, unlike many threatened local forms of otherwise numerous species, this goose is most distinctive and infinitely worth the effort to save it.

The nene is descended from one of the ancestors of the Canada goose, which must at some remote time have been blown from the North American continent to Hawaii. Thereafter it evolved very differently from the Canada goose. With no necessity for migration, the birds' wings have become shorter, and with much reduced aquatic activity (for they live among the lava on the comparatively dry mountain slopes), the webs of the feet have been partially lost. The body colouring is not unlike that of the Canada goose, but the beautiful buff-coloured neck has developed an extreme example of the 'pleated' arrangement of the feathers found in many other species of geese, while the smart black crown and face and the black ring at the base of the neck are strikingly handsome.

In pursuance of one of its main objects, the Severn Wildfowl Trust, soon after its formation in 1946, communicated with the Government of the Territory of Hawaii, inquiring whether steps could be taken to save the nene, and indicating the interest of naturalists all over the world in preventing the impending tragedy. But at that time, it seemed, nothing could be done. With so rare a species some form of artificial propagation was clearly desirable, particularly when it was known to take kindly to captivity. Indeed, a large proportion of the remaining nenes were living in a state of semi-domestication in the garden of Mr. H. C. Shipman, at Hilo on the east coast of the island of Hawaii.

Three years later, however, the Hawaiian Board of Agriculture established a breeding station at Pohakuloa on the saddle road between Mauna Loa and Mauna Kea, 6,000ft. above sea level, and here a few pairs of nenes, most of them lent by Mr. Shipman, were established in special aviaries: the project was under the supervision of Mr. J. Donald Smith, of the Division of Fish and Game at Honolulu. Mr. Smith was soon in communication with the Severn Wildfowl Trust on various avicultural problems connected with this project, and in December 1949, the Trust's curator, Mr. John Yealland, (now Curator of Birds at the London Zoo) went to Hawaii to advise and assist at the first breeding season. Only two of the eggs laid that year were fertile and both the young were successfully reared.

A secondary scheme for saving the species involved sending a pair of geese to England (where the species was successfully bred many times between 1824 and 1900). Mr. Shipman presented an adult pair to the Severn Wildfowl Trust and these were brought back to Slimbridge by Mr. Yealland. There is no plumage distinction between the male and female Hawaiian goose and in March 1951, both birds of the 'pair' made nests and laid infertile eggs. It is not altogether common for unmated geese to lay eggs, and that both should have done so in this case was great good fortune, for if only one of them had laid, the cause of the infertility would not have been immediately apparent. As it was, the eggs were removed and a cable was hastily sent to Hawaii. It was hoped that it might be possible to obtain a gander in time for the second clutch of eggs, which are normally laid by waterfowl if the first nest is taken away. Exactly seven days after the dispatch of the cable a fine male Hawaiian goose arrived at Slimbridge, having travelled by aircraft from the opposite side of the globe. Although he took up with one of the females—and indeed both were much pleased to see him—he was already in full moult (for January is the breeding season in Hawaii), and so the second clutches of eggs were once more infertile.

But in February 1952, both the females nested again and this time the eggs were fertile. The gander, with no more than a faint trace of embarrassment, undertook the care and protection of both females and their nests. The host clutches were taken and placed under bantam foster parents and in less than a fortnight both females had laid again. In all nineteen eggs were laid of which nine hatched. The goslings, which are purplish grey with a well-defined face pattern, are thriving— all nine of them, although three are less strong than the others.

The first five to hatch are now becoming feathered, and like their parents are quite delightfully tame.

It seems possible, therefore, that by his skill in rearing goslings under foster parents, Mr. S.T. Johnstone, the Trust's curator, will have increased the world population of this rare and lovely bird in one season by more than twenty per cent of its present numbers. This achievement indicates the part which aviculture can play in rescuing a threatened species at the eleventh hour. Such methods might have saved the passenger pigeon, the Labrador duck—even the dodo. The Hawaiian goose is not the only bird to which they should be applied today.

WILD GOOSE CHASE

by Peter Scott and James Fisher, *Lilliput*
(October/November 1952)

Stories of natural history adventure very seldom have a definite hero or heroes. When we rode out of the central desert of Iceland on 6 August 1951, and walked our horses on the last lap of their long journey through the meadows of Ásólfur, smelling of newly mown hay, we felt very happy and satisfied. But we did not feel like—nor, indeed, did we resemble–heroes. Perhaps the pink-footed geese were the heroes, those romantic birds whose last great secret was in our notebooks. But the pinkfeet of Iceland were the passive objects of our search.

If this story has to have heroes, they are the naturalists and explorers of the past: the anonymous Icelanders of long ago, whose discovery of the Thjórsá pinkfeet was forgotten, and who made strange pens on lonely grey hills to catch them.

This is the story of how the Severn Wildfowl Trust expedition of 1951 discovered what is probably the chief world breeding place of the pinkfoot, which no ornithologist had seen in the nesting season, how they caught and marked over a thousand of the geese, and how, as a result of this, they were able to make an estimate of the world population of this fine bird.

The expedition consisted of three English birdwatchers—myself the leader, Philippa Talbot-Ponsonby, and James Fisher—and the Director of the National Museum of Iceland, Finnur Gudhmundsson, one of the best-known and (he will not mind our saying so) *largest* ornithologists in Europe.

If the expedition began anywhere, it was not in Iceland. The necessity for it became evident on the stubble fields and pasture-lands of the Tay, the Solway Firth and the Wash, where nearly all the pinkfeet in the world feed in winter. And the plans for it were made in a hut in the Lapland mountains during the International Ornithological Congress of 1950. Occasionally during the winter of 1949–1950 and often during that of 1950–1951, certain favourite fields of the pinkfoot in England and Scotland were the scene of curious and unprecedented happenings. When the geese had been flushed gently from their feeding ground, half a dozen human figures would drive up in a couple of jeeps, rapidly unroll something from a cable drum, dig mysterious holes with narrow spades, and busy themselves on the ground for an hour. Then the jeeps would retire to the road, and the human figures behind a hedge or into a portable hide towed up behind one of the jeeps and parked in a corner of the field. Save for the tracks of the jeeps, the field would look as if nothing had happened. The watchers would watch and wait, eat their sandwiches, chat to each other in low voices. In the distance the double-honking of the pinkfeet would indicate that the geese were restless and becoming hungry. Perhaps after an hour or two the whole flock would rise in the air—skein after skein would come streaming in towards their favourite field. With the first party down on the field, the rest would follow, whiffling through the air and dropping down so close to each other that the centre of the field would become a solid mass of grey geese.

Gradually they would settle down to the contented buzzing of busily feeding geese. Gently the flock would drift over the field, across the jeep tracks, back to their favourite spot. All at once orange flashes, sudden black and grey smoke, a tearing swishing noise, and an apparition would leap from nowhere among the feeding birds. The flock would burst into the air, but a hundred of them would at once find themselves firmly enveloped in the meshes of an enormous net.

This net was propelled by rockets, touched off by a member of the watching party in the hide. A moment later the watchers would be running out into the field to free and mark the geese as soon as possible.

This rocket netting of geese was invented and perfected entirely by the Severn Wildfowl Trust (although a comparable method using small cannons to propel the net has since been developed in America). All those who have taken part in it agree that it is a more exciting sport than goose shooting, and it is infinitely more productive in scientific evidence about the habits of the birds and their numbers. All the geese are marked with a numbered aluminium ring giving the address of the British Museum of Natural History, and in some cases the rings are also coloured; the white rumps of the geese are also dyed some prominent colour by immersing the whole bird's tail in the bucket. The marked geese are, of course, immediately released.

During the winter of 1950–1951, Peter Scott and other members of the Severn Wildfowl Trust caught in their rocket nets no fewer than 634 pinkfeet, mostly in Scotland. It was only natural that while planning and executing this catch of winter geese, minds should turn to the possibility of tracing the marked birds to their breeding grounds, catching and marking them there, and arriving at all sorts of new and interesting conclusions not only about the age and migration of pinkfeet, but also about their family affinities, their local movements, their attachment to particular nesting sites and feeding grounds, and, above all, their numbers. For when a substantial part of a population is marked, and that population is again sampled (and in the case of the geese, perhaps at the other end of its range), the proportion of marked birds in the second sample found to have been already marked can, theoretically, lead the sampler to a mathematical estimate, within calculable limits of probability, of the size of the total population.

However, the question of following the pinkfeet to their breeding headquarters was made more complicated by the fact that nobody was quite sure exactly where the world headquarters of the breeding pinkfoot was. In the chief, western island of Spitsbergen, where the breeding pinkfoot was first discovered in 1855, its distribution among the Arctic poppies and saxifrages of those high, cold valleys is now well known. Indeed, the information from thirty or forty expeditions to Spitsbergen has made it possible to compile a map which probably marks the parts of the island inhabited by pinkfeet with some truth.

Nearly twenty years ago, James Fisher, as an Oxford undergraduate, visited Spitsbergen on a vacation expedition and saw the pinkfeet. The birds were often nesting on the steep sides of cliffs and ravines cut by rivers. But all that was known of the pinkfeet in Spitsbergen led to the conclusion that only a small fraction of the world population nested there: perhaps just about enough to account for three or four thousand birds which go to North Germany—the only large flock wintering outside England. Of course, we are not yet sure that the Spitsbergen birds are the ones that winter in Germany, for none of them has ever been marked, nor has there been a recovery in either place.

Since it was first discovered nesting in Greenland—in the vast inlet, Scoresby Sound, in 1891—the pinkfoot has been found by subsequent expeditions to have quite a wide distribution wherever good stretches of tundra become snow-free in the summer along the Northeast Greenland coast. Indeed, from the southernmost to the northernmost known Greenland breeding point is a stretch of some six hundred miles. Further, the geese nest right up to Scoresby Sound, which is almost another two hundred miles. But everywhere in this Greenland distribution the groups of breeding pinkfeet are small—never

more than a few hundred. Between Greenland and Spitsbergen
there were not nearly enough pinkfeet to account for the
winter population, which Scott believed to be between twenty
and forty thousand. It seemed possible that the bulk of this
population, perhaps two-thirds of it—certainly over half of it—
might nest in Iceland.

It was not until 1929 that the grey goose, breeding in the
interior of Iceland, was discovered to be the pinkfoot. It then
became clear that the goose of Iceland's coastal farmland,
lowland meadows, and the quieter lower reaches of its rivers
was the greylag. Most of our wintering greylags in Britain come
from these parts. Icelanders had always known that there were
plenty of geese in the interior. They called them 'heidhargæs':
heather geese. Egg collectors Congreve and Freme's 1929
sample had shown that these were pinkfeet; it had not shown
the main breeding grounds.

There is no doubt that what held up the identification
of the inland geese of Iceland was the inaccessibility of the
interior. Iceland is an oval-shaped country, the size of Ireland,
almost wholly of volcanic origin, heaved up by the great earth
movements of the Tertiary Period. Volcanic activity still
continues. The interior mostly consists of a plateau at about
two thousand feet above the sea, from which great rivers
radiate in almost every direction of the compass, the largest
of them to the north and to the south. Special parts of the
interior are much higher than two thousand feet. Large areas
are entirely covered with permanent ice. The largest ice cap,
Vatnajökull (which is larger than any English county except
Yorkshire), occupies over three thousand square miles of the
southeast, and three other largish ice caps occupy the centre
and south. One of these, the Hofsjökull, is a round boss of ice
over twenty miles in diameter, which marks the very centre of
Iceland's central plateau.

The summer melting of the Hofsjökull ice cap feeds a big river
which runs to the north coast, the Skjálfandafljót, and another,
river, the biggest in Iceland, the river of the Viking god Thor,

the Thjórsá, which flows approximately southwestwards to find
the sea on the west side of Iceland's south coast. As it reaches
the fertile coastal region, it passes through lands once owned by
heroes of the sagas—Gaukur Trandilsson, hero of the lost saga
of Thjórsárdalur, whose great farm at Stöng was drowned in ash
by the great eruption of Hekla in 1104; and past Hlídharendi,
the home of Gunnar, the hero of the saga of Burnt Njal. The
great volcano Hekla dominates the region. The district between
the Thjórsá and the southern ice cap Eyjafjallajökull, one of the
most beautiful and fertile in all Iceland, was covered with three
inches of dark pumice in a couple of hours on the first morning
of the latest eruption of Hekla, on 29 March 1947.

The courses of the two great rivers, the Skjálfandafljót in
the north and the Thjórsá in the south, form a natural route
for travellers across Central Iceland. The pass runs between
the ice caps Hofsjökull and Vatnajökull, and in almost exactly
the topographical centre of the island involves the crossing of
a sandy desert called the Sprengisandur, which lies between
the main sources of the two rivers. It takes laden ponies
about twelve hours to cross the Sprengisandur—twelve hours
without food, though there is plenty of water. The route, which
is undoubtedly the swiftest across Iceland, was discovered by
the farmer of Íshóll in 1810. Íshóll was the highest farm up
the valley of the Skjálfandafljót; it is now a deserted ruin.
Perhaps the route should be described as rediscovered, for there
is plenty of evidence that the farmers of the Heroic Age of the
Icelandic Sagas thought nothing of crossing the interior, and
some evidence that they used the Thjórsá route.

The first British traveller to make this crossing was
W.L. Watts in August 1875, and in the next year another
Englishman, C. le Neve Foster, made exactly the same journey.
When he reached the wonderful oasis beyond the Sprengisandur
desert (he started from the north), he camped under the mountain
Arnarfell and rode on the following day across a great plain of
tundra vegetation formed by the melt-rivers of the Hofsjökull as
they flowed to the Thjórsá—seeing, as he puts it, 'various lakes
and ponds and plenty of swans and wild geese'.

This casual statement was the first indication of the real whereabouts of the world's greatest breeding ground of the pinkfoot. But it was not until 1951 that it was proved to be so, and only after the four Scientific members of the expedition had spent an exciting and profitable six weeks in those tundra meadows under the Hofsjökull ice cap, eighty miles from the nearest farm.

Congreve and Freme, the egg collectors, found the pinkfoot in 1929 at a place where the River Krossá flows into the Skjálfandafljót. This is in a deepish gorge.

On the terraces of the gorge they found, all told, about twenty nests, on most of which pinkfeet were incubating eggs, though some had been robbed, probably by foxes. Since then, several further journeys have been made into the interior by ornithologists or goose-minded travellers, as a result of which the following places became at least suspected of harbouring breeding pinkfeet, if not in every year: four oases towards and in the upper reaches of the Thjórsá; six in the upper and middle reaches of the Skjálfandafljót and its tributaries and one in an upper reach of a tributary of the neighbouring River Laxá; seven in the upper and middle reaches of the big River Jókulsá á Fjöllum, which drains most of the northern part of the great ice cap Vatnajökull and runs north to the sea past the vast lava-desert of Odádhahraun, paralleled with the Skjálfandaljót and about forty miles east of it, and two near the source of the Jókulsá á Brú, which rises from Vatnajökull just east of the other Jókulsá and flows to the east coast.

The most promising line on the still unknown headquarters was given by a journey of the late Magnús Björnsson. At the end of July 1932 he found deserted goose nests on the terminal moraine of the southeast tongue of the Hofsjökull glacier, and encountered pinkfeet. This was just the place at which Foster had seen 'plenty of wild geese' in 1876. And across the Thjórsá from here, in a neighbouring oasis called Eyvindarver, or Eyvindarkofaver, Magnús met fairly large pinkfoot flocks, including young birds not quite yet flying, and shot a flightless adult gander on 27 July. But he did not find any empty nests.

Later (in 1947) the Icelandic geologist Gudhmundur Kjártansson visited the terminal moraine where Magnús found the deserted nests. It is called Arnarfellsmúlar. Gudhmundur also found nests...a lot. He estimated that there were about a hundred on the whole circuit of this deserted, overgrown moraine, from which the glacier has retreated over half a mile in the last fifty years. Gudhmundur told Finnur Gudhmundsson, now head of the National Museum of Iceland, who had already explored a good deal of the interior in the search for the missing goose ground, particularly up the Skjálfandafljót.

Finnur began with this process of elimination, and came to the conclusion that it was most likely that the breeding place was at the headwaters of the Thjórsá. His conversations with the farmers of the Thjórsá, who came upriver to collect their sheep and hunt foxes in the late summer and autumn, also led him to this view. The farmers had seen many heidhargæs in some boggy oases between a place called Sóleyjarhöfshi (which means 'Buttercup Headland') and where the Thjórsá can be forded when it is low, and the ice cap Hofsjökull on whose moraine were those nests. They said that the geese lived in some boggy flat meadows separated from each other by the glacier streams draining the ice cap—Tjarnarver, Oddkelsver, Illaver, Múlaver, and Arnafellsver. And there was the possibility of geese also in the meadows on the left bank of the Thjórsá—Eyvindarver (or the 'Meadow of Eyvindur'), and Thúfuver (or the 'Meadow of the Hillocks'). Altogether, these contiguous oases deserve the name of the *Thjórsárver vidh Hofsjökull*, which being translated means the 'Meadows of Thor's River by the Ice Cap of the Shrine or Sanctuary'.

The problem of getting to the Thjórsárver early enough in the season to be sure of finding the geese still nesting was a difficult one. It was essential to arrive before the end of June, and only possible to travel by horse train. Yet in June the snows would still be melting, and both snow rivers and glacier rivers would be full of water. Some of the oases on the way might still be snow covered, and none might provide enough fresh growth to satisfy the horses. It would be necessary to camp for some weeks, and to carry a good deal of equipment. It would be expensive.

On 22 June 1951, the members of the Severn Wildfowl Trust Hofsjökull expedition arrived at the farmstead of Ásólfsstadhir in a large bus full of equipment. Ásólfur, the farmer, arranged a good supper for us. Our objective was to reach the vegetation oasis under the Hofsjökull, eighty miles up the great river near its source, to camp there, and explore the place for pinkfeet. If we found any pinkfeet, we intended to catch and mark as many as possible.

All birds go through at least one annual moult. In most species, the big wing feathers used for flight are shed and replaced by instalments, so that the bird is always able to get into the air and fly. But among the geese and ducks this is not so: all the flight feathers are shed practically simultaneously, with the result that for an average of about three weeks in the year the adult birds are quite unable to fly. They can, however, run fast, swim, and dive. The stage of flightless moult of the adults coincides exactly with the period when their own young are between one and five weeks hatched. For most of this period the young can run almost as fast as the flightless adults. Their leg muscles grow amazingly fast in their first few days out of the egg: much faster than their wings. Thus, on their breeding grounds, geese spend nearly a month in flightless family parties which often pool together and form great pedestrian flocks.

In the equipment which the members of the expedition packed in special bundles to fit the ponies were nets and stakes and a thousand rings. With this supply we were certain that we were prepared to meet any number of geese in flightless flocks under practically any circumstances. As things turned out, this proved to be wrong, but in making our plans we decided that the expedition would be a failure if we marked a hundred, a success if we marked two hundred, and a complete or roaring success if we marked five hundred.

The journey on 22 June in the bus had been mostly in pouring rain, but 23 June dawned with improved and improving weather. The great volcano of Hekla dominated the other side of the valley, its sides black with the three-year-old lava of the last great eruption, which had had no time to find any clothing of vegetation. In the still air a thin cloud of steam rose straight and high from a crater on the southwest side of the mountain, for it was still mildly active.

We spent most of 23 June repacking our gear into three piles with the assistance—indeed, under the guidance—of our two farmer-guides, Jóhann Sigurdhsson and Snjólfur Snjólfsson. One of the three piles would be loaded onto the eleven ponies for the first trip in (making, with the riding animals, seventeen ponies in all); the second pile was to come in ten days or a fortnight later by a relief train. The third pile consisted of a very large number of things which the party was thankful to leave behind altogether! In the late afternoon the ponies set off, but without loads or riders, for people and gear were to go the first fifteen miles in two trailers, one towed by a jeep, the other by a tractor. It was about 5.30 in the evening before the expedition finally said goodbye to the latest of a long line of Ásólfurs and left Ásólfur's farm, Ásólfsstadhir, the jeep bulging with rucksacks and kitbags. At last the expedition was off.

That first evening produced a mass of impressions. The whole scene was dominated by the great volcano to the east of us, and indeed we never shook it off for the whole of the trip, for from our listed camp, seventy or eighty miles farther on, we could still see it, with its cap of snow and its plume of steam. We quickly shook off the last real woods. (Woods are not as rare in Iceland as the books tell you, and around Ásólfsstadhir was a pretty dense bit of woodland with birches ten or twelve feet high, with redwings and redpolls in them.) There was a level stretch of old lava desert flattened by wind erosion and crossed by hoofmarks and tyre tracks. We had a puncture. The tractor and the jeep, with their trailers, negotiated a little river, bumping over the big rounded stones on the bottom.

On a meadow of grass by this river we came across a bunch of sixteen pinkfeet feeding. The birds honked, took wing, gained height, strung out, and flew up the valley of the River Thjórsá in the direction the expedition was aiming for. We wished them *au revoir*, and from that moment began to believe that the expedition was going to find what it was looking for. A black dog from the farm ran with us all the way to the camping place, about fifteen miles, just for the fun of it. As we approached a fenced-off grazing place called Hólaskógur, three whooper swans rose from the edge of a stream, and nine pinkfeet from the grass above.

Camp was pitched in half an hour, which was not bad for our first tenting, in spite of a fresh breeze. Then we opened the first ration pack. We had brought with us British Army rations in compo packs of ten man-days each. These were very convenient, as four of them made a neat pony-load of just the right weight. Peter thought the food disappointing at first—but only for a few days. His previous expedition (to the Perry River in Arctic Canada) had been on American Army rations! But as time went on, we all found the British compo most excellently balanced and satisfying, and even the guides, accustomed to Icelandic food, came to like it.

Next morning Finnur said, 'I will now introduce you to your ponies.' Phil, the best rider of the party, had a fine grey belonging to the wife of our guide Snjólfur. Peter had a small, quiet chestnut mare with a mop of grey mane cut in a fringe. James had a rather difficult black pony. Finnur, in view of his size, had about the largest horse in Iceland, a splendid piebald gelding. We reckoned ourselves lucky to be sorted out and packed in five hours, while a fresh wind blew across the desert before us, whipping up little sandstorms into angry browny-yellow pillars which rushed across the desert quite close to the camp, often forming a curtain between it and the Thjórsá valley beyond it and the snow-dappled slope of Hekla. We set off to a chorus of trilling whimbrel, plaintive golden plovers, purring dunlins, across a patchwork quilt of desert and the dwarf campion *Silene*. There were masses of *Dryas*, the lovely yellow-white mountain flower, *Arabis*, and, thrift, and a little single white bell heather, *Cassiope*.

Our expedition was moving into the interior a full month earlier than most normal travellers in order to reach the geese at least before the majority of them should have hatched. This meant facing two difficulties, which are present in June but which disappear in late summer and autumn. The first of these was grazing for the ponies, the second, river crossings. To carry food for horses on an Iceland journey means a great expense, because the food can only be carried on more horses, which themselves require food. Thus, quite a small amount of horse food may double the length of a cavalcade. The expedition had to rely on natural grazing, and only in a good season is this ready for horses in the interior plateau in June—and then only in scattered oases, special grazing places: the good one always marked by a stone hut known as a 'kofi', in which the horses themselves can shelter and the men sleep on a stone ledge.

We camped by the kofis on the way both in and out of the interior. As things turned, the grazing was, quite adequate, as it had been a rather forward spring; so, although the horses sometimes got tired, they could always find enough to eat.

The river difficulty concerned the lateral streams and rivers that flowed into the Thjórsá, some of which were gathering water from large areas and many snowfields. These snowfields had been melting throughout a rather sunny June, and the guides foretold that some of the side rivers would he rather difficult to cross.

We spent the night of 24 June on a rich meadow, eroded into gullies, on a steep hillside Gjúfurleit overlooking the Thjórsá, which here had a considerable fall and flowed through a gorge. At a corner in this gorge the fast river was swept to the left and had deeply eroded a series of precipices, pillars, and pinnacles out of a bastion of black basalt.

Upon a buttress on this cliff over the river we found our first pinkfoot's nest—much lower down the valley than we had expected. Peter and Finnur saw it first, through powerful glasses, from a distance of nearly three-quarters of a mile across the valley; for a gander flying up the gorge went straight on to the nest, evidently to call the goose off to graze on a neighbouring hillside. For some time before the birds flew off, the watchers watched both together on the nest: the goose sitting, the gander standing close by, its bright summer-pink legs hardly showing through a dense mass of *Sedum roseum* (rose-root, midsummer men), the fleshy green and yellow plant that grows richly on many Iceland cliff ledges.

On 25 June, the pony train had its deepest and longest crossing of the trip across the River Dalsá, to the music of a chorus of whimbrels and plaintive golden plovers. No pony stumbled and nothing got wet. On the following day we started late in the afternoon, to avoid the heat of what was by then a Continental sun. Almost at once we were in the Nordhurleit, a real desert of sand and flattish, plate-like slabs of stone which tinkled and clattered under the horses' hooves. The desert was black, grey, and brown, mostly black, and it took over four hours to cross.

And then we were out of the desert and among the pinkfeet. As soon as the creeping willow carpet returned again the riders were among their nests, and it was about hatching time, for anxious parents were feigning injury to distract the humans from new goslings, and others were leading their broods (up to six) down to the river, and in one case even up a snow-hill. The expedition itself was amongst the scientific material it had come so far to gather.

The fact that brought home to us, more than anything else, that here was a special concentration of wild geese, was a slightly sinister one. On the banks of the Thjórsá stood half a dozen great black-backed gulls. A pair of dark forms of the Arctic skua moaned about the moor. The guides found a dead Arctic fox. These were the parasites upon the goose population, the snappers-up of neglected eggs or unconsidered goslings. And as the riders came up, a huge brown bird flapped across the river and alighted, yellow-legged, alert and cruel-looking, on the opposite bank: a young sea eagle, not yet in white tail.

On 27 June, after the first night at the edge of the tundra meadows of the Hofsjökull, the expedition realised that it was camping amongst one of the denser concentrations of breeding pinkfeet for miles around, and that the 'miles around' did in truth contain the missing breeding population we were looking for. No further decision was left to be made about travelling, save the actual choice of a site for the base camp.

Finnur kept watch over the ponies throughout the night of 27 June. In the morning it became clear that two of them were exhausted and sore after the hot journey; and while the guides were trying the crossing of the Blautakvísl, two other horses, although hobbled, suddenly charged off southwards down the way they had come before anyone could intercept them. So, when the guides had returned, there were only thirteen horses fit: not enough to move camp in one operation. This was the chief reason why we decided to stay at the south side of the oasis. As it turned out, however, it was the best place, for if we had camped in a more central spot we would have disturbed more geese.

The name of the camping place was Bólstadhur. It was on a dry, slightly elevated part of the oasis, a few yards from the River Thjórsá itself. Just at this point the Thjórsá gathers itself from a mile-wide complex of rather shallow branches, with gravel- and sand-banks in between, to a quarter-mile wide stretch of gentle rapids flowing between rather steep banks. The bank opposite the camp was the green hog's back of Sóleyjarhöfdhi (Buttercup Headland). Between Bólstadhur and the Buttercup Headland there is a well-known crossing place of the Thjórsá which the autumn shepherds ford on their horses. The other side of the ford was marked by a kofi. There was a pair of snow buntings just building in a crevice in its wall and a pinkfoot nest on its turf-covered roof.

On 28 June, Peter and James finished articles for *The Times* and the *Manchester Guardian*, and wrote letters home. The guides were hanging about, rather anxiously, drinking coffee, waiting to return. At last they were able to get away. Peter filmed the cavalcade of ponies as it disappeared over the little hill. The return visit, with the second instalment of our gear, was promised on or before 10 July. Peter and Finnur set to filming a nearby pinkfoot from a hide. The four of us had the centre of Iceland to ourselves for nearly a fortnight. Without horses it was not going to be possible to explore every part of the Thjórsárver, the meadows of Thor's River.

The first days were spent in exploring the home meadow, Tjarnarver. All over the place pinkfoot goslings, newly-hatched and dry, were running with their parents. They were very nervous and temperamental. Such goslings as were caught were, of course, far too small for leg rings, but were tagged with the new Swedish-type wing clips. These were fairly easy to handle: a bent stainless-steel pin with an aluminium label, folded at the edges to make an attachment like the clasp of a safety pin. The pin is threaded through the skin of the goslings forewing, behind the web tendon and in front of the bones opposite the elbow joint. This was quite harmless, and apparently quite painless, for this particular part of the gosling's anatomy appears to be devoid of blood vessels or nerves.

These were busy days, finding and counting nests, measuring eggs, tagging goslings. There were enormous individual differences between the geese. Some females went straight back to their eggs the moment the humans were out of sight; others took hours to return. One female was away from her newly hatched and hatching offspring for so long that a foster goose had to be found to take the deserted brood, and she ended up with no fewer than eleven goslings, which she looked after very well.

In a few days the main tent had been shifted to a new and more satisfactory position. We ran up an aluminium mast for the wireless receiver-transmitter, with which we made intermittent contact with Reykjavik, two hundred miles away. On the wireless mast we ran up the Iceland and Union flags, and their agreeable and familiar colours played and waved against the white of the ice of the Hofsjökull. Later we were to see these flags, and Peter to film them, against yellow sunsets and orange sunrises, against the red-brown and white of the

Kerlingafjöll (the 'old women's mountains') in the west and the black and white of the Tungnafell, the Hágongur, and Vatnajökull to the northeast, and Hekla to the south, against dark rainclouds and white cumulus. But in the early days of the camp the weather was hot and anticyclonic, the sky cloudless. The sounds around camp were always birds, and either wind or insects. There were many flies, including the black fly *Simulium*, an American species which gets no nearer Europe than Iceland. There was a bumble bee, and four kinds of moths. The expedition had brought effective insect repellents, so we were not much troubled by the biting elements of the insect population.

The area of this camp belonged to a meadow pipit, which sang its display song continually; and the camp was visited by the cock snow bunting from the kofi three hundred yards away. Sometimes he sang in flight, sometimes from a bank—a cheerful little song somewhere between that of a corn bunting and a hedge sparrow. Later, we put up a hide at the kofi, and filmed the male and female snow buntings as they fed their young.

The pinkfeet usually kept quiet at this time, unless they were disturbed, when we would hear their double-honk—'ang ang'. The whooper swans, when they were disturbed, uttered curious sad honkings that could be heard at a great distance. But saddest of all the sounds were those of the Arctic skuas, which cried like lost children.

On 29 June the weather was still fair, but the prospect was less promising—at least, from the point of view of comfort. From the point of view of communications, a cold spell was desirable, for the hot weather of the previous week had melted the glacier so rapidly that the *kvislar* were unexpectedly full and deep. This meant that the crossing of the Blautakvísl, which the ponies had failed to find, was going to be quite a problem on foot. Finnur contrived a level mark by the bank which told us when it began to drop. Peter thought of trying to cross at the place where it entered the Thjórsá itself. Here it spread out into a wide delta, and it looked possible to cross from sandbank to sandbank, in places more shallow than higher up. After two hours of pottering, Peter found it was quite possible to cross in thigh boots, and the rest of the expedition followed me. As we did not have thigh boots, we wore waterproof trousers tied round ordinary wellingtons. Phil got a trickle of water in one boot, but the rest of us got over dry and for the first time stood in Oddkelsver, after many nights' moves from sandbank to sandbank to find the shallowest elements of the much-split river.

At once we were among a near-colony of goose nests, and started quickly to find and note them. It began to rain (the first rain of the expedition) and we had a wet lunch in mackintoshes by a washout where Peter swore he saw a purple sandpiper: James said it was probably a dunlin, but it turned out afterwards that Peter was right. After lunch we worked over to the west side of the hill Oddkelsalda, and at once Peter recognised the note of a barnacle goose, and we presently saw it. It was flushed from a nest, over which it was evidently standing guard, and which was afterwards found. There were eggs—three heavily set, one rotten. The bird appeared to be a male barnacle mated with a female pinkfoot, and it was marked down for photography. Many dunlins and goldies were to be seen, and once we saw a dunlin pursued by three Arctic skuas at once—it got away. On the way back, Phil and James got their boots full crossing the Blautakvísl: they had become careless because of their first safe crossing.

There followed several days of bad weather, and for a good deal of the time the expedition was confined to camp, except for short dashes to inspect nests already found and to tag a few whooper cygnets. But 4 July was very fine, and we decided to walk to the ice cap at Mülaver, near Afnarfell. We walked about thirty kilometres in about fifteen hours, starting from camp at about 11.30 and returning at about 02.30 on 5 July just as the sun was rising. For most of the time there was sun and cumulus, with little wind. The reflected light and heat from Hofsjökull appeared on still days to create a patch of blue over it even when the rest of the surrounding part of the world was clouded. At times we could talk gently to each other at a hundred yards, and the absence of wind and rain made the cold night enjoyable, even though it froze.

The Blautakvísl crossing went like clockwork, and so did the slanting crossing of Oddkelsalda, which led us past the lunch-place of 29 June. We pushed on up a natural hill road over the water-parting, and down to the Miklakvísl, overlooking now the eastern corner of Oddkelsver, from a natural trough passage through which one could ride a horse unseen by the tundra geese on Oddkelsver. There were plenty of geese, some with broods; they moved off west, while the party plunged down to the crossing.

This was prospected by Peter in the usual style, and was followed by the others. We worked far out into the delta, so as to be practically in the Thjórsá. Peter carried Phil over the worst bit. James's mackintosh trousers stood up to several above-knee passages; Finnur's did not, and he went wet-foot for most of the rest of the day without complaint.

The crossing took half an hour. We staggered ashore at a mossy corner of Illaver and had a good lunch by a tarn of clear water. Before us stretched a great flat bog, in which we could see geese and swans, leading apparently straight up to the semicircular moraine—though we knew there was another river, the Fremri Múlakvísl, in between..

Illaver is a very sticky bog, and it was necessary to zigzag across it on the harder ridges between patches of ooze. Occasionally the supply of ridges gave out, and we had to plunge our way across *Carex* and *Sphagnum* growing in mud that sucked and spluttered and shook and sank under us. But we arrived at the banks of the Fremri Múlakvísl amid a chorus of purring dunlins, moaning skuas, plaintive goldies, bubbling whimbrels, and twittering phalaropes.

Another successful crossing, and we sat in shelter, illuminated by the slanting evening sun, at the farthest point reached in the past by the glacier (a full kilometre from where it now ends). A terminal moraine clothed with earth and vegetation.

The moraine behind this terminal tangled bank is barren and forbidding: a colourless, lifeless desert of hillocks with hardly a plant; giant's gravel of grey stones, for miles laterally and nearly a mile transversely. Here and there pieces of red stone (rhyolite) lie shattered and scattered into a score of fragments by frost. The country is hilly and dale-y, and in the middle exactly, between the glacier edge and the *ver*, is a chain of long lakes with shallow crossings between them, fed by meltwater streams from the glacier which cut down through the gravel hills of the moraine. The whole 'moon area' of gravel and gravelly hills is a desert; probably because the plants have not had time to colonise it.

Later on our guide Valli told us he remembered his first visit to the glacier twenty-six years ago, when the ice-front was only about thirty metres from the overgrown front of the moraine.

Finnur and James went right up to the ice cap and walked on to it, where a tongue came down between two morainic banks, about a hundred yards under a convex slope where the strain had forced the ice into blue and blue-black corrugations and crevasses of smallish size and depth but of incredible complexity. There were very blue tarns just where the ice cap ended, into which it was melting, and from them the streams cut down through the moraine.

At 19.25, after an evening meal, the party started out for home, taking this time a more easterly course, which gave us better footing across Illaver. Here, near hills much larger and longer than those marked on the map, we made an important discovery. We were working south to the Miklakvísl, along a moss-polygon flat, when we saw some geese and broods crossing a stream-mouth between them and the hill to the west of us and making up the hill. As we crossed the stream it was noticeable that one bird, which looked like a gander, had no white on its tail; and then, in a streak of evening light as it turned up the bank, it looked red. It was about three hundred yards away. There was some argument, for the gander had quickly reached dead ground before anyone had had time for more than a fleeting glance. If it was red (and in the end all agreed it probably was), then it had been ringed in Southwest Scotland in March 1951.

Past a lovely knoll the party went, with a natural moat on its south side and a platform covered with a tangle of *Sedum*; across the Miklakvísl, where the river had risen a little: back over Oddkelsver, and up the Oddkelsalda corridor and along the sands to the Blautakvísl. As we shook the water off our boots on the gentle slope from the river to he camp, it was 2.30 a.m. on 5 July, and there was hoar frost, a clear sky, and the audible quiet of windless frost. The dominant sallows had turned from green to almost white, changing the landscape entirely to a sort of Christmas colour, for in the frost their leaf groups had closed to show their lighter undersides, and upon them was white hoary dew. There was a film of ice in the water-bucket.

After this long walk the expedition settled down to a routine. In fine weather fieldwork; in bad weather writing up results. One day in camp we watched an Arctic fox, on Sóleyjarhöfdhi across the river, trot slowly along the bank and come to a goose's nest which we had previously observed to be occupied. Perhaps the nest had not hatched; perhaps the young were away, leaving a rotten egg behind. Whatever the case, the fox played with, and eventually ate, an egg in the most leisurely fashion, and afterwards curled up in the downy nest and went to sleep for twenty minutes. Finally, it sloped off over the hill in no kind of hurry.

One day Peter and Finnur found the remains of a ptarmigan surrounded by great footprints the size of Finnur's hand. The white-tailed eagle strikes again!

On 9 July, the first sheep reached the oasis. A ewe and her lamb trotted past the camp and swam the Blautakvísl. The old ewe seemed to know exactly where she was going, and Finnur said that each sheep had its favourite upland grazing spot. On the evening of 10 July, we saw the relief convoy between two hillocks to the south, and were ready with our cameras as it came in—thirteen horses, including those the men were riding. The men were Águst Svensson, the farmer from Ásar,

who was also the district postmaster; Fílippus Jónsson, the fox
hunter from Háholt; and Valentínus Jónsson from Skaftholt;
the last—Valli—was to stay with the expedition, together with
seven horses.

The guides made a lightning tour of the oasis on horseback
the following day. Fílippus found the fox earths blank and
had no opportunity to lay his poisoned baits. When they
came back on the evening of 11 July, the expedition decided
to keep the base camp where it was, as the grazing was good
for the horses. On the morning of 12 July, Águst and Fílippus
said goodbye and turned back for home, taking letters, and
newspaper despatches from James and me.

The five of us remaining, and our seven horses, had the
oasis to ourselves once again, this time for three or four weeks.
At once we began to explore it all over again on horseback, led
by Valli, who had a magnificent fast animal.

In the early days Valli had a good deal of trouble preventing
the animals straying away downriver, and he had a long chase
for them, lasting several hours, on 13 July, while the others
collected flowers in the marsh and tried not to worry.

We found it a little easier to catch the goslings with horses,
though the last stages of the chase always involved dismounting
and pursuing the birds on foot.

On 14 July we set a big V of rabbit netting on the hill
Oddkelsalda, in Oddkelsver, and tried to drive geese into it,
without success. We heard on the radio that a British aircraft was
going to try to drop mail for us, but it had to return unexpectedly
to Scotland with an ambulance case, and never came.

We found and tagged a brood of five whooper cygnets, much
easier to catch than goslings. On many of the shingle banks
between the arms of the glacier rivers we began to find the
blossoms of a beautiful flower called in Icelandic 'eyrarros'—
the 'shingle bank rose'. It is an American species found also
in Greenland, and in Europe only in Iceland; Peter had seen
it on the Perry River in the Canadian North. It was a kind
of willowherb, but growing low, and with flowers very much

larger than those of the common English willowherb. They were of a willowherb colour, somewhere between magenta and cerise, the colour of bilberries and cream.

One day we encountered a bird new to Iceland, fossicking for insects around a particularly fertile part of the oasis called Nautalda—one of the dark-headed forms of the yellow wagtail. In the same place we found the remains of an adult pinkfoot in a great splash of feathers on the ground. Amongst the feathers was one brown one, which could only have belonged to a white-tailed eagle.

Near the top of the hill of Nautalda was one of the drystone constructions which the farmers knew as 'goose pens'. There is only one reference in the rather lengthy literature of Iceland to the use of these pens. In 1638, the last year of his life, Gísli Oddson, the Bishop of Skaholt in South Iceland, wrote a treatise on the natural phenomena of Iceland in his native tongue. The original is lost, but a Latin treatise, *De Mirabilibus Icelandæ*, by one of his ministers, is in Bodley's Library in Oxford. This is what Gísli says:

'I am speaking of fowl which come from abroad; throughout the winter these do not dwell among us and are not even observed. Such are commonly the wild geese, the 'graagaaser', so called from their ashy colour. These are a little smaller than swans and in springtime they occupy the island in an almost countless number, in winter however they are nowhere to be seen. The common report is that every year in autumn they make for the neighbouring countries of England, Ireland and Scotland and in spring leave those countries and wait upon us. I must put on record the most remarkable usefulness of these birds. By the generosity of Providence they provide for us and leave like loot exceedingly tasty eggs, their own flesh to feed on and feathers to use. Our birdcatchers keep a careful lookout for the time (which appears miraculous) when the young geese, half grown and exceedingly fat and living for the most part in deserted places, have not yet become able to fly—the time when their parents are also unable to fly, having no strength left,

and their wing feathers being sucked down to the blood. Then,
I say, our hunters are at hand; they prepare beforehand fixed
fences, mounds or pens whither with no trouble they drive the
flocks of birds like sheep to the slaughter; when they are shut up
they kill all they choose, since the geese have no chance left to
them of escaping by the help of their wings.'

These statements are in many respects remarkable, since
they show that the catching of the flightless geese in these
pens, in the interior, went on up to the seventeenth century;
most people had thought that with the close of the Saga Age,
in the fourteenth and fifteenth centuries, the Icelanders had
given up going into the interior altogether. But certainly there
is no evidence that they went there in the eighteenth or early-
nineteenth centuries, and all the old interior crossings had to
be rediscovered in the last hundred and forty years. Gísli's
statement that the geese of Iceland are wintering in the British
Isles is also remarkable, when we consider the ideas then-
prevalent about bird migration.

The goose pen on Nautalda, which is one of the best
preserved of the dozen or more seen by the expedition, is about
twenty-five yards long and two yards across. Its walls, which
must have been over four feet high before they began to fall
down, were made of boulders just small enough for a strong
man to carry, and were of dry stone. The pen was shaped like
a very long and narrow U or the longitudinal section of a test
tube, and very cunningly sited about three-quarters of the way
up the hill, on a flat above a slightly convex slope so that the
geese going uphill would not see it until the last moment. For
a week or more the expedition wondered how the operators
persuaded the geese to go through the mouth of the pen, but
eventually we found the solution from our own experience, as
you shall see.

Meanwhile, we were concentrating on goose chasing and
goose hunting. Sometimes we were accompanied by other
hunters, on several days we encountered the young sea eagle,
and once flushed it from a newly killed gosling by the bank of

a stream. It had already eaten the head of its prey. At one time or another three different Iceland falcons were seen: they were also eating goslings. Unlike the eagle, these ate the breast and intestines first. And twice we met a bird which was new to the English members of the expedition—at least, wild and at close quarters—a magnificent, white, male snowy owl. Finnur, who had made the first discovery of a snowy owl's nest in Iceland a few year's previously—in the central desert about thirty miles north of where we were—thought it might well have been an off-duty bird operating from its nesting place.

A later crossing of the Blautakvísl was more spectacular than former ones. Crossing where the river was single, not at the delta, Valli went ahead on his own horse, towing the two pack animals. They splashed in, and he was soon up to his knees and his horse nearly swimming. So he came back, and the whole party floundered along the muddy bank down to the delta crossing—all but James. His horse, coming last, picked its own way along a mossy bank of the main river-stream, very near the edge. This was all very fine until it got bogged in the moss and began to flounder. It soon became clear to James that the floundering was getting out of control, so he rolled off to the left, still on the bank, just as the horse slid into the river. It then waded out into midstream, which was halfway up to its saddle, and started to walk downriver to the Thjórsá, in which, Valli told us afterwards, he thought it would end. The rest of us found a certain bizarre humour in the situation, overtaken as they were by a riderless horse in midstream. However, the mare soon thought better of its first idea and waded ashore to Valli's horse, whence it was returned by him to James, who forded the delta after all without having to get wet.

Another day we drove fifteen geese into the nets on Oddkelsalda: the first time we had used these successfully. Certainly we were finding the geese (even though the goslings were now big, and all could run faster than a man) easiest to catch on the hills, when we took advantage of the natural propensity of the geese to run uphill when cut off from water.

In a hunt on the fine hill Arnarfellsalda we rounded up twenty-four altogether: six adults and eighteen goslings. But as this was out of a pack of some hundreds, we were still pretty dissatisfied.

There is much individual variation in the behaviour of geese and goslings during a hunt. Some are very wary when crouching and run on when a rider is dismounting. Others stay put and are easy to pick up. When released in bunches, some become very calm, take humans or horses for parents and have to be pushed away; this concerns only goslings, for adults always rush off at once, though one or two occasionally crouch again about thirty yards away.

When the young go in little bands, squeaking to each other, they often walk slowly at first, their rings clinking on the stones of the hill, and then appear to reach a distance at which the humans suddenly become enemies instead of half parent-substitutes: for they suddenly accelerate and rush off into the dead ground, of which they have no sense, however, for they often reappear on ridges beyond. This is when the group straggles out, and sometimes the runts get separated.

On 22 July, the expedition caught thirty-seven geese. On 23 July, we rested the horses for the day, brought our diaries up to date, and washed—even shaving came into the day's programme! We discussed plans and results, and came to the general conclusion that we were doing something wrong. Although we had ringed no fewer than 268 geese and goslings, we felt we were not making the best of our opportunities: not catching enough of a population that was proving to be surprisingly large—working, in fact, in an exhausting and wasteful way. Such was the situation when the expedition decided to make a crossing of the River Thjórsá to taste the goose density on the other side, and to find a more efficient way of driving and catching the pinkfeet of Thjórsá.

It had been a very cold sunset and it was an unpleasantly cold night. James woke several times with cold and, in wriggling about to dodge the draught he tore the inner lining of his ancient sleeping bag. He came into the mess tent for breakfast looking like a snowstorm. During the night an Arctic fox barked several times in Oddkelsver, a triple coughing bark. The morning hoar frost made the glaucous willows a cold green, like crystallised angelica. But as soon as the sun had shaken off the skyline of the ice cap, it was bright, and soon it began to be warm. A swan flew past as Peter emerged from his tent, and over in Oddkelsver he saw three groups of geese and a few sheep.

We were now much attached to our base camp in this glorious place: the only disadvantage of this particular part of the oasis was the fairly high density of animals in the drinking water: no doubt they were very nourishing and full of vitamins. When the expedition got back to England, J. P. Harding of the Natural History Museum identified a dozen different sorts, of which by far the commonest was a Copepod called *Diaptomus castor*.

The main tent, the big white Scottish-made 'Iceland' tent, was extremely well organised (by Phil) and quite comfortable. The floor, which was moss and grass—to begin with— was now somewhat the worse for wear, and dusty; but otherwise the accommodation was very good. Just inside the door on the right was a group of ration boxes on their sides, their pigeonholes filled with food tins: this was the larder. Next came another box with the two Primuses sitting on it. In the middle of the tent was a wooden box full of biscuits with a cardboard tabletop attached to it, the corners carefully rounded off—all this the work of James. The dining room table was a source of great pride and gratification to all. The expedition sometimes sat down to meals with a tablecloth, and always with a vase (empty tin) of flowers in the middle of the table—sometimes thrift, sometimes thyme, very often the pinkish-mauve, orchid-like *Viscaria alpina*. Ranged around the walls of the tent were kitbags and more ration boxes, full and empty (or at least empty of food, and filled with films, books, and oddments). There was a string along the wall of the tent on which we hung washing up cloths and socks. On the far tent pole from the door hung Finnur's gun (scarcely used), and behind the pole he stowed his air mattress, as he slept in the mess tent. We sat on ration boxes, using various forms of padding. James had thoughtfully bought two air cushions, one of which was lent to Phil. Peter brought in his sleeping bag every morning, rolled up as a cushion. The last side of the tent was Finnur's department (collecting gear, plant presses); it contained also the toolbox, and the wooden box to which was attached the generator of the radio and beyond that was the transmitter-receiver itself, next to the door, so that we could lead in the aerial and the earth.

At breakfast Valli interrupted a general discussion of the relative merits of cameras to report (Finnur rapidly translating) great quantities of geese which he had seen south of the camp when he had gone to get the horses, including about sixty in the mouth of the iron stream quite close to the camp. We discussed setting a net here when we had come back from the other side of the river.

Although not more than twenty miles from its main source, the River Thjórsá as it flowed across the great plateau near the camp was in places quite a mile wide, ramifying intricately through sands and alluvium which it had brought down in past ages. Just by the camp, however, it narrowed to a quarter of a mile, to flow off the plateau down minor rapids between two headlands. The farmers' crossing was just above these rapids, and it was this that Valli had successfully tried on horseback the day before. It was now the time for the entire party to explore the mysteries of the left bank.

We all crossed at about eleven-thirty, on our horses, wearing outer mackintosh trousers fastened with strings to the tops of our wellingtons. The crossing was from camp to sandbank (up to the horses' knees), from sandbank to sandbank (bellies), from sandbank to stony island (bellies), and from stony island to the headland Sóleyjarhöfdhi (hocks, and in one place bellies). The last part of the crossing was difficult, with large round boulders on the floor of the river. But all the ponies behaved wonderfully well, and James's only stumbled once. So we were all over the famous crossing, dry and ready for anything. We rode up the green hill and looked over the valley beyond.

Down on our right a small party of geese was moving away. With the glasses, Peter could see a much bigger bunch half-hidden under the hill which had not yet begun to move. We withdrew, and trotted along the blind side of a ridge so as to come out opposite them. When we came over we found a large crowd of geese, fully fifty, and galloped down into the marsh. Phil and Valli were all among the young, but a big contingent went up the steep slope beyond, and we roared after them. It looked as though it should be a good do, but somehow, surprisingly, it was rather a failure. At the end, the catch was only nine goslings and three adults, but we got five more rather large goslings half a mile on down the valley, which were obviously a product of this hunt.

One of the adults, a gander, had a broken tarsus which had completely mended. This was the right leg, and although we could easily have put a ring on above the swollen joint, we thought that anyone recovering the bird later would be bound to attribute the injury to the ring, so ringed the left leg instead.

We rode along the bank of a tributary of the Thjórsá known as the Thúfuverskvísl, with a high ridge on our right, and presently we saw a crowd of thirty or forty geese going up it. It was a forlorn hope really, but Valli went crashing off. Already this same ridge, farther back, had tired the horses at the first stint, and this second climb finished them and yielded only fifteen goslings. But it gave us an addition to our technique. A gosling crouched far ahead of Peter; he approached it in a wide curve, leaned down with his net, scooped it off the ground, brought it up to the saddle, and transferred it to his sack, all without dismounting. The horse didn't mind this at all, and behaved with exemplary *sang froid*.

The Thúfuverskvísl was a 'clear' river—a snow stream, not a glacier stream; it made the water of the extreme left of the Thjórsá also clear for quite some distance below its entry, as we found on our crossing. There were many snow buntings about, some with flying broods, and meadow pipits; on dry patches of vegetation, whimbrels and golden plover and dunlins. Over a marsh flew a pair of Arctic terns. Presently we came round a headland into sight of the main marsh of the Thúfuver (which means the 'Meadow of the Mounds'). At once we were faced by a deep creek with tangled banks, upon which was much vegetation. Here we found some plants that we had not seen before, and James saw a bumble bee. It was certainly an area of eminently goose-worthy tundra bog, and following the creek, we counted thirteen empty, hatched nests of pinkfeet on its dry banks in a few minutes. All of a sudden James's horse shied and deposited him neatly on the ground.

The horse had shied at a brood of whooper swans under the bank—cob, pen, and three cygnets, two or three weeks hatched. The cob was still able to fly and went off, returning after a few minutes; the pen, however, had already moulted, and was bravely ready to protect her young. The creek was not very easy to cross, except for me in long rubber boots, and the swan kept in the stream, although it was only a few feet wide. Eventually, after a violent and wet chase, Valli caught it, while James and Phil caught the three cygnets. A remarkable feature of the pen was that the irides of her eyes were a pale grey-blue, and marbled—this was quite different from the eyes of Daisy, the adult whooper at the New Grounds in Gloucestershire.

We all photographed the swans in colour and black and white, and then let them go, and had an agreeable (if fly-blown) sunny lunch under the bank near the ruins of an old shelter hut. The horses had a good grazing place.

After lunch we continued along the cairned track and encountered another pack of geese, some distance away by the shores of a lake. It was here that we suffered from indecision. Valli for once did not spur madly on, as the horses were tired. Phil cantered off on her comparatively fresh animal after some of the geese, and Finnur and James, with me not far behind, chased a party up a col between two hillocks to the ridge, and came quickly upon a huge new pack of geese and goslings, in all over two hundred, by a tarn. We urged our ponies on to a fast trot, and gradually came up with the geese, losing a small party of adults to a hillock on the right, but edging the vast majority up a steep hill to the left, along which the ponies, fortunately, could trot. Over this hill we confidently expected to see Valli and Phil, for they had last been seen going in that direction.

Presently, over the hill, Finnur, Peter and James found ourselves the agents of a classic round-up. Our three ponies stood on three sides, and for a moment held, immobile and hunched solid, about a hundred and fifty geese, mostly goslings.

Then an adult ran downhill, and it was as if the key log of a dam had slipped, for the situation at once collapsed and the goose pack scattered in every direction, leaving us to gather what we could. James, probably wrongly, charged off downhill to grab a gosling at the edge of the marsh, where he got off his horse. Peter and Finnur stayed up the hill. Valli came up hastily from half a mile away in response to urgent signals. Phil was nowhere to be seen. We fought to glean what we could from the lost harvest. James returned uphill to field another gosling, chased it downhill with his net, and turned his ankle painfully. It was Valli who caught the gosling. By the time Phil rode back, having pursued and caught three geese of her own, we were all seething with frustration.

There were no recriminations, for it was not in the drill that Valli and Phil should have stayed back, and the separation of our forces was entirely a mistake of our own agreed policy. But Peter went so far as to say that never in the whole of his goosing career had he lost such a mighty opportunity.

We were exhausted and disappointed. The pack horses were out of sight. Phil had had to catch one of her goslings twice when it escaped from her bag, and during the ringing operations we all fumbled so much that two more goslings escaped and had to be caught again, and then an adult escaped and was finally recovered by Valli about three hundred yards away.

But how could we have exploited the situation without nets? A net in the right place, on what we now called Frustration Hill, would have landed us with at least a hundred geese and an hour's ringing—perhaps two hundred. If the five riders had all been together, could we have surrounded the pack and let them out a few at a time to be caught individually? Could we have rushed in among the geese, brandishing our hand nets, and kept them crouched? Could we have intimidated them by shouting? What the hell could we have done? Answer: at least better than five adults and ten goslings—which is all we got.

As the horses were tired, we started back from the Thjórsá, and on the next hill south immediately fell in with a pack of goslings, of which, for once, we caught nearly all we saw—eight—bringing the day's total to fifty-five, a record for a day's work but somehow a very disappointing record. But we got these goslings at some cost, for as a result of this hunt we lost one horseman, at least temporarily.

When James had twisted his ankle on Frustration Hill, Peter had warned him to be careful of it. This warning got forgotten in a headlong chase after a gosling. Twice it crouched and twice it beat his hand net, and on its third run James thought he had it, when it somersaulted down a bank of large loose stones. Instead he came over on his already weakened ankle, turning it over sole inwards and coming down on it with all his sixteen stone from a four-foot jump. He immediately dropped his net and sack and staggered, unable to stop, another twenty or thirty yards, and ended up below the once-more-crouched gosling, in a trauma, so that he could only wave to Valli and point wordlessly to the gosling, which Valli easily caught.

Somebody brought James his horse, but he had to get off it at the top of the hill and lie down for a bit, as the external world was beginning to withdraw. It came back as the others were rounding up the last goslings and ringing them, and afterwards he felt better and improved in health and spirits as the party went home. He kept his gumboot on as a tight messing, and his by then throbbing ankle was much cooled, in a very pleasant way, by the return crossing of the Thjórsá, which had risen two or three inches. The party crossed without mishap in the evening sunshine.

James's foot was pretty blue and swollen when the boot came off, and chasing geese on foot was out for him for the rest of the trip (of which we only had about a week left before we had to start back). With the total catch at 323, Peter doubted if we could make five hundred, which was the figure we had set ourselves as 'complete success'.

Back in camp James's (medicinal) ankle-brandy somehow became tots all round, and we all settled down to cheerful talk and nonsense, in spite of the frustrations of the day.

Radio conditions were hopeless in the evening, which was once more very cold, with a marvellous sunset lighting the snow peaks of Tungnafellsjökull with luminous pink. There was a chill north wind which blew all night.

Next day, Peter was woken at 3.15 by the distant drone of aero engines. Could this be the expected Sunderland to drop mail and films? He emerged to find the most brilliant red dawn going on, and a distant speck of an aircraft which looked like a Catalina crossing from Reykjavík to Seydhisfjördhur—though why at 3 a.m. seemed obscure.

At eight it was blowing hard, still from the north, and cloudy and cold. We were going over to Oddkelsver to try some catching in our rabbit nets, already set on stakes at the top of the grey hill there—all except James, who was confined to camp with his ankle. The rest set off about 12.30, crossing Blautakvísl and dividing up immediately. Finnur and Peter forked left across the marsh, while Phil and Valli rode up the Thjórsá bank. All had agreed to emerge upon the marsh (now known as Falcon Marsh) at 2.10 p.m.

Finnur and Peter found a party of geese at the exact spot where we had previously made our best hunt-catch. They moved onto the hill ahead. It seemed they might be driven into the nets, so just before the fox earth the expedition divided, Finnur with the pack pony going up over the ridge, while Peter rode round the foot of the hill. Near the Fox Earth these geese, and many more, came into view, and began heading for the north crest of Oddkelsalda, but they slipped out to the left and crossed the Miklakvísl. At the time, Peter thought Finnur was going too fast, and shouted and waved frantically (and successfully) to hold him back. But when the last of the goose families—two hundred strong in all—had crossed the stream into Illaver, he rode over and joined Finnur feeling already slightly despondent and frustrated. All our trust would now have to be placed in the marsh on the other side of the hill, where we could hear at least one goose calling.

Peter dismounted when he came to the point at Miklakvísl and peeped over. Not a goose was to be seen on the green marsh. When there were still two minutes to go he saw Valli ride out from his corner, so mounted and emerged myself. At first he could see nothing. Then he saw three or four adults and a few young making their way up to the top of the hill. It looked as though the party would not draw completely blank. Peter moved up onto the ridge to make sure the geese did not leak out. Phil was riding up and down far across the marsh, he could see. As he breasted the ridge an amazing sight was disclosed: coming towards me was a flock of some two hundred adult geese, and farther behind another flock of not-less-than three hundred mixed goslings and adults. The first lot saw me and turned up the hill Oddkelsalda. By working the ridge carefully, he could keep them in view while keeping out of sight of the second batch. Certainly many of the second lot went the wrong side of the wing of the net, but a great and awe-inspiring crowd of geese was already in the net. Peter rode over to Finnur, and together we moved up on to the summit, with Valli on our left. There, in the middle of the V of the net, the birds all stood, tightly packed, adults and goslings together!

From what we subsequently learned, there must have been at least five hundred birds. For one thrilling moment we saw them move down towards the cage. They came to the wing at one side of it. It held them for perhaps five seconds, then, under the weight of birds, it fell down and they all ran out down the hill. It was a bitter blow. But Valli was galloping round them, and soon many were on their way up again. Peter had put up the net again, but in a few minutes the geese were against it on the wrong side. Again in a matter of seconds it was down again and the stream of geese had run through onto the top of the hill; now they were back on the right side of the net but heading for the Miklakvísl.

Finnur and Valli came in and cut off the stream before any had gone, and once more a phalanx of geese was standing on top of the hill. Now the four of us were on all four sides of the geese, and a state of near-equilibrium had been reached. This was the critical moment. Could we keep them there long enough to repair and strengthen the net? How long would they be ready to stand in a bunch on the crest of the hill without making a determined effort to break out? Already some individuals were making minor sallies to test the siege. But the goose crowd seemed to offer some kind of refuge, for as soon as the breakaway geese were headed they ran back into the crowd and were, it seemed, relieved to be in the thick of the flock again. A few geese had become tangled on the wrong side of the net when they went back over it. These Phil and Peter now extricated, ringed, and released (five or six goslings and two adults). That got them out of the way. Then Peter went down to the end of the wings to get stakes, not now needed out there, to strengthen the cage and the wings near it. While this was going on, Valli and Finnur stood behind the geese, about ten yards from them. Finnur's horse and the pack horse came down one side of the geese, almost spoiling everything, but finally, instead, acting as additional stops.

At one stage Phil said they must take a photo of it. Peter agreed as long as Finnur didn't see, for poor Finnur was in an agony of mind about the situation and kept urging haste, saying that he did not think they could keep the geese in much longer! Peter kept calling to Finnur not to worry but just to keep them in—which he most skilfully did.

At last all was ready. The cage was as strong as it could be made. Phil drew back, keeping to the same side so as to hold the geese up if they began to break through. Peter moved round a little, and the whole flock began to move down the slope almost without knowing it was moving. It was at this stage that, for the second time, Peter remembered to look for blue rings (birds ringed by Phil and myself in Scotland or perhaps the Wash). The first time he hadn't seen any, but now, right in front, he could see a bright blue ring. He shouted to Phil, who also saw it.

The geese went into the cage, though it would scarcely hold them all. Peter was for bringing round one of the wings to enclose them from behind so as to have a much larger cage, but Finnur thought they might get them all into the cage, and they found when they were all in that there was just room for them. The cage was five yards by about three; more or less oval.

Now the mystery of the goose folds was solved. No wings had been necessary, no nets, nothing but the stone pen. A few more riders would have been necessary, but ten would be ample; the birds would be rounded up on the top of the hill, and then edged gently towards the fold. That was evidently the whole story, and it was very fascinating to have tested it in this way. With their geese safely in the cage, Valli finally pulled up one wing and brought it across to use as a door. With the cage so full they couldn't get at the door they originally provided.

Now the worst trouble was that if the party approached the cage the geese would crowd to the opposite side, climbing on each other's backs: there were at this time about three hundred geese and goslings in the cage. Another problem was that the top line of the net began to slip down the stakes as the net was bulged out by the weight. In this way, during the next hour or so, about thirty geese escaped in ones and twos. Some got out at the joint of the new door, one or two through holes in the net. Valli broke out a badly tangled bird, leaving a gaping hole in the net. These were all the difficulties, but by and large matters were under control, and we soon fell into a satisfactory drill. Phil got into the cage and caught the birds, adults one at a time, goslings two at a time, bringing them to me to be ringed. Finnur was on the opposite side writing notes, and Valli was free to move about, make minor repairs, disentangle birds about to hang themselves, and so on, while Peter ringed on.

In this account it has been said that three hundred geese went into the cage, but at the time we had no idea what the number was. Peter had 130 rings with me and whenever a bird escaped he said to Finnur—who was always much concerned about it—'Never mind: we have far more than we have rings for!' He was not even sure of that, but thought so, and eventually it became evident that this was the case. When he had no more than a handful of rings left on the string there was still a sufficient number of geese in the cage to make it worthwhile for Valli to go back to the camp for more rings.

While he was away the geese in the cage were rested. Most of the goslings sat down and went to sleep quite happily. We handled the blue-ringed bird: it was number 129984. In due course Valli came riding back. He had Peter's horse with him, which had wandered away a bit. He had been away for less than an hour. We got to work again and ringed the rest of the geese in the cage.

Meanwhile, in camp, James was finding his ankle standable but not walkable on, as expected, and was writing up his diary; trying to make some swan rings out of goose rings (the expedition had forgotten to bring any of swan size); screwing the radio dynamo on to a new stand; and washing. He had his first hot water bath for a month by instalments; washed some clothes; trimmed his beard; played a game of patience; and cooked a good lunch. When Valli came cantering up for what James quickly guessed were more rings, the situation became mysterious. It surely meant either splendid forgetfulness or a splendid catch; and the mystery deepened when James looked at the catching pen, three miles away on the hill, through his glass, and saw nobody. This was, as it turned out, because Peter, Phil and Finnur had sat down in a withdrawn spot. But an hour after Valli had left with a string of rings James saw the horses by the pen and human figures moving busily about. They were still there after a further hour and a half. 'Are they just taking up the nets?' he wrote in his diary. 'Or have they caught half the geese in the Thjórsárver? If the latter, why does this bloody ankle prevent me from being in on it!'

When Valli returned to the goose net, what Peter had thought to be sixty, perhaps more, turned out to be 118, and included another blue-ringed bird. When we looked the two 'blues' up later we found that one had been marked in October in Southeast Scotland, and the other in December on the Wash. Thus the total number ringed was 247 (ninety-four adults), plus six local recaptures (two adults), plus two recaptures of British-ringed birds. When the last geese had been released, we went down to the little pool to the west of the hill and had lunch. It was about 6 p.m.

Afterwards, we went up and reset the net with a larger cage of improved design.

One very curious thing had been happening. On the middle lake of the marsh from which our party had drawn the geese there had been a bunch of geese all through the ringing operations, although we were in full view and only about four hundred yards away. Many of the released birds must have gone down there, because the number steadily increased. They sat on the water, mostly, but after a while they began to feed quite unconcernedly on the far bank. This behaviour was in marked contrast to anything which we had seen before. After lunch we saw a possible cause. Sitting on a mound in the marsh beyond was a huge, pale bird—a very large Iceland falcon: so large indeed that at first it was taken for a female or immature snowy owl. A few minutes later, and quite close, a much smaller and darker Iceland falcon, mobbed by Arctic terns, flew out from behind the hill, but not towards the geese. This no doubt was the tiercel, the male. The falcon, the female, out on the marsh beyond, paid no attention to him. The whole behaviour of the geese was strange, and it may be that the presence of the hawks had something to do with it.

We trotted home well pleased with our great success, and arrived at camp just in time for the 10 p.m. radio sked. Communication was good, and we got a correct text for British Minister Jack Greenway's message of the 23rd.

*'Much regret due mistake in London Sunderland pilot received
no instructions re dropping. Am telegraphing London ensure
these issued for return flight approximately four days' time.
Please give exact map reference of your position. Greenway.'*

We passed our position as 64° 33' N, 18° 47' W on west
bank of Thjórsá, which he received O.K.

Then over supper the others retold the great doings of the
day to poor James, who had missed them, and went finally
to bed exhausted. Phil had handled every one of the 247
struggling, flapping, kicking, scratching geese—no mean feat
for a girl.

After that the net technique was used successfully five
or six times, and catches of over a hundred became almost
commonplace.

The first of August was our last day in the Thjórsárver.
That day the farmers were expected with the pony train to
take us back home downriver. It was a day which should have
been spent in packing up the scientific specimens, dismantling
the radio, breaking camp. But the number of geese which
had been marked fell short of a thousand by only forty-six.
It was in vain that we talked of the practical necessities and
the scientific insignificance of round figures. What was the
difference between 954 and 1,000? A mere bagatelle! But by
unanimous decision we were riding out, soon after breakfast,
heading south towards Eyvafen. To make it a thousand seemed
to be a real and worthy objective.

It was a silent, windless, sunny morning, after a still, warm
night. We did not have to go more than two kilometres from
camp, on the way to Eyvafen, to find and catch geese. Indeed,
we were ringing so many on what we now called Roundup Hill
in Lower Tjarnarver that the expected guides, arriving from
Kjálkaver round about 1 p.m., found us still engaged with the
remnants of a gosling crowd in the catching pen, and stood by,
while the ponies sniffed and blew at each other. So we returned
to camp a triumphant convoy of seven humans and eighteen
horses, with a specially warm feeling promoted by having,

in our first visit to the mysterious goose grounds of the Thjórsá, marked no fewer than 1,151 geese (346 adults, 805 goslings) and recovered two marked in the previous winter in Britain. Just as we reached camp it began to rain from a calm sky—a cosy kind of rain. We had a meal with the guides and counted our blessings; we felt really elated and satisfied.

What happened at the last hunt was this. Arriving at the low place between Red-throated Diver Lakes and the River Thjórsá, we spied carefully. From his horse James saw some geese pushing up towards the lakes. The geese had already seen us. We were discussing whether to lay on a drive, and James had just suggested that there might be other geese in the bog, when Phil drew attention to a big lot going along the marsh away from them, round the next riverside hill, on the landward side. At once the shape of the drive became clear, and it needed no orders for Valli to rush on along the riverbank, and the rest of us to follow. The grey stony Roundup Hill was easy to cover, for Finnur and James could get into position along the riverside unseen by the geese. Peter stayed at the end with Phil, ready to strike out into the marsh, and made signal contact with Valli, who by now had got most of the geese moving up the hill. Peter saw them arrive there just in time to signal James into a more downriver position; and when James turned inland and breasted a rise on his pony he found himself facing what he thought to be 180 geese (they afterwards turned out to be 206: 202 caught, two goslings escaped from pen, two adults flew).

James just managed to close with Finnur enough to prevent a river-ward trickle, led by an old gander, from developing into a pipe-off. The goose pack bunched at the highest point of the hill. The bunchers changed a bit at first; to begin with, Finnur and James on the Thjórsá side, and me to the northeast. Then Valli quickly unloaded the nets onto the ground from the pack pony which he had taken over from Finnur, and Finnur moved round to the west side, Valli taking his place on the southeast side. Peter called Phil to the job of making a net-pen and wings, which she did single-handed in under half an hour, in spite of snagged poles and tangled nets. It was amazing how well she sorted it all out and got it up, tight and good and stone-loaded. But we had to keep the geese entertained for half an hour. All the time it seemed to James that they were trying to get into the Thjórsá—that is, past him as he stood on his pony between them and it. Led by two big ganders, one at each end of the flock (either or both of which James would cheerfully have shot) slide movements began, sometimes into the gap between James and Valli, sometimes between James and me. These were easy to check provided there was only one movement at a time—a few steps of the horse to one side or another. But when such a movement started at each end simultaneously it was necessary to choose one and call a neighbour to cover the other. Everyone suffered from anxiety-neurosis, and James had an almost insistent exchange with Finnur as to whether Finnur was near enough. Valli kept taking his eyes off the geese to see how Phil, behind him, was getting on with the net. But we held the geese quiet, in spite of the ganders, though they began to get very bold at the end, and once James thought they had nearly all gone between him and Valli. The flock clucked and peeped all the time, and when the adult cackling got loud, we knew nonsense was brewing and that an assault was coming.

At last Phil said she had the nets ready, and Valli relaxed his pressure. One of the ganders immediately made a break and bashed over the wing of the net where it was too low, and disclosed itself as airborne (but only just). Phil, who had retired a bit, came in again to put in a new stake, and once more the flock was niggled along to the net. And this time they went in in fine style—straight and not too fast—and Valli came across with the short wing to close it, and the geese were penned.

We followed the usual routine. Phil and Valli (after the latter had been off to settle the horses) fishing out geese (first) and goslings (mostly later); Finnur writing down, James rescuing tangled goslings in the net and adjusting goose pressure in the net; Peter was ringing, and when he had run out of rings, tagging. James relaxed after an hour to rest his ankle, and took some colour photographs of the proceedings. Peter took some wonderful ciné shots of this herd and its entry into the cairn.

And so, when the nets had been taken up, a small calm built to mark the spot, the bridle of Phil's horse found and the cavalcade reassembled, we trippled back the twenty minutes to camp after surely the most successful climax to an unbelievably successful expedition.

As we ate lunch in the tent—varied by orange juice and pâté de foie gras (dropped by air)—the rain turned into a heavy shower lasting for an hour or two. It did not matter. Peter wrote in his diary:

> 'Now it is over and we can pack up. Finnur reports a white wagtail, and the boys (Águst, Snjólfur, and Valli) are bringing stones to make a little cairn and mark our camp. We are all in high spirits. We have marked 1,151 geese (346 adults). None of us, I think, ever dreamed that we might really break the thousand. It is immensely exciting to realise that, in the past five weeks, I have actually handled eleven hundred pink-footed geese. What a marvellous, valuable, and happy trip it has been!'

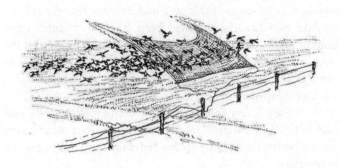

CATCHING WILD GEESE
WITH ROCKET NETS

Country Life (29 September 1955)

We caught our first wild geese with a rocket net over seven years ago—in February 1948. The catch was thirty whitefronts and one pinkfoot, and it was recorded in some detail in *Country Life* of 2 August 1948. Since then we have made 75 more catches, and caught over 6,000 geese by this method all told; yet this continues to be the most exciting occupation I know: combining the satisfactions of successful scientific research with the thrills of a new and unusually difficult kind of wildfowling. It calls for an even greater knowledge of the thoughts and actions of the quarry than ordinary wildfowl shooting. Since last December it has been necessary to hold a licence to operate rocket nets, which provides a useful safeguard: birds will be caught in them only for clearly specified scientific purposes.

Our first catch was made at Slimbridge, beside the Severn Estuary, where the largest numbers of whitefronts in Britain spend the winter. Subsequently we have travelled with our nets to many parts of England and Scotland, as our main interest has been in the pinkfoot, the most numerous of British geese, of which we believe there were about 46,000 in this country in October 1954. Formerly it also came to the Severn in thousands, but nearly twenty years ago the numbers at Slimbridge dropped abruptly, and now only a remnant of a hundred or so appears each autumn. Declines like this have occurred in several of the twenty main localities frequented by pinkfeet, while in others spectacular increases have taken place. We have been trying to find out why such changes occur, and whether the total numbers of the species are fluctuating violently too. So far, finding out has led us to catch pinkfeet for ringing and immediate release in 21 areas from the Severn to Aberdeenshire, and to set our nets in vain in at least five more.

The principle of rocket netting is simplicity itself. You hide two nets in a field where geese have been feeding, so that when they return they settle unawares close to the nets. You press a button and in less than a second the nets have spread out over part of the flock before they have had time to fly, and there they are, as the old fowlers used to say, 'ketched'.

The practice is far from simple. Our original nets were 25 yards square and were propelled by one-pound rockets, of the type used in ships and by coastguards for throwing lines. To catch more geese we wanted bigger nets. Bigger nets called for bigger and faster rockets. Bigger rockets needed stronger nets, and the mesh of the nets had to be reduced, so that the geese did not get their wings entangled, which made the job of extricating them a slow one. But when the mesh was made small enough to prevent entanglement, the geese ran about under the net until they reached the edge, when they flew away. To stop this, we had to fit flaps around the edges, and the nets were finally so much heavier that we needed yet bigger rockets. The endless-seeming problems of equipment called for innumerable experiments and the friendly cooperation of all sorts of inventors, experts, rocket-makers, net-makers, toolmakers, electricians, ballisticians and a host of helpers with no particular expertise. Our current equipment comprises two nylon nets, each 60 yards long by twenty yards wide, pulled over by six rockets made from 25-pounder shell-cases, using cordite as a propellant. The nets are set to shoot towards each other, like a giant version of the clap-nets used by the old birdcatchers.

Improving the rockets and nets has been a comparatively straightforward business, however many mistakes we may have made in the process. But, even with the best equipment, you cannot catch geese just when you want to. Geese are not mechanical toys, but living animals. Very mobile, keen-sighted and wary animals too: full of ideas of their own and with a language it takes long to learn.

At the end of last October we had begun to think we knew a lot about catching pinkfeet. In the course of twelve days we had made a catch near the Wash, another on the south-side of the Humber, two in Dumfries-shire and two in Southeast Scotland, and the total bag was 1,145. After a break for the full-moon period, when the geese often feed by night and become awkwardly unpredictable in their daytime excursions, we set off for another fortnight in November, believing another thousand to be as good as netted. Alas for our pride! There had been a lot of rain in the interval, causing unusually extensive floods in most of the goose haunts. We went first to the Loch Leven area, but there were few geese. One of the netting team, on his way to meet us, had found a promising-looking flock of over a thousand some twenty miles to the west. Next day we found them in the same place—a useful-looking oats stubble. (Stubble fields are the easiest in which to hide our nets—one of the reasons why we now do our goose catching in early autumn.) They were accompanied, most unexpectedly, by a herd of sixty whooper swans. We set the nets in the late afternoon, after the geese had retired to their roost, only about two miles away. The operation went smoothly enough, and the only question to raise doubts that night concerned the propriety of catching the whoopers, should they oblige us by visiting the catching area. We thought not.

We intended to be back with our nets at dawn, but were late—delayed by fog, but not much troubled because we knew the geese would be delayed by it too. They were. They sat on their heather roost nearly all day and did not come to 'our' field until after three in the afternoon. About half past three we thought there were 200 geese in the catching area. After a rapid but intense exchange of views by walkie-talkie between our hide and the rest of the party in the farmyard, we decided not to fire, because there was no hope of being able to extricate, ring and release a catch of 150 or more geese in the short time before dark. The next morning we were back, and so was the fog. The day dragged like the previous one. The geese came again in the afternoon, but rather fewer, rather less well placed and too late. No catch. The next day the pinkfeet did not seem to be trying at all, so, thoroughly frustrated, we packed up and retired hurt. Four days had been wasted.

The next three days were spent in moving north in a feverish search for pastures new in the shape of stubbles old, tolerably dry and packed with pinkfeet. These desirable anserine residences seemed to have ceased to exist. But at last we found a 'set' 100 miles northeast of our abandoned hope. By now we were beginning to feel desperate. Nine days out from home and not a goose. The prospect here was none too bright. Fewer than 500 geese in the most promising field, with another lot of about the same size using a field two miles away. 'Our' field was on the side of a hill; the slope was convex, with some awkward hollows. There were some stacks in one of the top corners, which served to cut down the effective area of the field, but would not do as cover for our trailer hide because of the slope. We decided to set well down the field and to place our hide by a fence two fields away, across the stream at the bottom. We set after dark. It was a beastly night: cold, windy and pelting with rain. Everything took twice as long as usual, but after just over two hours it was finished and we were soaked through. Next morning our luck changed. The geese came to the grass field next to ours. With communication through our walkie-talkies (which are the same as those used on Everest) it took only a few minutes to deploy our forces in such a way as to lift the geese and push them gently over to our stubble, where they settled just right, and in a trice we had 150 under the net. There was no prospect of a further catch thereabouts, so we set off south to Perth.

That night I travelled down to London for a day, leaving the others to search to the westwards in rolling country which is rather awkward for tracking flying geese from their roosts to their feeding grounds, especially, as it was then, in low visibility. When I returned, however, they had made a major discovery: a flock of over 3,000 geese living on floods in the bottom of a valley, so amply provided with feed in adjacent fields that they were scarcely flighting at all, flying only a few hundred yards. It took us two days to decide on the most suitable place to set. The field they seemed to prefer was almost entirely flooded and more or less useless for us. But on one occasion, when put off their favourite place, they had crowded into a very small field right on the edge of the floods on the opposite side of the valley: to be precise, it was a very small part of a field whose extent remained unknown because the rest was under water.

Having chosen this field for our nets, we had no difficulty in deciding where precisely to put them. Ruling out the immediate neighbourhood of the fences (geese rarely settle close alongside fences and feed up to them rather reluctantly) we found that there remained an area only just big enough, before the ground became too wet for digging in the rockets (and we cannot rely on our rockets going off under water). We had to leave the trailer-hide, from which the rockets are fired, rather a long way up the hill, so that, though we were looking down on the catching area it was from an angle, instead of along the length of the nets as we usually do. It was a good deal more difficult to visualise the outlines of the area from there. This might be difficult if the geese were tightly packed: an error of a few yards in tracing the outline of the catching area might cost us a large part of the catch. We tried for a catch that afternoon, immediately we had finished setting, but the geese did not come.

Early next morning we were back. Three of the team took up residence in the hide: one to look after the 'electrics' that fire the nets, one to take a film of the shot (if we should make one), the third to act as overseer, in a very literal sense. His job was to watch the geese after they settled in the field, count the number in the catching area, assess when the potential catch had reached a maximum and then press the button. He was also to act as radio link, hearing from the remainder of the party—500 yards away in the 'grandstand' (here the farm buildings, farther up the hill)—what was being done to bring the geese to the field. The value of this walkie-talkie intercommunication can hardly be overestimated. When the hide party may be confined for the whole of the daylight period, knowing accurately the situation round the net, but unaware of what steps are being taken to move geese from neighbouring fields, frustration can reach a high intensity. (Once geese were still being moved towards the catching field half an hour after the nets had been fired.) The introduction of a handy radio-telephone has revolutionised the whole technique.

On this particular morning the geese went first to their favourite flooded field, and fed while swimming. Gently, we put them up, one man walking across the neighbouring field until close enough to make them rise. They retired to the middle of the open water of the flood. An hour later they set off again to the same field and the process was repeated. After the third attempt they stayed on the open water, apparently no longer in any hurry. So a party drove off down the valley, over the bridge and back to as close as they could get. They had a walk of nearly half a mile across plough and a bank standing out from the water before persuading the geese to go about their business once more. It was no good. Most of them went off to a new field down the valley; a few resettled on the water. We left them for a short time in the new field, then put them up again. It was now half past two in the afternoon. They came streaming back up the valley towards their headquarters. They had to pass close to the set. In passing, some saw our decoys, checked, turned, circled and settled near them,

sad-looking stuffed apologies though they were. The settling
of the first bunch brought in others (the rotary wing-flapping
of alighting geese is the best possible decoying device) so that,
although most of the geese finished back on the water once
more, we had about 350 in the right place. But not quite right.
Despite the niceness of our calculation, few of the birds were
in the catching area, the majority being to the left of it (as seen
from the hide) and towards, or in, the water: and as they began
to feed they spread away from, rather than nearer to, the nets.

Now the only hope was to drive the geese into the area by
the most gentle disturbance possible (we call it 'twinkling')—
enough to make them stop, turn and walk away from you, but
not enough to make them fly. I set off down the hill to do
this most critical operation, under cover of a hedge three fields
away. After I had gone, a minor crisis arose, because the hide
party found that they could not see the markers of the catching
area properly. So one of the grandstand party set off, complete
with walkie-talkie, following the hedge behind me, until he
was able to look down the line of the nets, though rather
distantly. Thus in the last crucial minutes we were split into
four groups, kept in contact by a flow of messages by radio,
with the usual tendency for procedure to go by the board as
the tension increased.

Peter started creating his diversion and thought, with
horror, that he had overdone it. All heads went up, a few head-
shakes...they were going to fly...and a few started to flap away...
but no, the mass stayed on the ground. What was more, they
turned and walked quickly in the right direction. Slowly (it
may not have taken long, but it seemed slow) the numbers in
the catching area went up...90, 140, 160, 200, perhaps 210...
and then: 'Five, four, three, two, one, *fire!*' And up they went.
A swishing bang, a roar as the flock takes off. An anxious look
at the nets. Not many (there never seem to be many at first
sight), but well spread under both nets.

On to the field with all speed—all the gear in the jeep. The
keeping cages are set up (long rows of cells with walls and cover
of hessian stretched on stakes), and extrication begins. Two of

the team are extricating, four carrying geese to the ringer, one acting as clerk, one swabbing the throats of the geese (looking for a fungus disease), two taking geese from the carriers and stowing them in the keeping cages until the nets are empty. It was a catch of 140—modest, but useful. And, just over an hour after the shot, the keeping cages were lifted, the geese were free, and away they flew—our flock, ringed, and no doubt slightly surprised (except for the old hands caught once or twice before), but with such a story to tell us in the future of their movements and their numbers and their success in the struggle for survival.

There may be more exciting ways of doing biological research, but I do not know of them.

PAINTING WILD BIRDS

The BBC Naturalist (Rathbone Books, 1957)

I have painted all kinds of wild birds, but I tend to concentrate on the group of birds that interest me most—the ducks and geese—and inevitably you are inclined to give more loving care to painting a subject that pleases you intensely, in that way you create something which more easily comes alive. And for me a private pleasure is to paint a rare duck or goose in the setting in which I have seen it, in whatever part of the world it lives. If I can make it come to life again and recapture the atmosphere of the place, I recreate the enjoyment I experienced when I first saw it.

But of all the things that give me pleasure in painting, I like most trying to master the problems of light which comes from the other side of the canvas. I like to paint a picture in which I am looking into the source of the light—and if it is reflected in water, so much the better.

One of the special features of wild birds, as a subject for a painter, is that they compose themselves so easily. In painting a group of human beings, all at ground level, it is difficult to make an attractive composition; one of the classic devices for surmounting this difficulty is to introduce a flight of steps in order to give variety of height. But with birds in flight, you can move them about as they would naturally move in the air. You have to make the flock look characteristic of that particular species, but nevertheless you can group them in a pictorial shape; in fact, you can go on adding birds until you get the sort of composition you want, provided you stop before you ruin your canvas by overcrowding it. Nobody can say, 'There wouldn't have been one here,' or, 'There couldn't have been one there'. In that sense, birds give the artist a great freedom.

In other ways, though, they are not so cooperative! One of the great challenges that birds have always offered to painters down the ages is the challenge of movement. Unlike human beings, they do not sit for you. You need a quick eye to catch the changing shapes of a bird in flight, and you have somehow got to convey the sense of movement. One familiar device is to blur the wings, as the great Swedish painter Liljefors was the first to do. I have heard it said that this is merely an extension of photographic technique, at a time when photographic exposures were too long to arrest a movement of the wings. But it is a little more than this, because the eye does see a blur in a rapidly-moving object; and undoubtedly Liljefors was trying to represent what his eye saw as nearly as he could. However, I believe the real way of conveying movement is in the attitude in which you draw the bird, and in the grouping of other birds round it, so that the whole composition of the painting suggests movement.

Nowadays the artist has the photographer constantly at his elbow, as it were; and there is no doubt that the camera has helped to 'educate' our eyes. We are capable of seeing some things that we should never have seen consciously had it not been for the instantaneous photograph. A famous example is a galloping horse, which in the old days was painted with its forelegs sticking out in front and its hind legs sticking out behind, in a spreadeagled position. And presumably that was how everyone thought horses galloped. We now know, from instantaneous photographs and slow-motion movies, that at no single moment are a horse's legs in that position. The movement is much more complex, and the instantaneous positions have become familiar to us in every newspaper photograph of a big race. Nowadays, if you painted a galloping horse in that position, you would not get away with it, because people know that that is not what horses do. Our eyes have been conditioned to that extent by the camera. The same is true of birds in flight. In wild geese, for example, the tip of the wing is spread out on the downbeat, with the primary feathers separated like the fingers of a hand, and this movement is barely detectable to the eye. At least, I had never seen it; and I don't think anyone had ever drawn or painted it until high-speed cameras showed it to us. But now, every time I see a goose taking off or landing or putting any weight on its wing in the down stroke, I can clearly see the finger-like spreading of the feathers.

The photographer therefore has helped us to be more accurate by showing us things no painter had discovered; but that does not mean that artists should now throw away their brushes and take up cameras instead. I use both, and I think each technique has its different objectives and its limitations. You can pack far more into a drawing than a photograph can give, because the best photographs in the world do not say everything there is to say about a bird. In nearly all of them there is some one thing which is unsatisfactory: the bird's bill has just moved, or the shadow of a grass stem has fallen across its neck, or the reproduction of colours is imperfect. The artist can choose whether to aim at an impression of the general truth about a bird or whether to compete with the analytical quality of the camera and provide the precise literal detail of a birds appearance. If you are painting plates for books for the purpose of identifying species, every spot and stripe and tiny detail must be accurate; and here the artist can give an emphasis where it is needed, by ever so slightly accentuating some fine point of distinction. Even here, though, some degree of impressionism is not only permissible but in many cases actually a help to identifying the creature in the field, when the observer may be fifty yards away. In a decorative picture it is a mistake to paint in characteristics which you know a bird to have, when they could not be visible in the lighting conditions and the general setting you have chosen. For example, if I see a pintail fly past my studio window at The Wildfowl Trust against the evening sky, I may look for the white breast which I know it to have, but with the light behind it, the whole bird, breast and all, will look pitch black, or at any rate very dark indeed. A painting must be true as a whole.

Nowadays, many people occupy their leisure dabbling in paints, and discover that there are few things more satisfying. Those who are ambitious and try their hand with oil paints are likely, I think, to have the most fun. Oil paints do such pleasant things of their own accord—almost by accident. I know there are those who say there are already too many bad artists in the world and nobody ought to be encouraged to perpetrate more bad pictures; but I do not entirely agree. Perhaps too many bad pictures are *exhibited*; but that is a different matter. I would encourage people to have a go in their own particular way, not with a view to calling for admiration and showing how clever they are, but just for the delight of doing it while they are doing it. Whether your talent be great or small, the joy of painting is real and rewarding.

ON BEING A NATURALIST

Express Annual (Express Newspapers, 1957)

'You can make a start by keeping a few pets.'

One of the most prized books in my library is small with the rather unattractive sounding title of *The Minor Horrors of War*, by A. E. Shipley. The inscription on the flyleaf reads: 'To Peter M. Scott, F.Z.S., from the author.'

At the time, Arthur Shipley was Professor of Zoology in the University of Cambridge, at the head of his profession. He was also a great biologist (the combination is rather unusual). The book was presented to me when I was six years old.

There are several morals to this story. The first, and probably the most important, is that you can't begin to be a naturalist too young. I was a very keen naturalist at six. I had been for at least two years.

What were the 'minor horrors' in Shipley's book? Fleas, lice, bed bugs and such—the kinds of little animals that people prefer not to talk about and which nowadays we in this country don't have to worry much about either.

One of the main reasons why these and other parasites are now scarce is because scientists like Arthur Shipley have found out so much about them—so that it has been possible to destroy them.

I don't suggest that you start studying fleas, at any rate not until you are very experienced at keeping very small animals and have convinced your parents that the animals you keep don't escape. But I do think that keeping pets is a good idea.

I began by keeping caterpillars, especially those of the larger moths. Many of them are very handsome and it is fascinating to see how they transform themselves into chrysalids and then, after months hidden in a dead-seeming shell, emerge as beautiful flying insects.

To appreciate them you have to be prepared to look at them over a long period, feed them on fresh leaves of the right plants, but otherwise leave them alone.

If you live in the southern part of England see if you can find a privet hawk-moth caterpillar. Look at privet bushes during July and August for any bare stems where the leaves have been eaten away, and then search hard. If you're lucky you'll find a big green caterpillar with seven diagonal white stripes on each side, a pale green face with black markings, and a curious curved horn on its tail. A fully grown one is about three inches long.

Other insects, and small animals like spiders and woodlice, share the disadvantage of living in worlds so different from ours that you can't expect them to make friends with you. But you can get a lot of enjoyment from finding out how to keep them alive. Most of your finding out will have to be done by seeing where the animals live and what they eat.

One of the common British woodlice is known to be able to live for up to four years in the wild. You would be an extremely good naturalist to keep one that long in captivity.

Lizards and snakes, too, are not really able to be friendly though their worlds are closer to ours than the insects. But many of them make good pets because they like, or at least don't mind, being handled, and don't need very much care.

Mice and hamsters and other small animals are friendlier and livelier still. But you shouldn't keep them, or any other pets, unless you are really prepared to look after them, to find out what they need, and to give it to them constantly.

However interesting pets may be, most naturalists also want to look at animals and plants out of doors. There is so much more to be seen, so many different kinds, and often so many different individuals all adding up to a variety you cannot expect to equal even in the best homemade vivarium.

Of course, nowadays it is true that over most of this country the animals you see aren't natural in the sense that human alterations to the land have often very much altered the variety and abundance of the animals which occur. Though the animals are wild their communities are artificial. Perhaps the fascination of the really wild parts of Britain, the highlands and islands, is due not only to the scenery but also to the feeling that the animals and plants living there aren't doing so 'by our permission'.

Birdwatching is much the most popular kind of natural history in Britain, which isn't surprising because birds are found almost everywhere and there are lots of different kinds—but not too many.

I advise you to try and draw animals. Drawing is much the best way of describing animals, unless you're very bad at drawing and exceptionally good at saying or writing how things look. And if you've never tried you'll be surprised to find how much there is to see in every animal when you set about drawing it.

For me there is no job more worthwhile than looking at or listening to animals and recording what I see in pictures.

SLIMBRIDGE: WINTER HOME
OF THE WILD GOOSE

Meccano Magazine (July 1959)

The Wildfowl Trust was formed in 1946 to advance the study of wildfowl—ducks, geese and swans—many of which are in danger of extermination through the encroachment of civilisation. Its headquarters are on the south shore of the Severn Estuary at Slimbridge, in Gloucestershire.

The kind of wild country that wildfowl need is being steadily whittled away by the progress of civilisation. If they are to survive, certain steps will have to be taken, and in order to make sure that these steps are the most helpful ones, much research is still needed into the birds' habits and their life histories and migration routes.

For this kind of research the area known as the New Grounds, on the Severn Estuary, is almost ideally suited, and the Trust was therefore formed with the following objects: to promote the study of wildfowl and to undertake any activity which in the opinion of the Council is calculated to promote knowledge of and interest in wildfowl and, in particular, to establish and maintain a wildfowl research observatory at the New Grounds to make a close study of the winter flocks of wild geese and other birds; to ring wild ducks in the decoy pools and wild geese on the marshes for the further study of migration; and to study a comparative collection of live waterfowl.

The New Grounds, first so-named in 1470, consists of an area of flat alluvial fields reclaimed from the river, some four miles long and one mile wide, lying between the Severn and the Berkeley-to-Gloucester canal. These fields are protected from the high spring tides by a seawall, and outside it lies an area of salting, known as the Dumbles, which is the principal winter feeding ground for between two and five thousand wild geese. Along the seawall are a number of Observation Towers overlooking the salting, so that wherever the geese may be feeding it is possible for Trust members to watch them at fairly close range, sometimes less than ten yards. The thrill of watching wild geese at such close quarters is most easily appreciated by those who have had previous experience of their proverbial wariness, but even those who have never seen geese before cannot fail to be stirred by such an intimate view of these magnificent birds. They are mostly white-fronted geese, but a few pinkfeet arrive early in the season, and every species of goose on the British List has been seen at one time or another on this marsh.

It is important that the geese themselves should be totally unaware of being closely scrutinised. They have selected these marshes, and kept to them, chiefly because they have been carefully preserved from disturbance by the owners of Berkeley Castle for centuries past. This has been facilitated by the fact that the tidal waters to mid-channel, as well as the New Grounds, have been owned by the Berkeley estate, as indeed they still are.

Beyond the Dumbles lies the mile wide expanse of estuary sand and mud on which the geese and countless other birds roost. Some thousands of ducks spend the winter here and large numbers of waders pass through on migration. The broad estuary lying in the heart of Gloucestershire provides a sort of oasis for cross-country migrants, and a number of interesting birds have been seen there in recent years.

The seawall passes within 300 yards of the group of buildings which forms the headquarters of the Trust.

Between the buildings and the salting is a small spinney containing a decoy pool of about an acre. This decoy, originally completed in 1843, had fallen into disrepair, but it has been put into full working order again, and the annual catch has passed the two thousand mark. Each year more ducks are caught, ringed, and released again for the study of their migration routes. A gazebo, or summerhouse with a wide prospect, at the edge of the wood giving a view of the pool, is available to members of the Trust and to the public.

Parts of some rushy fields adjoining the decoy have been enclosed with a fox-proof fence, and special ponds have been dug to make a home for the largest collection of live waterfowl in the world. It is of great value both ornithologically, as an opportunity for the observation of breeding habits, and educationally, as an introduction to the study of waterfowl. Many of them breed and some of their offspring have been exported. In the summer months a hundred different kinds of ducklings and goslings are reared. Usually this is done under a hen or bantam foster mother, since many ducks and geese make poor mothers in captivity. There are, of course, exceptions and family parties can be seen in the grounds.

Special efforts are being made to breed species that are in danger of extinction. For example, the nene or Hawaiian goose, one of the rarest living birds, breeds well, and a flock of 53 now living at Slimbridge is descended from the original three birds given to The Wildfowl Trust by Mr. Herbert Shipman of Hawaii in 1950. The birds in the enclosures become astonishingly tame, and it is especially delightful to have a crowd of these beautiful creatures round one's feet, and feeding from the hand.

A wild goose chase is a phrase that has always been used to describe a fruitless errand, because geese are so difficult to approach in the open country they love. But the Trust has found a way to catch large numbers of geese and each autumn makes a trip to Scotland and northern England to ring up to three thousand pink-footed geese.

Large nets, sixty yards long and twenty yards wide, are thrown up, over and down on top of a feeding flock of geese. The nets are made of nylon so they are strong and yet light, and they have a small mesh so that the birds do not get their heads and wings through the holes, which would cause them to get very tangled. To carry the nets over the geese, smokeless rockets, six to each net, are used. These rush out from holes in the ground and are down again before the birds have had time to realise what is happening. Of course, those birds not under the net fly up, but they often come down a few fields away and start feeding again, and birds have been caught in the same place the next day.

The rockets are set off electrically by pushing a button in the camouflaged hide that we leave near the nets. Two or three people stay in there, the rest of the party go off to make sure that the geese coming in to feed do not go to the wrong field. The hide party is kept informed about what is happening outside by walkie-talkie radio sets.

By using this method much has been discovered about the migratory routes of the wild geese, their abundance, and habitat. Much too has been learnt of wildfowl behaviour. Although the Research unit of the Trust is based at Slimbridge, its work covers the whole country and close liaison is maintained with foreign organisations working on wildfowl, particularly those in North America. Expeditions have been undertaken to Arctic Canada, the United States, Lapland, Iceland, Patagonia, Bolivia, New Guinea, Australia and New Zealand.

In 1957 the Trust opened a branch near Peterborough in Northamptonshire—The Peakirk Waterfowl Gardens. This now carries the second largest collection of wildfowl in the world, and has brought to eastern England the opportunity of seeing a wonderful variety of wildfowl. The Wildfowl Trust includes full members, junior members under the age of 21, and associated members, all of whom have free access to pens and observation huts at Slimbridge and Peakirk, and there is a special grade of membership that will appeal to many of the younger readers of the Meccano Magazine who are interested in Nature study. For this all under the age of 16 years are eligible. The annual subscription is 7s. 6d., and members receive a Membership Card and a badge.

Members of this grade are known as 'Goslings'. They are entitled to free access to pens at the New Grounds and at Peakirk on Saturdays and Sundays, and an interesting scheme of promotions has been introduced. Any Gosling who in a test can name ten out of fifteen different kinds of duck, geese or swans pointed out to them becomes a 'Pinkfoot', and a red star is fixed on his or her membership card. By further tests advancement can be made through the grades of 'Whitefront' and 'Greylag', the latter being the senior rank of Gosling, and here again membership of the grade is indicated by stars, white for a Whitefront and blue for a Greylag.

Gosling members receive the present of an 'adopted duck' each time they renew their annual subscriptions. This means that to them is allocated a bird that has been ringed on behalf of the Trust. This may be given a name selected by the adopter, who is informed whenever the bird is recaptured, or recovered dead, so that he or she can follow as far as possible the life of the adopted bird.

A special leaflet explaining this grade of membership and including an application can be obtained by writing to: *The Editor, Meccano Magazine, Binns Road, Liverpool 13.*

FISH-WATCHING

The Second BBC Naturalist (Adprint, 1960)

For as long as I can remember I have been preoccupied with the study of living animals. My special interest has been centred in one family of birds—the wildfowl—the ducks, geese and swans of the world. Two hundred and forty-seven different kinds of them are known to science, and as soon as you begin to look carefully at the characters which separate these kinds one from another you cannot fail to wonder why and how the differentiation came to exist and you find yourself pondering upon the mysterious processes of evolution. This study was at one time largely the province of the museum worker who examined and compared the preserved specimens of the different kinds. But more recently the great importance of the differences in the behaviour of animals has been realised, and so the naturalist and his more scientific colleague, the ethologist—the students of living animals and their behaviour patterns—have come into their own.

At Christmas time in 1956 my wife and I were in the neighbourhood of the Great Barrier Reef off the northeast coast of Australia. A few months before, the distinguished pioneer of ethology, Dr. Konrad Lorenz, had told me, 'If you have not yet swum with a mask over a coral reef it is one thing which you *positively must do* before you die,' and now here was the opportunity. For three days we were free to go swimming over the most famous coral reef in the world. How, I wondered, would fish-watching compare with birdwatching?

When first put my mask below the surface of the crystal clear water at Michaelmas Bay I can remember shouting aloud with delight—so far as the snorkel in my mouth would allow—for the scene was a supreme and unimagined combination of beauty and interest. As an artist I was uplifted by the colours and shapes of the fishes and the corals among which they swam. As a naturalist I was amazed at the diversity of the living creatures I saw. In the clear sunlit waters I could see at one glance perhaps two hundred fishes. Some were in little shoals all of one kind, others in pairs, others swimming singly—not only a profusion of fishes but a profusion of different kinds, and a profusion, too, of invertebrate animals as well—bright blue starfish, orange sea urchins, sea cucumbers, green manic prawns, sea anemones, soft corals, giant clams. None of these creatures paid much attention to me as I cruised past lazily waggling my flippers in the balmy warm water. Little shoals of tiny sky-blue fishes which surrounded some of the coral heads withdrew into the branches when I came too close. Other bright blue and orange fishes about two inches long actually came out aggressively to try to drive me out of their territory. Fishes like vertical dinner plates with complex black and yellow patterns and comical turned-up noses swam in pairs and showed no fear at all. These I learned later were called butterfly fish. From one spot on the reef I counted up to fifty different kinds of fish within sight. Where above water could such diversity of species be seen together? But at once I wanted to know more about them. It was not enough to distinguish different kinds,

I wanted to identify them, put names to them, discover their relationships, study their feeding habits, their courtships, their aggressions, and above all to try to see how such diversity came to exist. About a month later we spent a whole week swimming on the reef at Korolevu in Fiji. Here we found more than a hundred species of fish, among them no less than fourteen species of butterfly fish or chaetodonts, swimming always in pairs and apparently living happily together at the same shallow depths on the same square kilometre of coral reef. How did all these chaetodonts, which mostly seemed to differ only in the patterns of their stripes and spots, come into existence? At first I was baffled; but then I began to see a mechanism by which it could have happened. Suppose that long long ago the widespread ancestral chaetodont species was hit by a great climatic change such as an ice age and could only survive in isolated shallow reefs where perhaps the sun warmed the water sufficiently. During this period the population on each reef might evolve different colour patterns under the selective pressure of slightly different conditions. Then when the climate improved again all these fishes might once more be free to travel between the reefs and indeed all over the oceans. But having been isolated long enough to become specifically distinct, and having a complicated courtship involving the striking colour patterns, they would not interbreed and become merged again, but would remain as different species all occupying the same habitat. Of course, this explanation may be quite wrong and many others are possible; for such things can never be known for certain. But for the fish-watcher, speculations like this are inescapable.

It was not until January 1959 that we were able to go fish watching again—this time in the Caribbean and later round the Galapagos Islands in the Pacific. There were new chaetodonts we had not seen before, and there were old friends too, familiar from the reefs we had swum over in Hawaii and Fiji and Queensland. Once more the profusion and diversity of fishes was fabulous, and once more we realised how little was yet known about them. What made the brilliant blue tang in one coral bay swim in shoals while in the next they went about singly? Why should some males of the blue and yellow damsel fish, which rejoices in the scientific name of *Abudefduf*, be aggressive while others were not? Were those small greenish perch-like fish the young of the larger groupers that we saw, or adults of a related (or even unrelated) species? Were the two types of bird fish with their long down-curved snouts really two species as the text books said, or were they, as seemed so much more probable, male and female of the same species?

Soon we came to realise that fish watching as a field study was at the stage reached by birdwatching about a century ago. The field is rich and now wide open to the naturalist. The aqualung is hardly necessary, the mask and snorkel—and perhaps a pad of plastic sheets, and some wax pencils with which to make drawings and notes—are all the equipment needed for great new discoveries in the study of animal behaviour and evolution. And as a delightful and stimulating occupation I can wholeheartedly echo Konrad Lorenz: 'If you are a naturalist and you have not yet swum over a coral reef it is something you *positively must do* before you die.'

NATURE OF FEAR

Argosy (March 1960)

In the summer of 1940, German bombers had command of the air. On a hot afternoon in the English Channel they came quite suddenly out of the dazzling haze round the sun. A spatter of machine gun bullets was the first warning; tracers drew thin blue hairlines round the destroyer; and then with a whining roar the first of the Ju87s pulled out of its dive.

Its bomb fell in the sea fifty yards away and a small spout of white water rose in the air to be engulfed instantly in the vast brown upheaval of the explosion.

Huge pinnacles of water shot upwards as the destroyer reeled and shook.

Ordinary Seaman McGill was knocked down by the blast and the jolt, and then nearly washed overboard by the deluge of water which fell like a cloudburst on the upper deck.

Dim through the brown mist of it he could see the next Stuka steep in its dive. Look out now, he thought, here's another. Quick now.

He scrambled up and scuttled for the protective cover of the galley flat.

The whine of the power dive was followed by a shattering explosion. The whole ship lurched and shook from end to end. The sound was as if the largest tin in the world had been whacked with a gigantic stick. With it came the roll of thunder and the crack of doom.

McGill was certain that, in this his first experience of action, the ship had been hit, that she must sink instantly; but outside the guns were firing still.

He had been on the way to his Action Station when the first bomb fell, but now he was back in the galley flat with the roar of aircraft and the bark of pom-poms in his ears and the fear of God in his heart. He crouched in a dark corner, the animal instinct to hide in complete control of his body.

The main armament had opened fire; the blast of the 4.7 guns blew into the flat through the ammunition hatches, and the crash of their discharge added to the shattering din. The ship heeled steeply under full rudder at high speed. Supply parties were handing up ammunition through the hatches; repair parties stood waiting.

No one noticed young McGill in the corner by the galley door. He crouched there with both clenched fists held against his head: his face was screwed up, lips apart, eyes half closed. His pulse raced but his mind was numb.

He knew there was something he should be doing but he could not think what it was. Could not think... If only there was a chance to think, but everything was noise—noise above anything he had ever imagined—noise that was more felt than heard, that shattered and stunned him.

From very far away he could hear the voices round him.

'Come on—keep that cordite going!'

'Near miss—lots of little holes in No. 2 Boiler Room.'

'More boxes of twelve-pounder, quickly!'

'...crashed about half a mile away.'

'Poor old Lofty.'

All these things he heard clearly, though far away as in a

dream; they did not belong to his world at all.

Suddenly the noise stopped. Someone shouted, 'First Aid Party—starboard waist,' and three hands shuffled past him with a stretcher.

McGill remained in his dark corner. Still he could not move. He was shivering violently. I must go... I must...

It was the final effort of his breaking will. He felt he was floating out towards the sunshine from the dark imprisonment of his terror. He was dazzled by the bright sunlight, but with it strength and self-control returned.

He met the stretcher party coming in and recognised the man they were carrying. It was old Hawkshaw, who had been teaching him boatwork from a book that morning. When you had grown up with boats and knew as much about them as McGill had learnt at home in Ireland, what with fowling in winter and fishing in summer—all these special names out of books were very bewildering. And what had books to do with this horror that he saw?

Old Hawkshaw! His face grey and twisted; the leg of his overall torn and blood-soaked; a long dagger of broken bone sticking from the mangled flesh; the hand that had held the book that very morning was not there now.

The stretcher passed, and McGill went out into the afternoon sun.

At the foot of the fo'c's'le ladder was a great pool of blood, and lying by the funnel was a headless body which someone had partly covered with a hastily-thrown duffel coat. The sea-boots projected grotesquely. There was movement under the coat.

'Poor old Lofty Reynolds,' said a voice at McGill's side.

'But he's still alive,' said McGill. 'I saw'm move, so I did.'

'Don't you believe it—that's just nerves.'

McGill went on up to the fo'c's'le and sat on a locker near the gun. The bright sun shone down on him. He felt very sick. The rest of the gun's crew were far too busy to notice him.

In the heat of the action the Captain of the gun had never missed one of his extra loading numbers, so no one but McGill himself knew that he had spent those four thunderous minutes crouching in the cover of the galley flat instead of feeding cordite to his gun.

The enemy did not return that afternoon, and when the protecting Spitfires arrived the guns crews fell out. Most of them sprawled about the upper deck in the sun in sudden relaxation.

McGill was stretched along the length of the locker gazing up into the deep blue of the afternoon sky with half-closed eyes. He was dazzled by the bright sunlight. His breath still came in choking sobs but the numbness was passing. As with cold hands, a terrible smarting pain took its place, filling every corner of his mind.

What difference did it make that no one else knew he had done it? He knew. Yes, he knew, but he did not understand. He had depended so much on being brave; he had been so certain that he would be.

It wasn't as though he had never seen fear before in all his eighteen years. They had met face to face in the short steep seas between his home and Chapel Island when he tried to cross on the ebb with a southerly gale.

Those were the nights when the wild geese flighted low and he loved to take the boat across, although they said he was mad to go. If it was dangerous he liked it more.

He would come back long after dark, soaked through, with perhaps a goose and a couple of wigeon to show for it, his hair wild and tangled with the rain and the wind, and his cheeks flushed, and Tim, his brother Tim, would give him a look... like that...

He had beaten fear many times, many fears: the fear of strong winds and strong tides, and fogs and quicksands, and leaky boats. The lough found new ones, but he had their measure—on the soft mud flats of the lough where others were scared to go.

The lough. And Chapel Island.

Just to think of them!

And the bright pastures of Green Island across the soft stillness of the bay; the golden brown of the seaweed and the smell of it; the sighing of the ash trees round the house, and the gentle curve of the grey pebble bank which joined their own island with the mainland shore, and was only covered by the highest spring tides. These were the real things, more real a million times than Ju87s and destroyers and HETF shells.

The green mound of the island with its tiny farmhouse among the trees on its sheltered side was his home and his life. He longed bitterly and desperately to be there, never to have left it, to wake up from the nightmare that was today.

There was aching pain in remembering his Irish home, for the last passionate sight of it, the whole last scene of departure was the clearest memory of all.

It was not anything they had said. His mother had been very quiet. He had loved her especially for that. 'It'll not be long, boy,' and she had smiled.

And then, just as his father took up the reins and the cart that was to drop him at the bus stop began to trundle out of the yard, he had looked down at Tim standing below. Tim, not quite two years younger than himself, who had shared every adventure until now.

He had looked very deep into Tim's grey eyes just for a second. In that second he knew that Tim was giving—giving in an agony of generosity all he could of his strength and love, an essence of his spirit. Take *my* sword, too—you may need it.

McGill, by meeting Tim's gaze, had accepted his trust— and now he had betrayed it in his first moments of fear.

Tim would make excuses for him if he knew. Tim would say, 'But you couldn't help it in all that noise. That wasn't your fault.'

But it was. He was a coward.

If only he could see Tim and talk to him. It would ease the shame...

'Don't you want no supper, lad?'

McGill opened his eyes and saw the burly figure of Ordinary Seaman Money standing over him.

'No,' he said.

'They piped 'hands to supper long enough ago.'

'I don't care,' McGill said fiercely.

'Ee, what's t'matter wi' you?'

'Oh, go away.'

Copper Money scratched his ginger head. Most people were pretty talkative this evening, and it wasn't as though McGill had been a special pal of Lofty Reynolds, though of course that might be it. But you never knew where you were with young McGill anyway—a proper Irishman he was, with his black hair and pale blue eyes. Copper didn't know much about Irishmen, but it was a convenient explanation.

He lit a cigarette and sat down on the deck with his back to the fo'c's'le screen. The sun was setting into a soft grey cloud which lipped the edge of the glass-calm sea. High streaks of mackerel sky turned from silver to gold and from gold to dull red, like hot iron cooling.

Copper puffed at his cigarette. Queer chap, young McGill. You never quite knew what he would say next. Then sometimes he had that faraway look in his eyes as though he didn't see or hear what was going on about him. Those were the times when the Petty Officers used to get mad at him for not obeying orders quickly.

Copper had once heard the First Lieutenant talking about him. 'What, *that* good-for-nothing? He can't even salute properly.'

Copper knew this was an injustice. Although the boy was long-limbed and clumsy there were things he could do— chucking a heaving-line, for instance. He just had the swing of it. And he was a marvel in the whaler, quick as a cat for all his long legs, and be knew how to pull and all.

Besides, he was somehow different.

Copper remembered the night he had first discovered it, on watch at the twelve-pounder. They had been looking towards the moon and its long sparkling lane reflected on the calm sea. McGill had begun to talk about his home. It was the first time Copper had ever heard him talk like this—even his voice seemed different, suddenly alive.

He had talked about the moonlight across Strangford Lough and the lapping of the flood tide over the soft mudflats and the stillness broken by the calls of the various birds—he knew the different ones too. Different names they all had. And he had talked a lot about the beauty of it, as though he'd taken special notice of it, like one of those artist chaps.

But he had liked most to talk about the wild geese—the barnacle he had called them—and the music they made when they fed right into the bay below the house. 'Oh, it was rare music, so it was.' There was a dreamy quality in his voice, soft like the rain, but with a secret urgency.

Copper, sitting on the Ready Use Locker with his legs dangling, had seen a vision. Something from a different entrancing world, something that you never knew about if you lived in a grey backstreet in Warrington. He listened happily, and when the watch was relieved and the spell broken he felt sort of flat.

Oh ah, he was a queer one, was young McGill. There he lay now on the locker, brooding, and thinking maybe of the first casualties he had seen—nasty ones to see too—of poor old Lofty perhaps. Who could tell what he was thinking?

As Copper looked at him, he saw the fingers of his hand curl into a clenched fist.

Three months later, on a wild November night, McGill was keeping the middle watch as a lookout on the bridge of the destroyer, now engaged in convoy escort duties in the North Atlantic. His eyes, long-practised in detecting the dim blackness of a pack of wigeon or a party of brents on a dark night, easily picked up the row of black lumps which were the ships in the starboard wing column of the convoy.

It was very cold. The gale howled in the foremast rigging and spray burst from time to time over the bridge, rapping viciously on the screen and on the sou'wester tops of the men who ducked to avoid the full lash of it.

Suddenly there was a dull explosion.

'See anything, port lookout?' asked the Officer of the Watch.

'No, sir.' Thick scurry of rain and sleet obliterated even the black lumps of the convoy.

'You heard an explosion, didn't you?'

'Yes, sir,' said McGill.

The Officer of the Watch moved to the voice pipe. 'Captain, sir.' A sleepy voice answered him.

'Explosion, sir. I think it was a torpedo.'

The Captain reached the bridge in time to see the rocket signals, dim and blurred through the rain, which confirmed that a U-boat had attacked the convoy. He thought, 'What a night for it, with this sea and these squalls and wind. The U-boat's bound to get away with it.' The enemy was developing surface attack at night in these early days of the Battle of the Atlantic, when the issue lay in the balance.

A hunt was carried out and many depth charges were dropped, with unknown result. McGill heard and felt their explosion almost unmoved. He was at his Action Station now at A gun. Great seas washed constantly over the deck, but he crouched to leeward of the fo'c's'le screen trying to keep dry. At any moment a torpedo might be running towards them—at this moment it might have started...or at this...He was not at all afraid.

The air was full of salt mist.

About an hour after the torpedo struck the Captain received orders from the Senior Officer of the escort to stand by the sinking ship. She was on fire.

McGill could see her through the rain as a big nebulous ball of orange fire. Below this the haze of spume was thick over the angry wave tops.

The destroyer crept up to leeward of the wreck and lay no more than half a cable away, rolling wildly in the trough of the sea. Her ten-inch searchlight swept the intervening blackness and lit upon a boat, low in the water and packed with men. It looked stark and white in the beam, the faces shining up into the light through the mist.

McGill heard the thin pipe of the Bosun's Mate above the howling of the wind, followed by a shouted order, 'A and B guns' crews muster in the port waist.'

That meant him, that meant a job to do. Up until now it

had all seemed far away, someone else's responsibility in which he could only stand and watch, shivering with cold and a vague detached excitement. Now there would be work for him, and he suddenly realised the strength of his burning longing to help—to help those blank white faces clustered together in fear—to get them at all costs, every one of them.

There was a crowd round the fo'c's'le ladder, filing down to the port waist, and when he reached the iron deck the boat was nearer, but it was also lower in the water—it was almost waterlogged. The wave tops were slopping over the gunwale.

McGill heard the sharp crack of a rifle shot, and a thin white line appeared in the searchlight's beam. The line-throwing gun had been fired over the boat, the thin cord flying out in a low arc. But the wind blew it away like gossamer, far astern.

McGill looked up to the pom-pom deck, where the Gunner's Mate was reloading the rifle. Presently he saw the figure poised, ready to fire again; then came the crack and a second line sped out far ahead of the boat to make allowance for the wind. For a moment it hung in the air, then slipped sideways in the clutch of the gale.

The men in the boat reached upwards, lurching, but it passed over their heads.

'Heaving-lines!' shouted the Petty Officer, who was in charge of the party waiting on the iron deck. 'Hey you, McGill, get a heaving-line, chop-chop!'

Swinging from one handhold to the next, McGill made for the fo'c's'le where the heaving-lines were kept in the fo'c's'le caboose. He knocked off the clips and opened the door, closing it quickly just before the next wave broke over the fo'c's'le.

In less than a minute he was back on the iron deck with a line, the specially-weighted one with a brass nut inside the Turk's head at its end.

The boat was much closer now. He gauged the distance and thought: 'I can just throw it that far.' All the time he was coiling the line on his left arm, ready to heave it.

When he was ready the Petty Officer said, 'Don't throw yet,' but McGill had gone far away into a world where his own capabilities were finely drawn like silver point. Far away and far ahead too.

He could see the men in the boat reaching up to catch his line; he could see them hauling over the heavier grass line that was now being flaked along the deck behind him; he could see the boat alongside and see the men being rescued, hauled up to safety.

It would all be done—if he could throw it that far. Just that far. He swung back, and with a great bowling action cast the coils out, aiming just ahead of the boat. The line spread itself smoothly, and the weighted end, falling like a trout fly, lipped the gunwale.

A strange murmur, half heard above the roar of the storm, ran through the cluster of men at the guard rail. Now they could help. 'Ah—now then,' they said.

The grass rope's end was bent to the heaving-line and passed outboard as the men in the waterlogged boat hauled in. At last it reached them and was secured.

McGill watched the boat being dragged towards the destroyer in angry jerks. Every time the ship rolled away the grass rope came taut, and when it rolled towards her they took down the slack and held on for the jerk. It was an unseamanlike method, but the First Lieutenant was giving the orders.

McGill could only gaze at the scene with fierce intensity, every muscle braced, ready to move when the opportunity came, to do anything he was told, or anything he saw that needed doing. He had never been so ready in his life, not even on those wild nights landing on the rocks of Chapel Island, or driving up the lough with the tiny sail which over-canvassed the duck punt to the point of breathless danger.

It was raining harder now, and with the squall the wind was whipped to new fury. The boat and the crowd on the tumbling destroyer's deck and the thick atmosphere of rain and spray were all lit by the pinkish-orange glow of the burning ship in the background.

Amidships she was a furnace, high flames leaping from the bridge and flickering from the ventilator cowls. The plating of the superstructure was already red hot. The hot pungent smell of burning blew down across the destroyer's decks in occasional waves: a stifling, menacing smell.

The crowded boat was nearly alongside now, heavy and sluggish in the great seas. About twenty men sat upright on the thwarts, and lines were being passed to them to haul her alongside the special clambering net which hung down the destroyer's side. Faces below were upturned, arms reaching already for the net, some of the men crouching, some standing.

McGill saw other figures in the boat down in the water, floating—swilling sickeningly back and forth with the rolling of the boat. Why didn't they pull them out of the water, give them a chance?

With a splintering crack the boat came alongside. A dozen jumped for the net and hung on. The destroyer rolled away and they were dangling against the ships side far above their boat. Then she rolled back, the water came up to meet them, and in a moment they were in it. The boat was caught by a wave and swept again towards the ship's side.

McGill saw what would happen, saw it helplessly, agonised. He shouted, 'Look out, now,' like most of the others watching, but it was too late.

The men in the water also saw, saw the boat high above them on the crest of the wave.

A terrible shout of despair that was almost a scream came up to the watchers and was blown away into the wild clamour of the night.

Then the boat crashed against the ship's side for the second time—a muffled crash as the human fenders took the blow.

At that instant McGill suddenly moved, his heart beating high, his brain crystal clear, his purpose defined. If he had felt fear at all that night, no trace remained to cross his mind. There were men in the water, helpless, injured, drowning; men who were within reach of safety but slipping away. It was for this he had been waiting—for just such a chance.

He took off his duffel coat and climbed through the guard rails and down the clambering net, past the survivors who were struggling upwards. A moment later he was on the gunwale of the boat which still bumped and crashed against the ship's side. Floating near the stern was a limp body. He seized hold of the kapok lifejacket and began to heave the man back into the boat.

In a moment he was being helped, and he heard the rich north country voice of Ordinary Seaman Money in his ear. 'That's the stuff, lad. In with 'im!'

'Get the other chap,' McGill said. He hauled the heavy man into the boat and propped him against the thwart, then turned and helped Copper with the second.

He had never been so strong, he could do anything. It was dangerous the way the boat crashed against the ship—oh yes, it was dangerous, but he was nimble enough to avoid the danger if he kept on his toes. The boat would break up soon so they must hurry, but he could be quick and strong, never so strong.

With a mighty heave the second man slithered into the boat. Two more hands were on the clambering net now, and coming down to help. Heaving-lines were passed and bowlines made round the bodies. Besides the crushed there were the three floating in the bottom of the boat who might yet be saved by artificial respiration. As they tied the bowlines, and struggled to lift the heavy burdens, willing hands reached down from the deck when the boat came up on a crest and dragged them on board.

'Below there,' came the First Lieutenant's voice. 'There's a fellow floating just clear of your stern there—can you get him?'

McGill saw him in the light of a torch from above, about five yards away, a white lifeless face above the lifejacket, almost as much under the water as above it. But there was a chance!

He slipped over the side and struck out for him.

It was breathtakingly cold, even though he had been wet through before, but it was easy now, no effort to try out his strength. His breath came in sharp gasps, the wavelets slapped into his face, half blinding him, but ahead he could still make out the white half-bald head, the thin hair washed flat across the dead face.

As soon as he reached him and started to pull him back,

a rope landed in the water beside him. He grabbed it and together they were hauled towards the boat.

'All right, I've got him,' said Copper. The drowned man was heaved first into the boat where the line was secured, then up the ship's side where the helpers clung to the upper meshes of the net to take the weight on the way up.

McGill was feeling so strong that he scarcely needed Copper's assistance to get back into the boat. He got a knee into the looped lifeline that ran round below the gunwale, and landed spluttering on one of the thwarts.

Copper said, 'That's the stuff, lad!'

The other two men shouted, 'Come on now—that's the lot.' They all jumped for the net and climbed it as fast as they could. Below them, the boat pounded again with a splintering crash, its last frustrated effort to crush them. At the top they were engulfed in the crowd.

'All right—let the boat go—cut the grass as far down as you can.' The First Lieutenant was giving the orders. He turned to go up on to the bridge. 'Well done, Chapman–and you, Piggott. Who else was down there? Oh, well done, Money! You'd better go forrad and get your things off.'

The Bosun's Mate came up to him. 'From the Captain, sir, He thinks there's a man still on the ship. He says will you speak to him about it at once, sir.'

A man on the ship. A man trapped there in that burning hell. The group stood gazing, and McGill, dripping and shivering, stood with them.

As they watched, a torch flickered at the stern of the ship.

The First Lieutenant came back and spoke to the Petty Officer. The survivors say that there may be two men still on the poop there. The Captain wants us to float a Carley raft away on the grass line. We're drifting so fast that it will float upwind to them quite quickly. No, no one's to go in it. We'll use No. 4 raft; better slip it at once.'

McGill heard all this; heard and understood it. But why was no one to go in it? With someone in it the trapped men could throw down a line from their quarter which could be caught on the raft. Otherwise it was pure chance if the raft went within their reach. These were the sort of things that McGill knew— much more than he knew about sounding machines, carpenters' stoppers, and the breaking strains of cables, and all the other things you were meant to know in the Navy. The very fact that he knew and understood it was a challenge. Being cold and wet made the effort harder, until the challenge was irresistible. He was exultantly ready to do much more than his share.

The raft was slipped and fell with a big flat splash into the smoky blackness below.

McGill followed quickly to the guard rail, climbed through and seized hold of the grass rope. Then he slid down into the sea and worked his way along to the raft at the far end of it. The water was desperately cold; much colder than before. He climbed eagerly onto the raft. Already it was drifting away from the destroyer's side, or rather the destroyer was being blown away from the raft, which floated low in the water, waves breaking over its rounded end. The centre of the oval raft formed a sort of basket, with its bottom in the water like a gigantic fisherman's keep net.

McGill sat on the cylinder with his feet in the basket, submerged to the knees. As he sat, he was suddenly seized with panic. Little feathers of spray burst over him. All at once he was tired and weak: his muscles went stiff, he was utterly done in the dark ocean between the two ships.

The weakness and the fear held him in a tight grip so that his stomach ached sickeningly. Now he would surely die, and for such stupidity, such stupidity, such mad vanity! People could not live long like that—all wet and exposed. He would be washed off the raft soon. Exposure—people died of it, he had heard about it, they went numb. Someone had said it was a comfortable, easy death, once you were numb. What nonsense some people did talk.

'Don't get above yourself,' his mother used to say. That was not nonsense. But this that he was doing was nonsense— folly—madness. Only Tim would understand why he had started out. Tim would understand. Like that night by Mount Stewart there, when they went on for the baits after the tide had turned just to show they weren't frightened. Well, now it was all over; he would surely die, surely.

The sea's ruffled blackness was velvet, the cloak of death. 'Is that a man in the raft?' called the First Lieutenant, as they paid out the grass line from the iron deck.

'Yes, sir,' answered the Petty Officer.

'Who is it?'

'I'm not sure, sir. I think its McGill.'

Half a dozen voices confirmed it.

'I said no one was to go.'

'I never saw him go, sir.' And then, after a pause, 'He was the first man down into the boat, sir, and swam to get that drowned fellow afterwards. Seems a good lad, sir, in an emergency, as you might say.'

The grass line floated away to the black outline that was only occasionally visible when a wave crest lifted it against the glow of the flames beyond. The raft was certainly working towards the bows. With the fire amidships there was no chance of the trapped men reaching it there.

The First Lieutenant went up to the bridge.

'Everything going all right, No. 1?' asked the Captain.

'Well—yes, sir. Actually, sir, there's a man gone over in the raft.'

'I said no one was to go. Who is it?'

'Ordinary Seaman McGill, sir.'

'Yeoman, shine the ten-inch on the raft.'

In the beam of the searchlight, the little raft and the figure perched at one end looked very white shining out of the mist of spray. The figure was moving—swaying rhythmically.

'What the hell's he doing? Paddling?'

'Yes, sir.'

Paddles were kept lashed to the floor of each raft. With one of these McGill was trying as hard as he could to work himself towards the stern of the sinking ship, so that as it drifted down on him he would come up against it on the sternward side of the midship blaze.

The exercise was warming him and with the warmth his strength returned. The grass rope was not floating and acted as an anchor to the raft, but every inch was worth the effort. He felt much better and despised his fear. He was well in the lee of the burning ship, and the spray was not breaking over him so much, but the pungent burning smell filled his nostrils.

He was out of breath soon but he saw that he had gained a few yards and paddled on with a second wind. He was very near the other ship now—close above, the fire raged. He could feel the heat of it, like the heat of a summer sun; oh, the deadly sweet taste of exhaustion and the fear of it! Then, from aft, he heard a thin faint cry. At the same moment the coils of a rope splashed down near him.

He reached out with the paddle but it was too far and he wondered whether he should jump in and fetch it. He decided to let them throw again, and at the second throw the line fell across the raft.

At once he made it fast and the raft was hauled towards the ship. The great stern fell with a thunderous slap and then rose high above him so that rudder and screw were clear of the water, the foam boiled around them as the ship pitched back. There was a Jacob's ladder hanging from the poop. If the raft was to reach the foot of the ladder, it would lie dangerously close to that plunging propeller, but there it would have to go. With the great waves the raft rose and fell past twenty or more rungs of the ladder.

One of the men had already started down, very slowly and hesitantly.

When he was a little more than halfway McGill shouted, 'Stay there now, and jump next time I come up to you.'

The man obeyed, and when McGill said, 'Now, jump!' he waited for about three seconds, and then jumped and missed. McGill reached out for him and pulled him into the middle of the raft; he sat on the edge, coughing.

It was darker now because they were shaded from the fire by the bulk of the stern. The searchlight had been doused, but even in the dark McGill saw at once that he had rescued a boy no older than himself. The boy was very frightened; he was sobbing with cold and fear, between fits of coughing.

This discovery made McGill feel suddenly old and competent and strong. With an effort he overcame the chatter of his teeth. It's all right, he said, we'll be back safe directly. He did not doubt that it was true, and he found that it encouraged him a lot to say it.

The second man was coming down now. As he came a huge wave lifted the ships stern high out of the water, showing again the rudder and the propeller.

McGill thought, 'What if a bight of the grass line should catch under the propeller, or a loop go under the rudder? It would pull the raft down.' He thought, 'It will do, it is bound to; and then it will really be the end.' He clambered along the raft and saw how the grass rope ran steeply down now into the water. It had sunk deep and the ship was drifting down on it. He tried to haul some of it in. Hey, give me a hand!'

But the boy did not move, he held on with both hands, too frightened to help. McGill had to give up. If the raft was pulled down, they would drown. There was nothing he could do. He was quite resigned.

The second man stepped off neatly into the raft. He was frightened too.

'Are there any more?' McGill shouted.

'No,' he heard the man say. 'No, we're the last.' With his knife he cut the rope which hung from the bulwarks far above. All that now remained was for the destroyer's men to haul them back the few hundred yards which separated the two ships. That was all, if the rope was not foul of the derelict. But how could they know in the destroyer that the raft was ready? McGill shouted, 'Heave in,' but the sound was drowned instantly in the fury of the night.

Then he remembered the flickering torch.

'Have you still got your torch?' he asked.

The man fumbled in his pocket and produced it. 'It's pretty well finished,' he said.

McGill took it and flashed once or twice. Then pressing on the button without pushing it forward he started to signal, out of the far off memories of the training establishment.

H—that was four dots; E—oh, E was easy, just one dot; and then A—a dot and a dash; V—that was difficult, he paused and then made a B—a dash and three dots instead of three dots and a dash; then E again. At the end of the word he had to wait to see if it had been read.

No answering flash came from the destroyer's bridge.

The torch was almost spent, showing only a dull amber light. He made the word all over again, but he was sure they could not see it. And then suddenly a point of light showed on the bridge. T, it said, which meant that it had understood. IN was easy to make: I—two dots, and N the opposite of A—a dash and a dot. The light answered again, paused, then fluttered quickly, far too quickly for him to read, but he guessed it meant that they had understood.

The man and the boy sat very still, clutching the rope strops of the raft. The boy was shivering; his breath came in quick sobs.

McGill climbed along to the other end of the raft and watched the grass rope which hung vertically under it. Suddenly, he looked up and noticed they were away from the ship's side, and at the same time he determined that the grass rope was not quite so vertical as it had been; it sloped away towards the destroyer; it was not round the screw of the wreck. They were being hauled back.

'Won't be long now,' he said quite cheerfully.

The man looked at McGill, for the first time aware that he was only a boy. He saw his black hair tangled across his forehead, and the glint of the fire shining in his eyes; he saw his shoulders hunched and shivering, and the thinness of him. 'Good,' he answered through clenched teeth.

McGill sat quite still, gazing back at the burning wreck.

'Look!' he said suddenly. Her back had broken and her two black ends were rising up. While they watched there came an awful hissing roar as the water boiled up and quenched the red hot plates. There was a muffled explosion and a great shower of sparks burst out of the centre of the fire. A pall of billowy smoke shone blood red for a moment, and then faded as the blaze was drowned. The stern and bows rose majestically into the air, almost touching as the ship folded in half. Then, quite silently, she slid down behind the black mountain of an intervening wave.

When next the raft rose upon a crest, nothing remained but a flicker of flame burning on the sea's surface. It flared for a moment and went out.

McGill looked back to the destroyer, a dim shape in the new darkness. He was utterly unmoved by the final plunge of the sinking ship. Too much had happened already. He was past caring about anything, numbed with awful cold and fatigue.

They came halfway down the net to pull the three of them from the raft. They had to hold McGill up and help him along to the mess deck. Copper was on one side of him. 'Ee—that's the stuff, lad,' he said.

They helped him off with his sodden clothes and rubbed him down with towels, and someone brought him a steaming cup of cocoa with too much sugar in it. The First Lieutenant was there some of the time, saying something about it being a good show.

McGill was too tired to remember it all. They wrapped him in blankets, and bundled him into his hammock. A rich glow came into his body and he curled his hands up to his face.

'Oh, Tim,' he said to his brother, 'it was all right this time, wasn't it?'

A moment later, he was asleep.

WORLD WILDLIFE FUND
ADDRESS TO THE POPE

World Wildlife Fund Yearbook 1969

Presented at the Private Audience granted by His Holiness Pope Paul VI to the Board of Trustees and Committees of the World Wildlife Fund, at the Vatican in Rome on 21 June 1969.

Your Holiness,

We are deeply honoured to be received in audience because of the organisation we represent and as individuals we are honoured that we are permitted to pay our respects to Your Holiness this morning.

Our organisation—the World Wildlife Fund—is international, with headquarters in Switzerland. It exists to provide for the *conservation of nature* and to bring to the attention of people all over the world the dangers which threaten nature. In eight years we have established National Appeals in fourteen countries, including Italy.

Your Holiness, we believe that nature is an important element in human environment, we believe that the delicate balance between the earth and its animals and plants in gravely threatened by mankind who has *responsibilities of trusteeship* over it—the responsibilities of this generation to future generations. We believe that a wise use of land, the conservation of nature, the protection of lesser creatures which share the earth with us —these things are essentially a moral, a spiritual issue.

St. Francis taught a reverence for the earth and its creatures. For him, all life had significance—all nature had intrinsic value. He treated nature as a friend deserving of man's love, not as an enemy to be subdued or a slave to be exploited. Alas, seven centuries later, too many people continue to treat nature as though it existed solely for their own material use, and to regard other forms of life as having no rights at all.

Our concern for the conservation of the earth is perhaps an extension of the teaching of St. Francis and it may even be a factor in human survival. The problems of *environmental pollution* are beginning to catch up with us—pollution of the atmosphere, of the fresh waters, of the soil and of the sea. The natural resources of our earth are for the most part grossly over-exploited. About a thousand kinds of higher animals are threatened with extinction. The earth itself needs the kind of reverence from all mankind that St. Francis felt and taught. This is a vast and noble conception and never more significant than it is today.

May we hope that Your Holiness can give *a message to the world* indicating the necessity for new awareness of the value of natural environment and wild nature to the spirit of man.

The Pope's Address to the World Wildlife Fund on the same occasion.

Gentlemen,

It is an honour for Us to receive such a distinguished group, representing the Directors of the World Wildlife Fund, the principal objective of which is the conservation of nature in all its forms: landscapes, waters, air, soil, flora and fauna, on a worldwide scale.

In principle, this objective may be accepted and approved. Man, the culmination of creation, always occupies the first place. To him was it said: 'Have dominion over the fish of the sea, and over the birds of the air, and over every living thing that moves upon the earth' (Gen. 1:28). Man was to dominate nature by his toil: 'God took the man and put him in the garden of Eden, to till it and keep it' (Gen. 2:15). Through his labour, man perfects and transforms all of creation. He extracts for his own use its resources and its forces. By cultivating the earth, he renders it useful and habitable.

Nevertheless, though he is the master of creation, man must not destroy it. He must admire it, he must explore and know it (*cf.* Gen. 2:20). He cultivates the soil and raises animals. How often Sacred Scripture refers to the human occupations of farming, fishing, herding flocks of sheep and cattle!

All of nature, created by a loving God, reflects the Creator. 'The heavens are telling the glory of God' (Ps. 19:1) and the earth and all that is in it proclaims His handiwork. St. Ambrose, Archbishop of Milan, was considered during the Middle Ages to be a great master of natural science. In his *Hexameron*, a study of the six days creation, and in many other works, he has beautiful pages on animal life, and the ways in which it manifests the wisdom and providence of the Creator.

'Manifested at the beginning of time, the divine plan is that man should subdue the earth, bring creation to perfection, and develop himself' (*Gaudium et spes*, No. 57). The perfecting of creation supposes its conservation, and this is the aim proposed by your meritorious association. The image of the Creator must shine forth ever more clearly, not only in His creature Man, but in all of His creation in nature.

We, therefore, wish you well in your admirable efforts, and We invoke upon you and your colleagues, upon the various national associations which you represent, and upon all who contribute to the great cause of preservation of natural riches and beauty, abundant heavenly graces and blessings.

Adelie Penguin.
Ecstatic Display, Torgersen Island. February 1968

EVERYMAN'S ANTARCTICA

Look (BBC, 1969)

On 4 February 1968 a party of sixty-one tourists left Punta Arenas, on the shore of the Magellan Strait, in the Chilean ship *Navarino*—our floating hotel—for a month's cruise. We were heading for the Antarctic with the Falkland Islands as our first port of call.

Similar cruises had been to the Antarctic in the two previous years, organised by an American tourist agency, but ours was the first to include British tourists. The possibilities of regular tourism in Antarctica have alarmed the hitherto undisturbed scientists from many nations. There are dangers from the point of view of wildlife conservation and these are my particular concern.

The Falkland Islanders are already conservation-conscious, and they have a rich fauna. Apart from a formal call at Stanley, the capital, time permitted us only one day on the outer islands to the west of the main group. The morning was spent on Carcass Island which belongs to, and is farmed by, the Bertrand family. It is about seven miles long and the party of *Navarino* passengers were divided into four groups. One went on foot along the shore to a small rookery of Gentoo penguins while another went in the opposite direction and found a wealth of bird life on the beach and in the tussock grass—all surprisingly tame and confiding, although the Magellan penguins which breed in burrows are less tame than most other penguins. A third party went over the hill to see breeding king shags, while a series of Land Rover trips took the rest over the rolling downland to the far end of the island.

Strange grunting sounds from the strip of tussock grass along the sand dunes revealed the presence of groups of elephant seals wallowing in the dunes and throwing dry sand over their backs. Below the tussock grass on the beach was a belt of rotting seaweed, then sand, then rocks. The area was alive with birds. There were flocks of crested ducks and yellow-billed teal, oystercatchers, kelp geese, flightless steamer ducks, kelp gulls, dolphin gulls, great skuas and upland geese. There were some Falkland thrushes digging in the rotting seaweed, and everywhere the delightfully tame *Cinclades* or tussac bird.

Next, across the sound to West Point Island. We ate our lunch on board, and by 2.30 p.m. we were ashore and all ready to see more of the wonders of Falkland wildlife. The main attractions here were a large breeding colony of black-browed albatrosses and a rockhopper penguin rookery. Our host, Roddy Napier, took some of the party across the island to the rockhoppers and a few went off in search of the big albatross colony. The rockhoppers were breeding on some bare rocky patches in the middle of a fenced-off area of tussock grass. They had well-grown babies and in among them was a scatter of black-browed albatrosses with pale grey fluffy young.

None of the birds paid the slightest attention to the ring of camera operators who now surrounded them. On the slope above the colony stood a black hawk—a 'Johnny Rook' or Forster's caracara—the worlds most southerly bird of prey and now very rare.

Sadly we left the Falklands. In the gathering dusk after an exciting day we headed south across the Drake Passage.

Bridgeman Island in Antarctic waters was our first sight of land on the third day after a rough crossing with force nine gales. Two icebergs with brown tops had presumably been showered with volcanic ash by the eruption at Deception Island ten weeks earlier. There were quantities of pintado petrels or Cape pigeons, an almost pure white giant fulmar amongst many browny-grey ones, some Antarctic petrels, a silver-grey petrel (or Antarctic fulmar) and a snow petrel.

We landed in Potter Cove on King George Island in the South Shetlands where those who had missed the elephant seals on Carcass Island were able to film them on the beach. In less than half an hour the sixty-one passengers in their special red Antarctic clothing were scattered along the shore and many had disappeared from sight, leaving a pile of orange lifejackets at the landing place. The jackets were compulsory in the shore boats and at the end of the day served as a useful check that all had returned.

There were a few odd penguins at Potter Cove—gentoos and some chinstraps. Round the nearest point we found Weddell seals and one leopard seal which made off fast. On top of a rocky bluff giant fulmars had well-grown fluffy pale grey young in nests of stones. Our first day ashore in the Antarctic was undoubtedly a success and it was encouraging to find that, with the sole exception of the leopard seal (they are apparently usually shy), the animals were prepared to allow parties of photographers to come close, one after another. In fact the disturbance had been minimal, and there had been space enough for the party to spread out and get away from each other.

Half Moon Island, at the north end of Livingstone Island, was our next stop and a chinstrap penguin rookery the chief interest. It was rather a long walk over snow and shingle to the rookery which was on a rocky promontory on the far side of the island. On the way we came upon a little party of moulting gentoos on the snow. It was very cold and even the gentoos managed to look chilled. Farther on a few scattered Weddell seals were well photographed. One was so perfectly camouflaged

on the large-stoned shingly beach that it was missed by most of
the passengers. An Antarctic tern's nest was found with one egg
in it, but we diverted the party round it as they are not common
and it seemed important not to disturb her.

We finally reached the chinstraps, they had a few sheathbills
among them. One pair of sheathbills had a young one in a
crevice in the rocks. They were extraordinarily tame and
confiding though not very beautiful because of their rather
small eyes and bare faces.

The chinstraps were dreadfully dirty. The earth round the
nests was reddish black. Both adults and young were stained
on their breasts with red from their diet of krill (a shrimp-like
animal that abounds in the Southern Ocean). Chinstrap babies
are two in a brood, and there were many moulting adults sitting
disconsolately among the nests. A few of the young were huddled
together in one place, clearly keeping warm. We appreciated our
luck in having a nice warm ship to return to, though it was here
that a boatload of passengers capsized on a previous expedition
and spent the night on shore in a disused hut.

By lunchtime we were back on board and steaming towards
Deception Island with a rising wind, intermittent snow-
showers and poor visibility. Deception had not been visited
since the eruption which occurred there on 4 December
1967 when the three scientific bases, Argentinian, British and
Chilean, were evacuated in a hurry. At that time a new island
was formed at the far end of the old horseshoe-shaped lagoon
which is five miles long and three miles wide and surrounded
by a wall of mountains. We found the island coated with ash
and lava dust—here and there some ice showing through.
With our ship anchored safely inside the crater on the lovely
sunny morning following our arrival, we were able to make an
extensive tour in one of the lifeboats to circumnavigate the new
island, with its steep cone and its crater lake at one side. Nearby
along the lagoon shore were steaming fumaroles and yellow
sulphurous water too hot to hold your hand in. Near the old
whaling station I walked right up to a leopard seal on the shore
and photographed it at five feet.

The large penguin rookery on the outer rim of the island was sighted from a hilltop and had apparently not been destroyed by the eruption.

From Deception we moved south to the Chilean base at Paradise Bay on the mainland of Antarctica.. We arrived on a bright day with a dead calm sea and the passage through the Gerlache Strait among the islands and icebergs was of incredible beauty. Chinstrap and Gentoo penguins were porpoising round the ship, and crab-eater seals lazed on the ice floes. The base was right in the middle of the Gentoo rookery but penguins and young were extremely tame and phlegmatic, indicating that they were well treated by the Chileans. But a new tourist/wildlife relationship problem presented itself—the desire of some of the passengers to handle the penguins. Several downy penguins were cuddled and photographed, struggling furiously and biting their captors. When put back the chicks received angry pecks from unrelated birds until they found their own parents. The disturbance was not serious but provided food for thought about future tourist trips, and a notice on the ship's noticeboard—*'Passengers are requested not to handle penguins.'*

At Palmer Station, the American base on Anvers Island, which we reached next day after passing through the dramatically narrow and beautiful Peltier Channel, the area available for walking about and photographing the Adelie penguins was considerably larger, there were many more penguins—perhaps 10,000.

Our now well-trained party spread out quietly among them on a low rocky island in the bay. The Adelies are the clowns of the penguin world and to me the most 'penguiny' penguins of them all. They too had young, many of which were in crèches. With a whole day in this beautiful bay everyone seemed to be delighted and for the specialist ornithologists there was a trip to next-door Humble Island, a nature reserve, where the lichens are being studied by scientists and there were more penguins, breeding skuas, giant fulmars, and Antarctic terns.

So far we had been incredibly lucky with the weather but as we left Palmer Station to approach the Lemaire Channel, perhaps the most famous beauty spot in the Antarctic Peninsula, it was a grey cloudy morning with a strong westerly wind. The forbidding mountain walls rose almost vertically into the clouds on either hand as we threaded our way cautiously among the icebergs—in some places so many that the channel ahead appeared to be completely blocked. The lack of sunlight produced one dramatic effect. In a world of black and white with a slate-coloured sea, the blues and greens of the icebergs shone out with incredible brilliance.

At eight in the morning we slowed and stopped opposite a tiny channel leading among low rolling islands. Through the crack we could just see the buildings of the British 'Base F', Argentine Island. But alas the weather was deteriorating and the wind was blowing the pack ice and icebergs into the channels amongst the islands ahead through which we must pass to reach the open sea. It was not possible to anchor the ship. The Captain permitted a small party to go ashore to post letters and to avoid disappointing the British scientists who had been awaiting our arrival. But it was a bitter disappointment to many of the passengers who were unable to visit this base. This sadness was to a great extent offset by the superlative beauty of the scene for the following three hours as we moved slowly forward among pack ice which looked as though it would bar our passage. We passed quite close to small groups of Adelie penguins resting on ice floes, once very close to a leopard seal and occasionally to crab-eater seals. So we crept through this wonderland of ice and out at last into the open sea for our dash to the Antarctic Circle, which we crossed at 9 p.m. in the gathering dark with a rough sea running and a rising gale.

We had spent nine days in Antarctic waters and been ashore on six of them. We had been, we felt, among the pioneers of a new kind of unforgettable adventure holiday which many thousands in the future will enjoy. With care and goodwill the spectacular and astonishingly tame wildlife need not be upset.

The birds and mammals of the seventh continent show a remarkable and hitherto largely misplaced trust in mankind. In the future, untrustworthy man must somehow contrive no longer to betray the tameness of the Antarctic wildlife. This is part of our responsibility to succeeding generations.

Peter Scott
1961

WORLD WILDLIFE'S
TEN YEARS

World Wildlife Fund Yearbook 1970–1971

I think the astonishing thing is that we have, in ten years, created a viable international organisation which already has National Appeals operating in fifteen different countries and will fairly soon have twenty.

I think the other thing that is astonishing is the enormous change in attitudes to nature and environment that has taken place in almost every country and at all levels of influence during those years.

The history of our organisation starts really with our sister organisation, the International Union for Conservation of Nature and Natural Resources (IUCN)—which itself only started just after the Second World War. There was, and still is, a tremendous need for the technical and scientific work of IUCN. It is doing a magnificent job, working to a large extent through Governments and international agencies. Ten years ago, it was practically without financial support, and it became evident that a professional fundraising effort throughout the world was needed to see that its work did not collapse.

And so we created a separate fundraising organisation to work professionally—because these days fundraising requires very professional handling—and on an international scale. So it was that, like the hero in a Western, the World Wildlife Fund rode in to the rescue. And the two organisations run in harness together—IUCN as the scientific and technical arm—World Wildlife as the campaigning and fundraising arm.

Among the most important of IUCN's international activities is the preparation of conventions and treaties between nations. For instance three years ago an African Convention was concluded which binds the signatory nations to certain conservation standards. It replaced the outdated London Convention of 1931, and has been accepted by the Organisation of African Unity (OAU).

IUCN is now working, with World Wildlife support, on a Wetlands Convention for Europe and North Africa. This will mean that marshes which are important to migratory birds will be declared by different countries to be of international significance. We are working on a Convention for the Export, Import and Transit of Certain Species of Wild Animals and Plants to which we are hoping all the countries of the world will become signatories in time.

IUCN has been trying with World Wildlife to make sure that in future great development projects shall have a sound ecological basis, as a condition of financial support. In the past many major projects have met disaster because this was not done—the Aswan high dam, the Mekong River Project and many more. The principle has now been accepted by the World Bank and by the UN Development Programme.

Then there is the Survival Service Commission (SSC) which is concerned with the survival of species, and of which I happen to be the Chairman. The prevention of species extinction—through greed or carelessness—is something which many people believe is worth some effort. I think it is the irrevocability of extinction which catches the imagination. 70 kinds of animals have become extinct since 1900 and the rate has tended to accelerate. 800 kinds are currently threatened.

Here are a few facts and figures about these first ten years of the World Wildlife Fund. I said when we started: 'If we can get a hundred projects going in the world, we will be doing well'. Well, we got them going in a little over a year. International project numbers are now up to 701, but that does not mean that we have supported that number. By the end of 1970 we had supported 358 *international* projects. Most of the National Appeals have also fairly long lists of their own national projects which they have supported. Altogether there must be more than 700. Many of these are quite small, and by themselves you may think that they are not very important. But if you add them all together, it seems to me that they amount to a very considerable conservation achievement.

We have pushed out on the international projects alone £2.5 million, and we have attracted an almost exactly similar amount from other sources which would probably not otherwise have supported the projects. Thus we have been instrumental in promoting some £5 million worth of conservation. We have also established capital endowments, both for the International operation in Switzerland and for the British National Appeal. People often say: 'I want every penny of my money to go to the animals'. Well, of course animals can't use money. It's no good tucking a five pound note into the pouch of a kangaroo. But clearly people want their contribution to go as much as possible into field projects. With enough endowment of the central operation, any money subsequently contributed could go direct to the field. We have made a start. Our International Capital Fund Stands at £291,000 and the BNA Capital Fund at £205,004. It should be noted that this has been done with special donations which would not have been given for immediate spending, but were given specifically for this kind of endowment, which gives a solid foundation to our work and a promise of continuity into the future.

I do not want anybody to think that we are in the least bit complacent about what has been done in these ten years. Starting from scratch, the success has been fantastically better than I expected, but our performance has got to be better still. To achieve this we accepted an offer by the well-known firm of McKinsey to examine the affairs of the World Wildlife Fund free of charge. They are doing this because they believe in our cause, and they wish to see it prosper. I do not need to remind you that they are the people who have examined, among others, the efficiency of Shell, the BBC, the GPO, the City of Liverpool, and the Vatican.

We believe that the two most important activities in conservation nowadays are first what can be called 'fire brigade action'—the saving of nature—animals and plants and wild places—which are under immediate threat. And second, education, because in the long term when people understand the principles, then conservation action will automatically follow.

In the first category one of the most important uses for money is to acquire land for National Parks and Nature Reserves and Refuges. Our biggest project in ECY 1970 was the acquisition of a wetland area at Marchauen in eastern Austria. During the first ten years we have bought land in the famous Coto Doñana in the Marismas of the Guadalquivir in Spain, in the Dombes in France, in the coastal marshes of New Jersey, in the coastal prairies of Texas (where the last of a subspecies of the prairie chicken survives). We have helped to buy a part of the Arusha National Park in Tanzania, a plant sanctuary at Mutomo in Kenya, an area adjoining the Lake Nakuru National Park, and an extension of the Mlilwane Reserve in Swaziland. Other significant areas where we have played a part in land acquisition and reserve promotion are the Manu Park in Peru, the Seewinkel in Austria, the Ouse Washes in England.

Rescue operations for species threatened with extinction include the Javan rhino, the Arabian oryx, Hunter's antelope, wild cattle in the Philippines and in Cambodia, the polar bear, the orang utan, tigers, spotted cats, giant tortoises in the

Galapagos, marine turtles, the monkey-eating eagle, Swinhoe's pheasant, the Western tragopan, the white-winged wood duck, the Hawaiian goose, the Hawaiian duck and the Laysan teal.

We started off mainly concentrating our attention on animals, but we very soon realised that plants were intricately involved, and from this we soon discovered that the totality of the ecological scene was a part of our business. This landed us in the environmental arena and from there it is a short step to the survival (or extinction) of the human race. Rightly or wrongly, when it came to the great international Congress which we held in London last November we felt that this was the area on which we had to concentrate—to point up the interdependence of the ecosystems of our earth—the interrelationships between 'all life on earth', and we used that as the title for the Congress. I think in this way we linked our Fund with the environmental awareness which has suddenly arisen in many parts of the world, notably in the United States.

There are of course some who say, 'If the prospects of human survival are so slender as the scientists tell us, why are we wasting time and money on trying to save the whooping crane'.

The answer to this is that whooping cranes and humans all have to live in the biosphere, and if we wreck the biosphere both will die out. We have to recognise that the earth is of finite size, that neither the human population nor economic growth can go on for ever. We hope and believe that World Wildlife has played some part in alerting people to these basic truths. Meanwhile looking ahead we have to keep on with the fire brigade action as well as the education.

WORLD WILDLIFE'S
TEN YEARS

World Wildlife Fund Yearbook 1971–1972

**Address given as Chairman of the World Wildlife Fund
at the Tenth Anniversary Celebrations,
11 September 1971**

Ten years ago today the World Wildlife Fund came into legal
existence, but the idea had been born many months earlier. As
often happens, the initiative came from several directions at
once. One suggestion came in a letter from Mr. Victor Stolan,
who is with us here today. He wrote to Sir Julian Huxley, who
got into touch with Mr. Max Nicholson, also with us today.
Max was already thinking of some international fundraising
effort to bring urgently needed support to the International
Union for Conservation of Nature and Natural Resources,
with its headquarters newly set up in Morges.

IUCN, itself only formed in 1948, had been sadly starved of funds and I was at that time one of its Vice Presidents. After much thought it was decided that the fundraising organisation should be an independent entity, though the two bodies must obviously run in double harness together. And so World Wildlife Fund was formed, as the Campaigning and Fundraising arm of the operation, with IUCN as the Scientific and Technical arm.

Looking back over the first decade it's clear that we hadn't much idea then about the difficulty of the job we were undertaking. We thought we should just have to tell people the story and the money would come rolling in. Unfortunately it wasn't quite like that. And now it seems astonishing to me that in ten years we have managed to create a viable international organisation at all. International organisations are not easy things to create, but here it is, with its International Headquarters in Morges and National Appeals in sixteen countries; and there's a chance of nearly double that number in the foreseeable future. But there is no merit in creating an organisation unless it produces results. What can we say the World Wildlife Fund has achieved in its first ten years? Well, it has made grants totalling 31½ million Swiss francs, which is seven and a half million dollars or just over three million pounds sterling. This money has gone out to 392 international and 158 national projects in 59 countries, each project duly screened by IUCN scientists. These grants have stimulated financial support from many other sources—often from Governments—which have almost doubled the total sum made available to conservation bringing it to over ten million dollars. I can't tell you about the 392 international projects. Just to read out their titles alone would take 64½ minutes— and I don't intend to keep you that long. But it may be helpful to look briefly at the ways in which money can be spent for wildlife conservation—because the animals themselves have no use for the stuff. It is no good pushing a ten franc note into the pouch of a kangaroo and telling her to get on with saving herself from extinction. Money can only be used by people.

But how? Well you can buy land with it for a nature reserve or a National Park, you can buy equipment—a Land Rover, an aircraft, radio equipment to beat poachers and so on. Or you can pay for certain services—for wardens or rangers, or for scientists to do the necessary research to make sure that the conservation measures are the right ones, or for specialised teachers to tackle the immense education problems involved.

You can—and we do and must continue to—spend money or education—on documenting the case for conservation, or producing literature which explains what we're trying to do. One such document, which is available to you all, lists a number of our specific achievements so I'll do no more than draw your attention to a few of the more important ones.

Here are some of the grants World Wildlife has made: taking Europe first: one of our earliest and biggest projects—the purchase of the Coto Doñana, and later of Guadiamar, to make the Doñana National Park in the Marismas of the Guadalquivir in Spain, with the Spanish Government contributing almost half the price. Projects of land acquisition for a National Park at Skaftafell in Iceland, for riverine wetlands at Marchauen/Marchegg in Austria. Support for seven wetlands on the Project MAR list of European marshes of international importance. Land acquisition at two unique wetland areas on the Ouse Washes in England. A grant to start some very important research on polar bears in Spitsbergen.

Then by high level representation World Wildlife played a part in preventing the destruction of the Vanoise National Park in France.

In Africa grants have been made to the Congo National Parks, to the Arusha National Park in Tanzania for buying Momella, to the Meru Park, the Shimba Hills Reserve, the Nakuru National Park and the Mutomo Plant Sanctuary, all in Kenya, and to the Lochinvar Park on the Kafue flats in Zambia. Eleven projects have been supported in Ethiopia, eight in Madagascar, eleven in Indonesia, five in the Philippines, six in Pakistan (including four reserves), seven projects in the Galapagos Islands, four in Ecuador, five in Peru, including the vast National Park of nearly 16,000km^2, five projects in Mexico, two in the Seychelles and Indian Ocean Islands, and ten for the protection of marine turtles in various parts of the tropics.

In North America three great land acquisitions have been undertaken and almost completed by World Wildlife Fund (US)—an area of brush country on the borders of Mexico in white-winged wood dove country, an expanse of coastal prairie to save the last remnant population of Attwater's prairie chicken and a substantial block of coastal wetlands in New Jersey which would otherwise have been destroyed by development.

I have scarcely time to tell you of the successful part played by World Wildlife in the spotted cats campaign, in the ban on killing tigers in Nepal and importing vicuña hair into England; in the protection of crocodiles in Australia, birds of paradise in New Guinea, in the reduction of catch quotas for harp seals in Canada.

We think that, as a direct result of World Wildlife action, the future is now more promising for a number of endangered species such as the aye-aye, the orang utan, the Javan rhino, the vicuña, the Arabian oryx, the Hawaiian goose, the koloa or Hawaiian duck, the white-winged wood duck (not dove this time), the noisy scrub bird, Morelet's crocodile, and many more. These projects looked at singly may seem to be mostly rather small and unimportant. No world-shaking significance in a good many of them. But I submit that taken in aggregate they amount to solid conservation achievement.

During the ten years, World Wildlife has brought reinforcement to numbers of national and local conservation organisations which are so manfully 'holding the line' against the human pressures. Most important of all we have been able to give support fairly solid support, although not as much as we should have liked, to our sister organisation—the International Union for Conservation of Nature and Natural Resources— whose work is absolutely vital for the future. And we regard our grant aid to the International Council for Bird Preservation, and to the International Wildfowl Research Bureau, as also of high importance. Making the key organisations effective by adequate funding is a most essential element in the total conservation effort. Make no mistake, there's plenty to be done, and so often when you think the specific battle has been won you find yourself having to start fighting it all over again against some new threat—or the same threat that's been lying dormant.

World Wildlife has held two World Congresses during the ten years. The first, in Amsterdam in 1967 under the title 'Nature and Man', ended with a solemn undertaking by the delegates and members of the Congress to—and I quote—'to apply ourselves with renewed vigour to the task of making all people, including the Governments of the Nations, aware of our joint responsibility for the common heritage, and to work with redoubled energy for the integrity of our earth through the conservation of nature for the long term social, cultural and economic benefit of all mankind'. No more, you may say, than a pious hope—a New Year resolution. Yet the broad principles need to be stated, and many who were at that Congress have done exactly what they undertook to do. This gives me the chance to salute the gallant band of conservationists, still pathetically few, who have given their energies so unstintingly to our cause.

The second World Congress of the World Wildlife Fund was held just under a year ago in London. Its title was 'All Life on Earth' and it dealt mainly with root causes. Its resolutions were on the population explosion, development planning, environmental monitoring, trusteeship for Man's heritage in the biosphere, disposal of waste products and oil pollution. But there were also resolutions calling for action towards the survival of endangered species and of especially threatened habitats. One resolution introduced by our President's daughter, Her Royal Highness Princess Beatrix, called on the women of the world to renounce the wearing of endangered animals' skins. The accent on environment was deliberate, because it seemed important to us to stress the idea that the conservation of wild nature was part of the same environmental dilemma which is at last beginning to be recognised. The oneness of the problem was movingly brought home to us by the first man to set foot on the moon. Addressing the congress on what he calls 'The Blue Planet', Neil Armstrong said, 'To stand on the surface of the moon and look at the earth high overhead is certainly a unique experience. Although it is very beautiful, it is very remote and apparently very small. We have been struck by the simile to an oasis or an island. More importantly it is the only island that we know is a suitable home for man. The importance of protecting and saving that home has never been felt more strongly. Protection seems most required, however, not from foreign aggressors or natural calamity, but from its own population.'

All in all we believe that World Wildlife's two Congresses were useful and successful exercises. But I wouldn't like you to think that we are any of us complacent about what the Fund has achieved in these first ten years. Quite the opposite. We've got to do much better, and Dr. Luc Hoffmann will tell you later this afternoon what measures we have taken to that effect.

One other remarkable thing has happened during the last ten years—there has been, it seems to me, an enormous change in attitudes to wild nature and environment—in almost every country and at almost all levels of influence. Of course the conservation message contains a significant measure of self interest. Wild animals and plants may be indicators of a healthy environment and give warning of danger to mankind; they may be a latent reservoir of as yet undiscovered successors to penicillin; they, and the wild country they live in, may be the best therapy for the stresses of urban life; they may be the main spring of a successful tourist industry and local prosperity; they may be at one end of a problem of environment and resources which, at the other, threatens the very survival of the human race. In short there may be all sorts of compelling *material reasons*.

But there is another more philosophical element in the conservation message—the *concept* of responsibility to future generations, the issue of principle, the right and wrong of destroying the irreplaceable, or extinguishing the unique species. Many people believe that the material arguments are the only cogent ones in this day and age, but whatever the cynics may say, vast numbers of ordinary people are motivated by their principles—motivated to do things they believe to be right. And it's in that direction that I see so much change during the last ten years, and so much prospect of even greater change indicated by the youth of today—change which, in my view, has to come swiftly if there is to be any hope for the survival of life on our earth. And swiftly believe it will come.

I have always been an optimist. There are times when it is difficult, but lately I've become greatly encouraged by the way in which the younger generation in many parts of the world is turning away from ruthless materialism. If the trend continues and if human populations can be stabilised there may yet be hope for the survival of the miraculous diversity of life that has taken twenty million centuries to evolve on our blue planet, and which if we do not succeed may be blotted out in a mere instant of geological time by the stupidity and irresponsibility of the cleverest animal of them all.

THE POND

From *The Twelfth Man* (Cassell, 1971)

The mother duck swam across the pond surrounded by eleven newly hatched ducklings. In the window overlooking the water a two-year-old child laughed with joy. 'Babies mallards!' she cried. The tiny balls of brown fluff foraged busily along the shore of the pond within a few feet of the window—held invisibly together by family ties and the soft quacking of their mother, who kept watch over them without having the slightest idea how many there should be.

The pond was a hundred yards long and fifty yards wide, specially dug at the same time as the house was built, so as to be in front of the great picture window. The pond was home for the mallard family, and for hundreds of other waterbirds, some confined to it by enforced flightlessness, others free to come and go as they pleased, some like the Ross's geese and barheads and mandarins native of faraway places, others like the mallards and pintails and shovelers natives of England, and joined in wintertime by hundreds of their wild brethren.

The girl was eight years old when the very important visitor came to stay. Floodlights were installed so that the pond and its ducks could be seen after dinner. The bright whites of the pintails' and shovelers' breasts, and of the Ross's geese, shone golden in the glow. The lights had come to stay.

In February 1964 when the girl was eleven years old, the first wild Bewick's swans, coming from faraway breeding grounds in the Siberian Arctic, were persuaded by four tame Bewick's swans to land on the pond. Twenty-four of them spent a month there, coming daily to the wheat that was put down for them in the shallow water in front of the window. Then they flew off to the northeast towards their summer home on the tundras of the Yamal Peninsula and the Kara Sea.

In the following winter they came back to the well-remembered feeding pond, and were themselves remembered by the watchers in the window, who had found in the previous winter that the yellow and black bill patterns of Bewick's swans are infinitely variable and much more obviously different on each individual than fingerprints. The discovery had led to the naming of the individual swans—Pink and Rebecca, the Owl and the Pussy Cat, Lancelot and Victoria, the Major and Ethel—and when darkness fell, the swans fed on along the foreshore under the window, shining brilliantly in the floodlights. The plumage of all the birds looked wonderful against the dark water, but the white plumage of the white birds was most beautiful. As they swam the bright reflections of their ripples moved endlessly up their necks in flickering parallel lines. The duckling pond had become Swan Lake.

Not all of the original twenty-four swans came back the following winter but those that did brought their families and encouraged other passing families to come down and join them. By the end of the season seventy-two swans had been recorded by the watchers in the window. Already the girl knew them best. One pair she named herself—Leo and Stella—and they were, from then on, her favourite swans. On Christmas Eve 1966, although many swans were already assembled on Swan Lake, some now for the third winter, Leo and Stella had failed to turn up. There was talk about Christmas presents and the girl said the only one she wanted was the arrival of her special swans. Next morning, miraculously, they were there, and they have come each winter since.

The number of swans increased dramatically every year, their presence being recorded daily on a chart in a kind of 'roll call'. Their heads were drawn and photographed, their behaviour noted, and from time to time odd individuals were caught, usually by flying into minor crash landings in the garden or the small pens. Thus a slowly increasing number could be weighed, measured, ringed and released again on Swan Lake. The birds seemed to care little about such indignities and rarely if ever flew away on release.

The study of the swans became the full-time occupation of a scientist, for the girl was often away at school, although she had special dispensation to watch and record the swans each weekend. At Christmas 1968 her Christmas present was a conversation piece in oils of her second favourite swan family— Peasant and Gypsy and their cygnet—painted specially for her.

That winter 439 different Bewick's swans visited Swan Lake and in the following year the number was 570, although the highest number on any one day was 404, and for most of January and February there were more than 350 together with three whooper swans and about sixty of the non-migratory mute swans. Also on Swan Lake daily was a great crowd of ducks, perhaps three hundred each of shovelers and pintails and a leavening of tufted ducks and pochards. On one morning of frost there were, including gulls and coots, not less than three thousand birds all within seventy yards of the great windows.

In the earlier part of the winter most of the swans stay on the pond but by the turn of the year most of them are going to the Severn Estuary to roost, flighting out in the late dusk, lit gloriously by the floodlights that were installed for the very important visitor, whose son came to see them in the spring of 1970.

That spring some of the swans left early on the first stages of their 2,600 mile flight to their Arctic breeding grounds. The girl, now seventeen, got a grant from her school to follow them as far as Holland. She arrived there on 22 March, and visited the known haunts of Bewick's in a car driven by a Dutch friend. The swans were mostly concentrated along the flooded meadows beside the River Yssel, and the first swan she recognises was Karroo (a son of Sahara and Gobi). He was a long way off and she could not be quite certain that day. Next day Gypsy swam into the field of her telescope and a moment later she found Peasant—her familiar special pair here 350 miles from Swan Lake. It was a moment for exultation.

Two days later she found Raquello. She knew he had a tall white plastic leg ring with large black figures that could easily be read through the telescope. The distinguished Dutch professor who had come to see how she was getting on was himself asked to read the number, which provided the proof that all good scientists need that the recognition system really worked.

The fifth old friend was a swan ringed originally as a cygnet (and therefore unnamed). He carried a metal ring of an earlier type and was too far away for the number to be read, though by a process of elimination he was almost certainly a son of Pepper and Amber.

On her last day in Holland the girl picked up Booster (a son of Boosey and Hawkes). Booster, she knew, also carried a metal ring, and being a male, it would be on his right leg in accordance with standard practice. But now he sat sleepily in the water, and in due course tucked his head back into his scapulars and slept. For more than half an hour the girl's eye was glued to her telescope, until at last the swan awoke. As he swam his right leg appeared briefly and it had no ring on it. In a flash she remembered that he had been ringed by mistake on the left leg, and as he turned, there sure enough was his ring.

The girl returned to her home beside the now empty Swan Lake in Gloucestershire, while the swans headed on northeast perhaps by way of Denmark, the Swedish islands, Matsalu Bay in the Estonian Soviet Socialist Republic and away to the Siberian Arctic. By late-October 1970 the first of them were back in England. On 7 November Bewick's swans were pouring into Swan Lake—fifty-three came during the day, which constitutes a heavy 'swanfall'. It being Saturday the girl came post haste, sixty miles from school. At teatime she was sitting at the binoculars in the studio when a pair of swans with two cygnets planed down out of the eastern sky on to the lake and waterskied to a halt. They were Peasant and Gypsy and their family, less than five months old, who had flown with them the 2,600 miles from the breeding grounds. They swam fearlessly up to the window to start feeding within less than ten yards of the girl who was watching them.

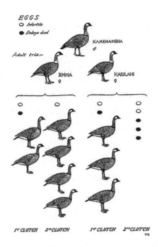

SPECIES EXTINCTION
IN BIRDS

Witherby Memorial Lecture, delivered at the
BTO Annual Conference, Swanwick, Derbyshire

2 December 1972

It is a great honour and a particular pleasure to have been
invited to give this lecture in memory of the great H. F.
Witherby. As an ornithologist I first became known to him
when I misidentified a ruff as a greater yellowlegs. After that I
was astonished when he invited me to illustrate the wild geese
in *The Handbook* and allowed me double space for each picture.
When the third volume came out, in 1939, we had not yet
described the Greenland white-fronted goose—*Anser albifrons
flavirostris*—but a footnote above the initials 'H.F.W.' quotes
my opinion that whitefronts from West Greenland might prove
to be the same as those wintering in Ireland and to belong
to a different race. After the incident of the Ruff that wasn't

a yellowlegs, I've always regarded that footnote, from one of the most meticulous ornithologists of his day, as an astonishing act of faith. Thank goodness the theory turned out to be right.

But I am to talk about 'Species Extinction in Birds', and although the Greenland whitefront has a pitifully small world population of perhaps no more than 15,000 it is not yet listed as an endangered subspecies. This raises the point, which I shall come back to, that my title 'Species Extinction...' also includes subspecies, because they represent the birth of species, and that is very relevant when talking about the death of species. I am well aware that the BTO is mainly preoccupied with the study of the British avifauna—and indeed that most of this country's ornithologists, birdwatchers and bird lovers (I use the last phrase reluctantly, for want of a better term, for those who know little but care much about birds and who are extremely important for the future of birds). I know that most of the bird people in this country are, reasonably enough, interested mostly in British species. Of course the great auk *Pinguinus impennis* was on the British list, but that is the only species we have lost to global extinction. Nevertheless I hope you will allow me in this lecture to range more widely over the birds of the world.

It seems likely that the last dodo, *Raphus cucullatus*, was killed on Mauritius in 1681—a large and eminently edible flightless bird that had evolved without predators—and, in particular, without the arch predator, man. Whether it was the sailors themselves, or the pigs and dogs which they released on the island, which directly caused the extinction will probably never be known. But either way the dodo was gone for ever. It was—in the ubiquitous phrase—'as dead as the dodo', and until recently it was convenient to measure the rate of extinction of species in terms of those which had died out since the dodo.

Our greatly lamented friend James Fisher, who did more than any other ornithologist to integrate living birds with their fossil ancestors, became the foremost authority on the accelerating rate of extinction. He persuaded the Survival Service Commission of the International Union for Conservation of

Nature and Natural Resources that for a number of reasons 1600 was a better date to calculate from than 1681—the dodo date—because virtually all the mammals and birds known to have become extinct since 1600 are identified by adequate descriptions or portraits, nearly all of them by skins, and a considerable number also by sub-fossil bones. All but two have acceptable Linnean or scientific names. So 1600 was adopted by the Survival Service Commission as the reckoning date for modem extinction.

I need, at this stage, to follow James Fisher a little further into his scholarly study of extinction, because I believe all of us here are concerned to prevent or at least slow down the rate of future species extinction, and by studying what happened in the past we can the better learn what to do and what not to do in the future.

James believed that in the year 1600 there were approximately 8,684 living species of birds and that since then 94 (or 1.09%) have become extinct—and incidentally that at least 187 more (2.16%) are currently in danger of extinction. Now there's nothing new about extinction. Since the dawn of life, species have been born and species have died out. The rates at which they have done so have no doubt varied widely down the twenty million centuries. But since 1600 man seems to have increased the rate of extinction in vertebrate animals— so James Fisher held—by at least a factor of four, and some regard that figure as an underestimate, believing that a factor of twelve would be more realistic.

'This,' as James wrote in 1969, 'is a state of affairs that is quite without parallel in the former span of man's life with nature, that is to say, in his less-civilised history before 1600...'

What has brought this about? What are the underlying principles? To explore this I hope you will forgive me if I take the train of thought onto a wider stage than that of birds alone. I should like to propound to you a simplification—not, I think, an over-simplification—which may give an insight into what has happened and is happening. It is that all species extinction comes about because of changes in the environment, whether in the form of climatic or other elemental change, the evolution of a new predator or competitor, or the failure of food supplies. Inability to adapt quickly enough to such changes is the only cause of species extinction. If we look at the impact of man since 1600 in these terms we may perhaps get a new perspective, because man is, after all, a product of natural selection—inescapably a part of nature, and still, in spite of his much vaunted technology, subject to natural laws. But man has fought against nature for so long that he has come to regard himself as the antithesis of nature. Objects or problems are described as 'natural' or 'man-made', as if the words constituted a distinction. If we accept that man is a part of nature, it follows that man's influence on the environment is 'natural'? By the same token the capacities evolved in man—to reason, to plan ahead, to communicate and to record past experience—give us the chance to assess the consequences of our actions, and in particular those which affect the environment. They also give us the possibility (and the responsibility) to minimise the damage and disturbance to the environment which we're causing.

Following this line of thought we emerge as the most dangerous and destructive animal the world has ever known— the arch-predator, the arch-competitor, the arch-disturber of the environment. Yet the selfsame process of natural selection which made us into all these things, also evolved in man a conscience, and with it a school of thought and pattern of social behaviour which leads some members of the species to be labelled 'conservationists' and to find and use all kinds of arguments—ethical, aesthetic, scientific, economic, and 'skin-saving'—for redressing the baleful balance of our current impact on the planet.

If environmental change is the root cause of all species extinction, then, in today's context, we should carefully examine all those aspects of environmental change that impinge on bird species.

Inorganic or elemental environmental changes which may affect the course of organic evolution include sudden catastrophes such as volcanic eruptions, earthquakes, tidal waves, hurricanes, floods and droughts; or, in the longer term, climatic changes, whether of accountable or unaccountable origin. Very long term changes such as continental drift, chemical balances in air or water, perhaps even wobbles in the earth's rotation, may have influenced evolution by natural selection (profoundly). But the accumulated genetic changes in the plants and animals themselves have had a far greater effect on the other plants and animals.

Successful species—notably invertebrates such as locusts, termites and ants—have by their very numbers made large scale environmental changes. Even smaller organisms have made much larger changes, and plants have made the largest of all. Local overpopulation by elephants and rodents and some birds may change the vegetation and thus greatly alter the biotope. But by comparison with all these, the impact of *Homo sapiens* on the global environment is of an entirely different order.

As a ruthless and efficient predator, Stone Age man was probably responsible for the extinction of quite a large number of species like the European woolly rhino and the sabre-toothed tiger. The development of weapons capable of killing or wounding from a distance—the spear, the sling, the arrow, and eventually firearms—each in their turn tipped the scales against man's prey and against the predators which hunted him and his domestic animals. Deforestation and capriculture in the 'cradle of civilisation' altered the climate of the Mediterranean region, creating widespread desert. Down the centuries the destruction has escalated exponentially. Over-exploitation and pollution threaten the biosphere today on a scale so vast and so ubiquitous that to most people it is incomprehensible.

Only in a few cases is the damage to the environment calculated and deliberate—and even then the reasons are supposed to be so vital to human progress as to justify the actions. The verdict of history on such destructive practices as the use of biocides as defoliants in the Vietnam war will clearly fail to provide such justification. Nuclear test explosions in the atmosphere, since the fallout implications became fully known, seem likely to be judged equally unjustifiable.

But the vast majority of environmental damage is caused by unintentional and inadequately understood side effects of human actions which have acceptable and even laudable objectives. Of these the most obvious example, of course, is pesticide used in disease control and in agriculture—often very effectively, though in some cases to deplorable excess. The fallout from the burning of certain synthetic substances such as polychlorinated biphenyls (PCBs), used for their insulating qualities and the gloss they give to paints and varnishes, has also been shown to affect predatory species at the top of the food chain (including man). Then there is lead from high octane fuel, and the wide spectrum of atmospheric and water pollution caused by industrial processes. In the oceans there are the general problems of effluents from land-based human activities, and two special problems—the disposal at sea of chemical and radioactive wastes, and oil spillage whether by accident or design. A principle which is emerging on industrial pollution is that whoever makes it should pay for clearing it up. As one industrialist exclaimed, '*this pollution is costing us the earth.*'

It remains to be seen whether the newly developing countries of the Third World will be so mesmerised by the questionable benefits of our industrial civilisation as to accept pollution as an inescapable concomitant of prosperity. Until the poverty gap can be narrowed it seems likely that the cry will be 'Pollution means prosperity', and until human populations become stable on a global scale the poverty gap must continue to widen.

Sheer numbers of human beings can alter wildlife habitat, quite apart from the effects of their activities. Many shy species, especially of birds, cannot live their lives and reproduce successfully if the density of human beings in their habitat rises above a threshold—which may be quite low. In such cases inviolate refuges or reserves may be the only chance for their survival.

Even more serious has been the introduction of predator or competitor species, often for reasons which future generations will brand as grossly irresponsible. Examples are legion, especially on islands. Crude and simplistic attempts at biological control, with cats, mongooses and owls; ill-conceived introduction of potential sporting quarry such as foxes and many birds; goats, pigs and rabbits as food for shipwrecked mariners; rats, cats and dogs as a result of carelessness and ignorance; and escapes from commercial fur farming ventures (mink being the most notably disastrous).

Whether man's activities, based on unlimited positive feedback, will inevitably lead—as some hold—to irreversible damage to the biosphere, is still widely debated. Some scientists predict 'the greenhouse effect' produced by an excess of carbon dioxide in the atmosphere. Others are more concerned about the effects not only of plutonium radiation, but of plutonium poisoning. Plutonium, the basis of 'breeder reactor' nuclear power, is a synthetic element, known to be exceptionally hazardous to life. It is likely to be in great demand and susceptible to human greed and human error. The point here is that whereas mercury, for example, has been with us all along and species have evolved with resistance to it, plutonium is entirely new and evolution has had no time to protect plants and animals from it. Resistances are simply not there.

Then there is concern about particulate pollution of the stratosphere. It has already been shown that increased 'dust' and water vapour produced by jet planes and other sources of pollution in the northern hemisphere have reduced the amounts of sunshine reaching the earth's surface, by comparison with the amounts getting through in the southern hemisphere. Consider, for example, how this will affect the navigation (and therefore the survival) of northern night-migrant birds which depend on star patterns that may be progressively less frequently and less clearly seen. Consider whether Concorde will improve that—or for that matter any other situation. It may be that the lack of orders for Concorde will curtail the supersonic aircraft programme and this may well be the time when there will be some rethinking about other expensive and unpopular proposals. Then it will be important to keep up the pressure against the third London Airport at Foulness.

Indeed if there is a message in this lecture it is that we must KEEP UP THE PRESSURE. I believe that we should produce plans for a Nature Reserve at Foulness, complete with facilities for people to see the birds. And whatever happens we must not concede defeat until the runways have been laid down. We are up against formidable odds. Alexander King—one of the founders of the Club of Rome—described what we are up against as, 'the arrogance of the economists, the naïveté of the natural scientists, the bloody-mindedness of the bureaucrats and the plain ignorance of the politicians.'

What seems likely is that the processes of environmental attrition will grind on, and that eco-catastrophes of various kinds originating from man's actions will continue to assail the biosphere, some with great, some with lesser effect. Man will continue to play the role of the environmental arch-disturber because of his preoccupation with short term advantage and his inability to take the long view. In that case the question may increasingly be asked: 'With global pollution and environmental disaster looming over us, why waste time and money trying to save the white-winged wood duck?' A simple answer might be that at every possible point we must concern ourselves with 'holding the line'. A more important answer would be to establish the vital value of genetic diversity, because it is an essential element in maintaining due stability of healthy ecosystems. The greater the diversity of species in a natural community, the greater its stability. And there is reason to fear an impending massive loss of diversity as a result of man's disturbance of the biosphere. This is the concept which led the U.N. Conference in Stockholm in June 1972 to make no less than nine recommendations designed to maintain the genetic diversity of the living world. Of the scientific reasons for preventing the extinction of species and incipient species, this is probably the most powerful. Reproductively isolated populations, clines and subspecies are of no less significance than full species if recruitment of new species is to keep pace with the 'normal' extinction rates of pre-human eras. Species-birth is as important as species-death.

But what should be the attitude of the conservationist to a species which is thought to have become an anachronism, and is judged to be 'due for extinction'? It seems doubtful whether any such subjective judgement could justify a course of action leading, either deliberately or by default, to the extinction of a species, even if all its known habitat has been, or is to be, destroyed. No one can tell what the attitude of a future generation may be, nor how much effort, time and money it may be prepared to expend in recreating a suitable habitat at some future date. But the probability is that it will be much more enlightened than the present attitude. Thus the responsibility must, I am convinced, remain on all conservationists to fight for the survival of each and every living form. Value judgements may have to be made when resources for human survival are in short supply, but the scientific principle persists that no species is expendable.

In addition to the scientific reasons, there are, of course, the ethical and aesthetic arguments—that we have no right to exterminate, and that the diversity of nature gives pleasure, inspiration and a sense of wonder to mankind. No doubt Professor Denis Gabor had these aspects in mind when he wrote to me in 1971: 'I have never seen either of them, but it makes me happy to think that there are still wild elephants in Africa and whales in the Southern seas.' Most of us here would surely echo this in terms of birds. No other animal but man has ever before known or cared about the avoidance of species extinction, but nowadays to many people it is no longer acceptable that man should deny existence to any other members of the crew of our spaceship.

There are economic arguments, too. Tourism to the Galapagos Islands, to Aldabra, to the Seychelles and to many other out-of-the-way parts of the world is largely based on natural history, and in particular on the endemic, and in many cases endangered bird species. Once more, diversity is the keynote.

Some domestic animals and certain others have adapted themselves to living with man so well, whether he likes it or not, that they seem to be assured of a place in the sun. Species like rats and mice, starlings, house sparrows, Indian mynahs, wood pigeons, even collared doves perhaps, have almost accidentally been allowed into the category. Others, such as predators, have been described as 'environmental litmus paper'—indicators of the health of the biosphere, like the canaries in the coal mines—a mere mechanism to help man save his skin. Yet the world attitude to the plight of the great whales—reflected in the overwhelming vote by the national delegates at the Stockholm Conference in favour of the proposal for a ten years moratorium on all commercial whaling—seems to have been primarily motivated by ethical consideration, with an ancillary element of resource wastefulness. Although whales are not part of our subject this morning, it may be of interest to some of you that the moratorium proposal is not by any means dead. It was turned down by the International Whaling Commission soon after Stockholm, but I believe within the next three years they will have to accept it.

In the past, man's interest in the impending extinction of species has centred round the higher vertebrate animals—largely mammals and birds. Perhaps inevitably this trend continues, and for those of us with a special interest in birds this seems rather a satisfactory situation. It stems of course from that very special appeal which birds seem to have, and which in turn makes far more people into bird lovers than into lovers of any other kinds of wild animals.

Attention has been directed to the plight of various bird groups, notably the cranes, the bustards, the swans, geese and ducks, the seabirds, and perhaps most of all recently the BOPS—the birds of prey. Flamingos are to come under special scrutiny shortly, and there has been concern about island forms—especially the flightless ones like the kagu *Rhynochetos jubatus* of New Caledonia, and the many island species of rails.

There are, of course, lessons to be learned from the species that have gone from the passenger pigeon *Ectopistes migratorius*, for example, which up until the 1860s had a population of perhaps three thousand million. It was probably the most abundant migratory land bird species in the world, and represented something between 25% and 40% of the total bird population of the United States. In the 1870s its numbers declined precipitously, by 1900 they had all gone except for one, called Martha, which lived until 1913 in the Cincinnati Zoo. Now she sits stuffed upon her perch, and not long ago she accompanied me to a fundraising dinner in New York and helped to raise $70,000. Incidentally, those of you who are interested in the survival of endangered species should read A. W. Schorger's scholarly book on the passenger pigeon, published in 1955 by the University of Wisconsin Press in Madison—especially the quotations from people in the 1870s and 1880s who were opposed to any measures for protecting the passenger pigeon because they were convinced it could never become extinct.

One might think that such an example—and with the Carolina parakeet *Conuropsis carolinensis* becoming extinct in 1914—the Americans would have quickly become sensitive about extinction. Yet they were not in time to save the heath hen *Tympanuchus cupido cupido*, the eastern subspecies of the prairie chicken. In 1890 there were no more than 200 left of a population which formerly occupied several of the eastern states. These 200 were all on the island of Martha's Vineyard off the Massachusetts coast. By 1916 the numbers had built up to 2,000 and it should have been fairly safe, but by 1921 they were back down to 414. By 1926 they were down to 50 and the last one died in 1932.

Well, maybe this is why so much attention is being given now to the survival of the whooping crane *Grus americana* which was down at one time to18 individuals. By 1959 they had crept up to 33—by 1968 there were 50. Last March the world population consisted of 59 wild birds and 21 in captivity—a total of 80.

All these are or were continental birds, and the only extinct bird which I personally ever saw alive was also a continental species—the pink-headed duck *Rhodonessa caryophyllacea* of India. I saw ten of them on a pond in Surrey about 1937—imported from India into the collection of an old friend, Chips Ezra. Alas they never bred and no pink-headed duck has been seen alive since 1944.

We tend to think of island species like the dodo *Raphus cucullatus*, and its relatives the solitaires *Raphus solitarius* of Reunion and *Pezophaps solitaria* of Rodrigues, as having been more vulnerable than the continental species, yet environmental change over vast areas is becoming a familiar patter in terms of pollution, and birds of prey with wide geographical distributions have, as we all know, been badly hit. Many of you here will know more about this than I do, but it seems to me that without for one moment relaxing our vigilance, we can be modestly pleased with the most recent British record on the conservation of raptorial birds. The decline of the peregrine *Falco peregrinus*—at least the inland peregrines—and of the golden eagle *Aquila chrysaetos* seems to have been checked, the kite *Milvus milvus* situation seems moderately satisfactory, and the return of the osprey *Pandion haliaetus* is positively encouraging. I had better return to a subject I know more about before displaying my ignorance any further—but not without a word of warmest congratulation to all those organisations and individual people involved in the effort to save our BOPS and in particular to the splendid work of the RSPB This is the sort of time when I ask myself Piet Heim's famous question: 'Do you sometimes feel you know more than you need to know about more than you need to know about—and not enough about what you know you need to know more about?'

I have been extremely lucky in being able to visit a number of remote islands and see many of their endemic birds—in Galapagos, in Hawaii, in the Seychelles, in Aldabra, in New Zealand and in the Auckland Islands—where we failed to rediscover the Auckland Island merganser *Mergus australis*, but saw at close quarters the now very rare flightless teal *Anas aucklandica*.

At The Wildfowl Trust at Slimbridge, as many of you will know, we have been concerned with propagating various species of endangered *Anatidae*. The story of the nene or Hawaiian goose *Branta sandvicensis* is fairly well known. In 1950 only 32 were known to exist with a possible further ten in the wild. At that time three were sent to Slimbridge. Later two males were sent for fresh blood, and later still two more. From these seven birds 729 have now been raised in England and 200 have been sent to the Hawaiian Island of Maui where the species had disappeared from its former habitat in the Haleakala Crater. There were said to have been 25,000 nenes in Hawaii in the middle of the last century. The world population, thanks to an admirable breeding programme in Hawaii, is now over 1,500, so the species is at least out of the most immediate danger.

We have also had some success at The Wildfowl Trust with the Hawaiian duck or koloa *Anas platyrhynchos wyvilliana*, with a world population of between 200 and 400; and with the Laysan teal *Anas laysanensis*, whose last known population on Laysan Island (1,000 miles west of Hawaii) was 200 birds.

Two continental species in some danger which we are now breeding at Slimbridge are the Mexican duck *Anas platyrhynchos diazi* and the white-winged wood duck *Cairina scutulata* of Southeast Asia. Last year we raised eight baby white-wings to maturity and this year eleven.

Some of you may have heard of the Red Data Books of the Survival Service Commission of IUCN and I should like to end by telling you how those books and how the Commission itself works. I know a little about it because I have been Chairman of the Commission for the last nine years.

The SSC has a comparatively simple objective—to avert the extinction of living species and subspecies—and when it comes to birds we work in close liaison with ICBP. We believe that whenever possible the species should be helped to survive in its natural habitat, but measures such as translocation and captive breeding may have to be used as an additional safeguard, and in desperate cases as the sole prospect for survival. The Commission's operations are broadly divided into fact-finding, communication, and action programmes. First we have to discover which species are endangered, and for each of them try to maintain some sort of inventory of their world population, keeping it as up to date as possible. Further research concerns reproduction rates, minimum viable populations, factors limiting population increase, the carrying capacity of the available habitat, the possibility of rehabilitating degraded habitat, the minimum viable size of habitat areas, the possibilities of captive breeding, and the prospects of subsequent successful release into the wild.

Specialist groups of people who are enthusiastic and knowledgeable about particular species or groups of species provide basic data from which the loose-leaf summary sheets of the Red Data Books are compiled, and used as a method of disseminating information on endangered species. Red Book volumes have so far been issued for mammals, birds, reptiles and amphibia, freshwater fishes, and the first of a series of plant Red Books—on the subject of angiosperms. Replacement loose-leaf sheets are issued from time to time bringing the information up to date.

The degree of threat to each species is indicated by the colour of the sheet—pink for the most endangered, white for others at risk, amber for those which are suffering galloping depletion and must be watched, grey for those on which there is limited information, and green for those formerly endangered which are now held to be relatively secure. Broadly, the objective is to reach a situation in which the Red Books contain nothing but green sheets.

At present the Red Data Book for birds contains 67 pink sheets—those most in danger—and nineteen green sheets—out of danger. In between these categories are 214 more birds on white, amber and grey sheets. So 281 species or subspecies of birds are considered to be sufficiently in danger to justify their inclusion in the Red Book, which I may say is now increasingly being used by Governments as a basis for their import restrictions, and other legislation.

It is interesting that no British bird species is so far in the Red Book. Maybe the British red-backed shrike *Lanius collurio juxtus* should be. The St Kilda wren *Troglodytes troglodytes hirtensis* is certainly in low enough numbers, but there is no immediate threat to its survival. The same applies to the Fair Isle wren *Troglodytes troglodytes fridariensis*. Island species will always be vulnerable, but their populations are generally easier to monitor than species living in ecological islands on larger land masses. Tropical rainforests, for example, thousands of square miles of which disappear each year through man's ignorant improvidence, may well hold remnant populations not only of birds, but also of amphibians, fishes and plants which may be on the verge of extinction without anyone knowing it. Indeed it is possible that many such will be exterminated by environmental changes caused by man without ever having become known to science.

May I leave this thought with you. If the behavioural evolution of mankind leads to a general acceptance of the principle that human progress demands the maintenance of genetic diversity by preventing species extinction, then the efforts I have been talking about this morning may lead to an altogether better break for the birds, as well as a bit of a breakthrough for our own species, and for our one and only planet.

RECONCILING
THE IRRECONCILABLE—
WILDFOWL AND PEOPLE

International Zoo Yearbook, Volume 13
(Zoological Society of London, 1973)

In the more thickly populated lowland areas of Europe, the
pressures on land are such that it is no longer feasible to set
aside large tracts simply for the benefit of its wildlife. Nature
reserves must be made to serve the people by providing them
with recreation and education. This is as it should be, for such
facilities are sorely needed. But there is an additional advantage.
The reserves then acquire an Amenity Value in the sight of our
master-planners. A piece of desolate wetland is an 'obvious' site
for a noisy airport, a polluting factory or a garbage tip. It is a
different matter if it has become a famous tourist site, clearly
to be seen as a money-making enterprise, or even as a place
drawing significant numbers of parties from schools.

At Slimbridge, we have been quite successful at attracting the public during the winter—some 40,000 people see the wild geese, swans and ducks in the six winter months—but there is no doubt that the uncommitted public are reluctant to penetrate into the country except in summer. 160,000 visitors come during the six months from April to September. The wild birds are away in their Arctic breeding grounds then, so a collection of tame birds is maintained to interest and educate the visitors and to persuade them to return in the winter to see what we really want them to see. To this end carefully- (and briefly-) worded pictorial wall displays in a lecture hall or entrance hall are of great assistance. So, too, is an attractive guide book.

To walk among the tame birds, to feed them from the hand, to photograph them with ease is the beginning of the educational process whereby the town dweller is brought to appreciate wildlife. It is fortunate that ducks, geese and swans settle well in captivity and look happy and contented even though one wing must be cut to prevent them flying away. And for this reason the collection must be surrounded by a high wire fence to keep out predators such as foxes and cats. This needs careful siting to make it blend as much as possible into the landscape. Yet even the fence has its role in saving the wilderness; it not only keeps the foxes out, it keeps the people in.

Many wildfowl breed readily in captivity and their progeny can be used to rebuild depleted native stocks. They can be left full-winged and remain in the proximity of the collection, providing, throughout the year, the added educative thrill of the massed flight of wildfowl that is otherwise to be enjoyed only in winter.

But will not the many thousands of visitors destroy the very wilderness we are seeking to preserve, and drive away the wild, shy animals whose habitat it was? At The Wildfowl Trust we think we have worked out an effective compromise. We have applied the principle at our reserves at Slimbridge on the River Severn, at Welney in Norfolk and at Caerlaverock on the Solway Estuary. These were places long famous for wintering flocks of thousands of wildfowl, respectively white-fronted geese *Anser albifrons*, wigeon *Anas penelope* and barnacle geese *Branta leucopsis*—as well, in each case, as many other species of wildfowl and waders

While the wilderness and its inhabitants are left undisturbed, the public is still enabled to view the wonderland at close quarters by going along screened access routes to observation hides. These can be small, holding five people, or large enough for ten times that number—a bus load. We build our larger hides with a concrete base and wooden superstructure, though, for small hides, precast fibreglass cabins have proved relatively cheap and maintenance-free.

The most effective, durable and natural-looking way of screening an approach route is by an earth bank about three metres high. Although the initial price is high, there is virtually no subsequent maintenance cost. Earth walls have the added advantage of muffling sound, needful when one is conducting a party of schoolchildren. The wall should, if possible, be along the southerly edge of the wilderness, so that the sun is behind the observers, not shining in their eyes. By building double earth walls, people can be safely conducted into the heart of the Wilderness—a particularly exciting experience. At certain key points we erect towers which may be as much as fifteen metres high. These obtrude more onto the landscape and should be used sparingly. However, they are very valuable to show large numbers of people the general habitat, and to enable wardens both to police the area and decide which route a conducted tour should follow to get the best views of the birds wherever they may happen to be feeding or resting. With experience, it is possible to concentrate the birds where it is most convenient, by the judicious use of baiting and by the presence of tame waterfowl. We have been especially successful in this with the beautiful little Bewick's swan, *Cygnus columbianus bewickii*, hundreds of which congregate a few metres from the plate glass windows of the main observatory buildings at

Slimbridge, and at Welney. The spectacle of truly wild birds alongside our captives is thrilling. It is also a reminder that zoo collections depend upon and are at best pale reflections of the wild populations from which they are drawn. Yet ours serve their purpose if they arouse the interest of public and politicians and ensure the conservation of the wild wetlands on which the waterfowl depend.

Manuscript received 8 May 1972

THE OBJECTIVES OF THE WORLD WILDLIFE FUND

STATEMENT IN 200 WORDS by PS.

which I was asked to submit to EXCO.

■ The concern of the WWF is the natural environment- its animals & plants and the ecological web which binds them together with climate, soil & water into those healthy ecosystems which for centuries Man has characterised by the word "Nature".

■ WWF pays particular attention to endangered species & those which have been seriously depleted by the impact of Man, & to endangered natural habitats.

■ At the same time WWF is acutely aware of the causal factors which make nature conservation so necessary and urgent - the problems of human population increase, of high Technology agriculture, of industrialisation and urbanisation, of pollution, of misuse & waste of resources and energy, of famine and poverty.

■ If solutions to these problems can be found WWF's aims will be more easily achieved, for it is clear that the conservation of nature cannot be dealt with in isolation from the human condition.

■ But in view of the limited funds at present available, WWF's priority projects are mainly, though not exclusively, directed towards wildlife- defined as animals and plants and their wild habitats, and towards the promotion of public awareness of the immediate dangers that threaten nature and the steps necessary to avert them.

SPEECH NOTES, 1980

SPEECH NOTES FOR THE
PEKING LAUNCH OF THE
WORLD CONSERVATION STRATEGY.

W.C.S. (Start)
 The object of DEVELOPMENT is to provide
for social and economic welfare.
The object of CONSERVATION is to ensure
the planets capacity to sustain development
and to continue to support life.
THE W´C´S´ shows, for perhaps the
first time, that
 CONS. is ~~shown to be~~ an aid to DEVPMt.
and that DEVPmt is ~~shown to be~~ an essential
element in CONS.

NEED FOR A CONS. STRATEGY in a
GLOBAL WAR ON WASTE
          and UNNECESSARY DESTRUCTION.

A COMMON STRATEGY involving
    COOPERATION between CONSERVATIONISTS
             and DEVELOPERS

Despite the efforts of conservationists over the last
thirty years, the destruction for short term gain
goes on virtually unchecked..... (examples opposite)
◀ We should establish three essential criteria:
1. The EXTENT of the LOSS that is occurring or is about to occur.
2. The IMMINENCE of the loss or damage.
3. The CHANCES of preventing the loss for a significant
                                                    time.
PRIORITIES   (over)

* TRF : 30 hectares per min (= 75 acres)
   Lowland rainforests going even faster.
   Lowland forests of Malaysia Indonesia & the
   Philippines gone by 2,000 – A loss without precedent
   in recorded history.

* Desertification: More than ⅓ of land surface is already
   desert or semi-desert. 19% more about to go.

* Wetlands, Estuaries & Shallow Seas: drainage,
   dredging, dumping, pollution, & 'shore improvement?

* Erosion & Loss of fertile land

* XTN of SPP   1000 Vertebrates
              Unknown number of invertebrates
              25,000 spp of Plants.

* Genetic Diversity of domestic animals &
                          crop plants.

* Depleted Fisheries   25 of worlds major fisheries
                       are seriously depleted

This list of waste & destruction is only part of
a much larger problem. We don't seem yet to
have learnt HOW to conserve — or if we have,
we haven't passed our lessons on to others.

We must adopt a strategy — a World
Conservation Strategy to win the war
against thoughtless destruction & waste

PRIORITIES

The longer we leave it, the more costly to repair damage.

☐ Man's dependence on habitat or species.

☐ Give priority to spp with low reproductive potential.

☐ Tackle the problem before the 'point of no return' is reached.

☐ Deal with causes not symptoms

Four basic human problems :
① There is a lack of **facts.** (Gaps in our knowledge)
② There is a lack of **understanding** even when the facts are known.
③ There is a lack of **will.**
④ In most developing countries there is a lack of **money.**

The **money** must be provided
The **will** to conserve will emerge with greater **knowledge and understanding.**
The DECISION MAKERS, & those who advise them, must develop the **will** and the **vision** to act.
The WCS' has indicated guide lines, but a new generation comes along every 25 years — so the need to communicate is unending. The effectiveness of law and policy must be continuously reassessed.
The strategy will need continuous UPDATING

CONS is most urgently needed where UNDERDEVELOPMENT prevents any real understanding of the need.

So DEVELOPMENT is the dominating prerequisite ~~for~~ GLOBAL CONSERVAT^N.

CHINA:
- March to be Month of CONS. EDUCAT^N.
- China's CONTRIBUT^N to WORLD CONS.
- China's TREE PLANTING.

- Whales + Whaling. IWC Membership.

ECO-DEVELOPMENT provides mans basic needs + satisfies his cultural aspirations, without depleting resources or destroying the systems that support Life.

ECO-D^t. conserves rather than depletes
maintains rather than degrades
     the quality of air, soil + water.
exploits indigenous materials + skills.
evolves with the help of the people
               involved
aims to meet ~~their~~ needs ~~rather than~~
     generate profits for others.

ECO-D needs a new kind of aid + a world order that respects the economic independence of communities as well as their rights to political self-determination.

ON WHALING

London, July 1979

Quote by P.S.

" What we have done to the great whales
in the sacred name of commerce is ~~a gross~~ an affront to
~~debasement~~ of human ~~dignity~~ & sensibility.
↳ a debasement of human values
These magnificent animals — almost certainly
the largest that have ever existed on earth,
and now recognised as the possessors of
outstanding intelligence — have been brought
to the brink of extinction by killing methods
of appalling cruelty.

I have personally witnessed and timed
the death-throes of a Minke whale — the
smallest of the baleen whales — which was
still active 4½ minutes after being hit by
an explosive harpoon, and was probably
in its rear end
still alive 8 minutes after being struck.
In the case of larger whales the time
may be 30 minutes or even more.

Consider your reaction if you watched
someone go into a field & harpoon a cow
in the rump, which then took that long
to die.

In the light of present knowledge of
these intelligent mammals, no civilised
person can contemplate the whaling
industry without revulsion and
our
shame at the insensitivity of ~~their~~ own
species. "

THE ANIMALS OF LOCH NESS

Lecture Notes

Truck driver.... _ NICKY

From 1812 for several years Michael Faraday, the discoverer of electricity, gave lectures at the Royal Institute in London. He once said: "The lecturer should give the audience full reason to believe that all his powers have been exerted for their pleasure and instruction - "

WHY DO I BELIEVE IN NESSIE?

Although ~~this~~ Phil & I have watched the surface of the loch for long periods & I have twice dived in it, we've never seen one of the animals ~~ourselves~~.

But we've been interested in the subject for nearly 20 years.

As I ~~have~~ told you, I think, I am a _painter_ by profession but i'm also a _biologist_ by _training_. And a _naturalist_ by inclination as well.

I like to think I have an open mind.
Or at least half open.   Like the
Irish railway crossing keeper...... who was half expecting a train

I find that after dismissing the _hoaxes_, the deliberate _falsehoods_, the _hallucinations_, the _misidentifications_ and the _honest errors_,

THERE REMAINS A HARD CORE OF EVIDENCE WHICH CANNOT BE EXPLAINED IN TERMS OF KNOWN PHENOMENA OR ATTRIBUTED TO KNOWN SPECIES OF LIVING ANIMALS.

So I think there's something /that deserves
further study.

I'm appalled by the attitude of some
scientists who are afraid to study the Loch
Ness phenomena because it might damage
their reputation.

SCIENCE IS ABOUT FINDING
THE TRUTH — NOT ABOUT REPUTATIONS
and whether or not you will be elected to this or that learned societ.

I'm appalled that a young scientist should
have lost his job with our leading museum
(at least in part because he studied the Loch
Ness evidence. "Taking the night Train to Inverness"

I'm also appalled that a great many reputable people,
who've seen what they are convinced are large
animals in Loch Ness, don't dare to talk
about it for fear of ridicule.

That is not a healthy situation.

The first recorded sighting was by
St Columba in the 6th Century: A.D. 565.
Since then, there've been several thousand documented
sightings, culminating in the recent
photographs coupled with sonar — underwater
echo-location.

ENDPIECE

Leigh Yawkey Woodson Art Museum,
Wasau, Wisconsin, 1990

I have been a naturalist at heart ever since I can remember. And, I have always drawn or painted. I tried to be a biologist and abandoned that about halfway through my academic career to become a painter.

I was likely, I thought, to paint best those things which moved me most. That meant my wildfowl. They had never been painted in the way I saw them... What I wanted to do was extraordinarily simple and easy. I had only to put on to canvas to the best of my oil painting capacity the birds as I had seen them at dawn or dusk or moonlight, or in storm or frost or snow, and I could not fail to be doing something original.

When I paint birds, I like them to be the right shapes and the whole effect to be as seen in nature. It is important to me to make an attractive composition which suggests the forward movement of their flight. Flocks have such beautiful composition. My style and technique are usually governed by my zoological training so that I try to avoid distorting what I know to be the correct shapes of the animals or plants that I am drawing or painting.

I draw quite a lot from nature. I also do a great deal of drawing from what I hold in my memory. (Sometimes) I go straight to the canvas and start putting paint on. Of course, an oil painting is the most wonderfully malleable thing.

But more often I set out to paint a commission, which means that the picture must have some preordained elements—some features which the commissioner required in the picture. This may involve a series of rough pencil drawings, usually smaller than a postcard, to get a basic composition into my head before I start. It may call for aids of various kinds, field sketches and photographs to remind me of the place and the creatures I am going to paint, although most of my painting is done from memory.

My pictures have been sold in my own country largely to the shooting fraternity—wildfowlers in particular. They want to be reminded, in the comfort of their homes, of the excitement of their sport. Having been a hunter myself for many years, I can easily understand the appeal which leads to this steady demand. But the trouble with such a situation is that it dictates a limited number of subjects—the quarry species of waterfowl—and leads, in the end, to a type of picture in which the birds are not too large nor yet too small, the sky is 'interesting' and the marshy landscape is attractive, while neither is allowed to detract from the quarry. There is room for some artistic creation in the sky and the landscape and in the positioning of the birds to suggest movement, but the upshot is a kind of formula which guarantees a sale but limits invention and innovation. It begets a degree of slavery to commissions.

I quickly discovered that if I worked too long on a painting, I was quite capable of ruining it. Working fast was the secret of quality as well as quantity. But I was also brimming over with new ideas. I could not wait until one picture was finished before starting the next, and I soon found that this was, in fact, a practical method; the first stage of one picture could be drying while the next was started. It also gave me the chance to adjust my work to my mood. If I was feeling creative, I could start on a blank canvas; if not, I could go quietly on with the chores—putting on a large area of blue sky, or laboriously painting up flocks of birds whose shapes and patterns I had already determined.

If beauty is truth and truth beauty, how much freedom is left for the imprint of the artists individuality? When colour photography was invented, what was left for the bird painter who believed, as I did, that nature had achieved a perfection that was sacrosanct? Who was I to distort the shapes, to exaggerate the colours, to try to improve on nature? Yet when an artist sets out to paint three-dimensional nature in two dimensions, the process of interpretation has begun, and consciously or subconsciously some part of the artist's personality creeps in. There is composition—where and how the shapes and colours should be related to each other. There is economy—what to put in and what to leave out, what must be stated and what left unsaid, what should be underlined, and what merely suggested. And there is always the possibility that 'caricature' can convey a basic truth more succinctly. These are the justifications for artistic license in the painter's continuing effort to make pictures that give pleasure to the people who look at them.

I am sometimes asked about my motives in painting. Why do I do it? What am I trying to do? What are my objectives? Well, I do it because I like doing it. I do it because I can't help doing it. I like to draw or paint something every day of my life, though I don't always manage to do it. And the first of my objectives is to give pleasure to people—as many people as possible, some possibly not yet born. I like to draw things that have excited me, to reflect my own enthusiasm for nature in general and especially for birds (and fishes and whales). I like to record, whenever possible, aspects of their behaviour and their biology as well as their appearance. I like to help to educate others to enjoy them, thereby enriching their lives too, and at the same time advancing the cause of conservation. And finally, I have to earn money in my profession, and to have been able to do so for almost half a century has been another piece of good fortune.

Birds were a very early interest, from the age of four onward—especially the shorebirds to be seen from our cottage at Sandwich. I saw my first wild geese there, which led to a general interest in wildfowl, and ultimately to Slimbridge and The Wildfowl Trust.

Art and science, or perhaps science and art (for that was the order in which I was trained in the two activities), have been twin preoccupations all my life; and the furtherance of scientific research has always been one of The Wildfowl Trust's prime objectives. However, research was not the only consideration I had in mind for Slimbridge. There was also education, and I had for long been concerned about conservation—concerned for the prospects of survival of many of the wildfowl species in a hostile world. I was anxious not only about the wildfowl, for it was clear that all over the world a great number of other animal species—and plant species too—were threatened with extinction. These species were the current end products of forty million centuries of evolution—four billion years. This is how long it has taken for all the diversity of living creatures on our earth to evolve into what we know today, and, of course, the process is continuing.

My biological training told me that an environmental crisis was on its way. It was becoming abundantly clear that all was not well with Planet Earth. It was not necessary to be an environmental expert to realise this... [So] we persuaded the world's leading conservationists to sign a solemn declaration called the Morges Manifesto, and soon thereafter we formed the World Wildlife Fund.

Conserving what is left of the world's wildlife and wild places belongs to the mainstream of civilised human progress... I do not believe that man could survive without the rest of nature; but most important, what good will it be if we live to inherit a barren world devoid of the natural things, the wild things, that make life worth living?

Being able to put a name to an animal or a plant has a special appeal, and if the differences are small and require careful observation to determine them, the activity is all the more appealing, taking on a kind of 'crossword puzzle' fascination which can easily become compulsive. With luck it can, and often does, lead to a lifelong enthusiasm for the subject, making Roger Peterson's field guide a major contribution to the relationship between man and the rest of nature... I am not sure whether he realises the extraordinary revolution that he was about to create by publishing this book... In my view, this invention was a major step in human progress.

The science of ecology had not been invented when I was learning biology; yet the instant its principles were enumerated, I immediately realised the essential truth that all nature is interrelated, that we are a part of it and need contact with it. Furthermore, because we are, as a species, the direct cause of so much of the environmental damage, we have a clear responsibility.

In my opinion, this puts conservation as a philosophical imperative—not merely as a device for saving our own skins—out in the mainstream of human progress. How much of it we can achieve, on the ground and in the oceans, is of course, another story. As the American conservationist Aldo Leopold once wrote: *'Conservation is a state of harmony with a friend; you cannot cherish his right hand and chop off his left.'*

One thing is certain: Conservation is only meaningful in the long term. I once rather sententiously dreamed up a '100-years rule'. It said that for work you should seriously consider whether your activity was likely to make life better for someone in a hundred years' time. Any time spent doing anything else was play or spare time stuff, of no real significance.

I hope the viewer derives as much pleasure out of seeing my art as I, as an artist, have derived out of seeing my subjects.

CHRONOLOGY

1909
- Born 14 September, at family home at 174 Buckingham Palace Road, London (on site of future Victoria 'Greenline' coach station).

1911
- Father—Captain Robert Falcon Scott—set off for the Antarctic. (*Terra Nova* expedition 1910–12)

1912
- Father and his comrades—Wilson, Evans, Oates and Bowers—reached South Pole (17 January) but tragically all died (29/30 March) on return journey.

1917
- Mother—Kathleen Scott—took job in Paris and moved there with Peter.

1918
- Went to West Downs Preparatory School in Winchester.

1922
- Mother married Edward Hilton Young (later to be Lord Kennet of the Dene)

1923
- Went to Oundle School near Peterborough (until 1927).
- Wayland (half-brother) was born.

1924
- First illustrations published. *Everyday Doings of Insects* by Evelyn Cheesman

1925
- Birdwatching forays to River Nene floods between Aldwincle and Lilford. First grey geese found: 200 mainly European whitefronts with family parties of pinkfeet.

1926
- *Illustrated Adventures Among Birds* by 'Three Schoolboys' privately published.

- Family moved to 100 Bayswater Road, London
  (where previously J.M. Barrie had written *Peter Pan*).

1927
- Left school and went to Trinity College, Cambridge (until
  1930) to read Natural Science. Switched to History of Art and
  Architecture in final year

1928
- Shot first goose on the Wash at Terrington.

1929
- First articles written (and illustrated) for *Country Life* magazine:
  'Wild Geese' (24 August issue) and 'Wild Geese and Ducks'
  (30 November issue).

1930
- Gained degree in History of Art and Architecture.

1931
- Studied at the Munich Academy for a term. Joined Royal
  Academy School as a pupil (15 December) until 1930.

1932
- Won pairs-skating championships at Westminster Ice Rink.
  Went to live at Borough Fen Decoy.

1933
- First exhibition of paintings held at Ackermann's Gallery, London.

- Moved into East Lighthouse at Sutton Bridge where the
  Nene runs into the Wash.

- Two paintings accepted by Royal Academy for Summer
  Exhibition.

1934
- First short story published, 'Mr. Spriggs and the Crane'
  in *Cornhill* magazine (October).

1935
- Book *Morning Flight* published by Country Life.

- 'My involvement with conservation began one day in 1935,
  when "Chips" Ezra, the distinguished aviculturist, invited me
  to his Surrey home to show me a group of pink-headed ducks,
  newly arrived from India.'

1936
- Visited Hungary as special correspondent for *The Field* magazine.
- Represented Great Britain in single-handed sailing in the Olympic Games at Kiel. Won bronze medal.
- Illustrated stepfather's book, *A Bird in the Bush* (published by Country Life).
- First broadcast for the BBC—15 minute talk on dinghy racing.

1937
- Won Prince of Wales Cup for International 14ft dinghies for the first time, in Lowestoft.
- Visited Persia and the Caspian Sea in search of red-breasted geese.

1938
- Won Prince of Wales Cup for International 14ft dinghies, in Falmouth.
- Designed trapeze wire to support a crew member outboard. It was then banned but reinstated some 30 years later.
- Book *Wild Chorus* published.
- Exhibition in Arthur Harlow's Gallery in New York. Did series of five etchings.

1939
- Volunteered for the Royal Naval Volunteer Reserve at outbreak of World War II.
- Visited Northern Ireland to check on his theory of another race of white-fronted goose.

1940
- Joined HMS *Broke*, appointed First Lieutenant.
- Invented camouflage scheme for ships in Royal Navy.

1941
- Promoted to First Lieutenant of a destroyer.
- Mentioned in despatches for his efforts in the rescue of the crew of HMS *Comorin*.
- Flew with RAF on two bombing raids over Germany.

1942
- Married Elizabeth Jane Howard on 28 April.
- Awarded the MBE (for inventing the night camouflage scheme for ships in World War II).
- Mentioned in dispatches for his part in the Dieppe Raid.
- Appointed Lieutenant Commander.
- Moved with Jane into 105 Clifton Hill, St John's Wood, London (in December).

1943
- Daughter Nicola born.
- Became senior officer of a flotilla of steam gunboats.
- Awarded Distinguished Service Cross for his gallantry in a raid into the Baie de le Seine.
- Mentioned in dispatches for his part in a Cherbourg raid.
- Won a bar to his DSC for gallantry in a Channel action.

1944
- Joined planning staff of Coastal Command to prepare for D-Day.

1945
- Appointed to command a new frigate, HMS *Cardigan Bay*.
- Book *Battle of the Narrow Seas* published.
- Resigned from Royal Navy to stand as Conservative Candidate for Wembley North constituency.
- First post-war exhibition at Ackermann's Gallery (November).

1946
- Won the Prince of Wales Cup for International 14ft dinghies, Brixham.
- Founded the Severn Wildfowl Trust. Inaugurated 10 November.
- Became joint-presenter of 'Children's Hour' radio programme, *Nature Parliament* (until 1967).
- Exhibition at Arthur Harlow's Galleries on 57th Street, New York. A series of five etchings were produced, the only ones of his career.
- Illustrated *The Snow Goose* by Paul Gallico.

1947
- Mother Kathleen died of leukaemia aged sixty-eight.
- Employed Philippa Talbot-Ponsonby as his Secretary and Assistant Secretary to Severn Wildfowl Trust.
- Severn Wildfowl Trust membership reached 1,000.
- Television commentator for Royal Wedding.

1948
- With Christopher Dalgety described the Greenland white-fronted goose *Anser albifrons flavirostris* as new subspecies
- First testing of rocket nets for the capture of wild geese.
- First Bewick's swan dropped in to the pen of whistling swans at Slimbridge. Caught for the collection and named Mrs Noah.
- Visited Delta Waterfowl Research Station near Winnipeg, Canada.
- Sold his London home (8 Edwardes Square) and moved into the cottage at Slimbridge.

1949
- Expedition to Perry River region, Canada.
- HRH Princess Elizabeth's first visit to Slimbridge.
- Book *Portrait Drawings* published.
- Book *A Key to Wildfowl of the World* first published in Second Annual Report.
- Mother's memoirs published: *Self-Portrait of an Artist*.

1950
- Two Hawaiian geese arrived at Slimbridge for captive breeding programme.

1951
- Married Philippa Talbot-Ponsonby in Reykjavik, Iceland.
- Expedition to Hofsjökull ice cap in central highlands of Iceland to study pink-footed geese (ringed 1,100).
- Book *Wild Geese and Eskimos* published.

1952
- Daughter Dafila born June.
- First Hawaiian geese breed at Slimbridge.

1953

- Awarded CBE for work connected to the Severn Wildfowl Trust.
- Further expedition to Iceland—ringed over 9,000 pink-footed geese.
- Presenter of first Natural History programme on British television: a live outside broadcast from Slimbridge— *Severn Wildfowl*. (Forerunner to *Look*—see 1955).
- Book *A Thousand Geese* published.
- Became Vice President of the International Union for the Conservation of Nature (IUCN)
- Gave first public lecture—'Wild Goose Chase'—and presented his colour film, *Pursuit of Pinkfeet*, at Royal Festival Hall, London (13 January).
- New house built with studio at Slimbridge to own design.

1954

- Son Falcon born.
- Broke sailing speed record at Cowes.

1955

- Severn Wildfowl Trust became The Wildfowl Trust.
- Presenter of new television programme *Look,* 14 June. (*Look* ran until 1970.)
- Voted President of the International Yacht Racing Union.

1956

- Report, *The Geography, Birds and Mammals of the Perry River Region* with Harold C. Hanson and Paul Queneau published.
- Took up sport of gliding.
- Introduced to world of coral fish on suggestion of Konrad Lorenz: snorkeled on the Great Barrier Reef. (This became a great passion.)

1957

- Book *A Coloured Key to the Wildfowl of the World* published. (Still in print.)
- Book *Wildfowl of the British Isles* (with Hugh Boyd) published.
- The Wildfowl Trust's second centre at Peakirk in Cambridgeshire opened to the public.

1958

- Completed his Gold C for Glider flight (only thirty-fourth time issued to a British pilot: the flight requirements are 5,000m height, 500km distance & 300km distance with a declared landing site).

1959

- Visited Galapagos Islands to help found the Charles Darwin Foundation. Whilst there made film for the BBC.
- Awarded the British Ornithologists Union Medal.

1960

- Elected Rector of Aberdeen University by the student body.
- Books *Faraway Look One* and *Two* (with Philippa Scott) published
- Invited HRH The Prince Philip, Duke of Edinburgh, to be President of The Wildfowl Trust (1960–1965 and again from 1972–1979).

1961

- Co-founder of the World Wildlife Fund. Designed its panda logo and became first Chairman.
- Invited HRH The Prince Philip, Duke of Edinburgh, to be first President of the World Wildlife Fund.
- Autobiography *Eye of the Wind* published.
- Awarded La Société Nationale de Protection de la Nature Medal.
- With three colleagues, set up the Loch Ness Investigation Bureau to report and study sightings in Loch Ness.

1962

- Book *Animals in Africa* (with Philippa Scott) published.
- Originator of Red Data Books for WWF (identifying endangered species).
- Became Chairman of Survival Service Commission of the IUCN (until 1981).
- First 30 Slimbridge-reared Hawaiian geese released in Hawaii.
- Appointed Admiral of the Manx fishing fleet.

1963
- Won British Gliding Championship.

1964
- Selected as helmsman of *Sovereign* for the America's Cup, Newport, RI.
- Became grandfather when Nicola had first child, Daniel.
- Bewick's swan study starts: Peter moved the closely related whistling swans into the Rushy pen outside the studio window, in the hope of enticing wild Bewick's in. On 11 February one dropped in; next day six wild Bewick's land and Peter noted that the bill patterns were all different. 23 Bewick's were regulars that first winter. Since that first discovery over 9,000 Bewick's have been recognised.
- Society of Wildlife Artists formed. Became first President (until 1974).

1965
- Edited first Annual Report of World Wildlife Fund— *The Launching of a New Ark*.

1966
- Visited Antarctic to make film for the BBC.
- Awarded Zoological Society of San Diego Medal.
- Awarded Cherry Kearton Medal of the Royal Geographical Society.

1967
- Land purchased at Welney in Cambridgeshire and reserve established.

1968
- First of twenty-six cruises as guest lecturer for the Eric Lindblad cruises.

1969
- To Danube Delta in Romania in search of the red-breasted geese.

1970
- Booklet *The Wild Swans at Slimbridge* (with Philippa Scott) published.

- The Wildfowl Trust Centre in Welney, Cambridgeshire opened to the public.
- Awarded Albert Medal of the Royal Society of Arts Manufacturers and Commerce (for his work in the conservation of wildlife).

1971
- The Wildfowl Trust Centre in Caerlaverock (near Dumfries) opened to the public.
- Became Director of Survival Anglia and started his commentaries on their wildlife films.
- Story 'The Pond' published in *The Twelfth Man*, an anthology put together for HRH The Prince Philip, Duke of Edinburgh.
- Awarded the Cornell Laboratory of Ornithology— Arthur Allen award for outstanding services to ornithology.

1972
- Book *The Swans* (with The Wildfowl Trust) published.

1973
- Awarded CBE—the first knighthood for conservation.
- Book *Waterfowl* published.
- Wrote conservation plan for Mauritius.

1974
- Appointed Chancellor of the University of Birmingham by the senate (served ten years).

1975
- The Wildfowl Trust Centre in Martin Mere, Lancashire opened to the public.
- The Wildfowl Trust Centre in Washington, near Newcastle-upon-Tyne, opened to the public.
- Awarded New York Zoological Society Gold Medal for contribution to the cause of wildlife the world over.
- Awarded International Conservation Award of the National Wildlife Federation of America.

1976
- The Wildfowl Trust Centre in Arundel, Sussex opened to the public.

- Awarded Commander of the Netherlands Order of the Golden Ark.

1977
- Received United Nations International Pahlavi Environment Prize along with Jacques Cousteau. Each received $25,000.

1978
- Travelled to Siberia in search of the breeding grounds of the Bewick's swan.

1979
- Co-founded Falkland Islands Foundation.

1980
- Book *Observations of Wildlife* published.

1981
- Awarded Master Wildlife Artist by Leigh Yawkey Woodson Art Museum, Wausau, Wisconsin.
- Awarded IUCN John Phillips Medal for outstanding conservation achievement.
- Awarded WWF Twentieth Anniversary Special Award for distinguished service in the field of international conservation.

1982
- International Whaling Commission agreed to phase in a moratorium on whaling.

1983
- Book *Travel Diaries of a Naturalist, Volume 1* published.
- Awarded the Royal Geographical Society Founder's Medal.

1984
- Suffered mild heart attack at home.

1985
- Book *Travel Diaries of a Naturalist, Volume 2* published.

1986
- Awarded RSPB Gold Medal for services to bird protection.
- Awarded J. P. Getty prize of $50,000.
- Awarded WWF Gold Medal at WWF's 25th Anniversary Celebrations.

- Awarded WWF Member of Honour.
- Party at Slimbridge to celebrate The Wildfowl Trust's 40th birthday.

1987
- Appointed a Companion of Honour by Her Majesty The Queen. (Limited to 65 people).
- Made a Fellow of the Royal Society.
- Book *Travel Diaries of a Naturalist, Volume 3* published.

1988
- Coral fish, *Cirrilabrus scottorum*, named after Peter and Philippa Scott.
- Awarded National Zoological Park, Washington Medal for outstanding services to zoological sciences and conservation.

1989
- Sixteenth exhibition held at Ackermann's Gallery in London. Opened by Prince Philip.
- The Wildfowl Trust changed its name to the Wildfowl & Wetlands Trust.
- Retrospective exhibition of artwork put together by Cheltenham Art Gallery, accompanied by book *Sir Peter Scott at 80* as exhibition catalogue.
- Exhibition travelled round the UK.
- Awarded *Wildlife Art News* magazine's International Conservation Award for excellence in the field of international conservation.
- Taken ill at home and died in Bristol hospital, 29 August, a fortnight short of 80th birthday.
- Memorial service to celebrate his life, St Paul's Cathedral, London (20 November).
- Memorial service to celebrate his life, Church of St John, Slimbridge (30 November).

BIBLIOGRAPHY (1909–1989)

Compiled by Paul Walkden

Sir Peter Scott's output as an artist spanned some sixty-five years. The talent that he portrayed in oils and pen and ink meant his finished works were constantly sought after and indeed are still highly collectable. His illustrations in pen and ink were outstanding and were much regarded and popular with authors to enliven the text of books and journals.

His first illustrations were published in 1924 when he was only fifteen years old, in *Everyday Doings of Insects*, a book by Evelyn Cheesman, in which seven of the artist's drawings were used. The first books in his own name were *Morning Flight* and *Wild Chorus* published in 1935 and 1938 respectively; these were stories of his time on the marsh as a wildfowler and were lavishly illustrated with his paintings. They are now classics.

Prior to these, however, two books were published which made reference to Peter Scott: the first *Like English Gentlemen to Peter Scott* was a children's story of the heroic Captain Scott, published in 1913 and sold to raise funds for the relatives and dependants of Scott and his comrades. So successful was this fundraising initiative that when the dependants had been taken care of financially the residue monies were put into the founding of the Scott Polar Research Institute at Cambridge University. The second book is *Princess Marie-Jose's Children's Book*, published by Cassell in 1916, which had a colour plate of Peter leading a bear, painted by G. Spencer Watson. This book had the purpose of raising funds for the child war victims of Belgium.

Illustrations by Peter have appeared in many books including twenty-five of his own. The long running *Wildfowl*, the Wildfowl & Wetlands Trust Annual Report, bears special mention. This publication first appeared in 1948 as *The Severn*

Wildfowl Trust Annual Report; the 1990 copy was number forty-one and was the last to feature a colour painting by Sir Peter. A colour reproduction of wildfowl in their habitat had been used on the cover of every report. This in itself had been a record. In the early days this report related the happenings at the Slimbridge centre and the reserve. However, as the years passed, still produced in house, it became a collection of scientific papers, reporting on all wildfowl matters. Over the years more than a thousand illustrations of Sir Peter's have been included and these are some of his finest pen and ink drawings. The largest single-volume collection of drawings is to be found in the Seventh Annual Report, 1953/54, in which there are one hundred pen and ink drawings.

To my mind the best book in which to find a complete cross-section of the artist's work is *Observations of Wildlife*, published in 1980 by Phaidon, with a reprint in 1987 and a new edition in 2011. It contains a collection of works covering a period of forty years, and has thirty-nine colour plates with sixty-six other illustrations. But what makes it so special are the notes and jottings of Peter about the paintings, conservation and other matters that arose in his mind at the time of its writing.

The final books published under Sir Peter's name were *Travel Diaries of a Naturalist* volumes one, two and three, published in 1983, 1985 and 1987 respectively. These were lavishly illustrated with watercolours painted on his many journeys around the world. They also contain photographs by his wife, Lady Scott, who accompanied him on trips. The text was selected from his personal diaries which make fascinating reading. We follow his work as an ambassador for the World Wide Fund for Nature, for which he tirelessly campaigned. These trips saw Sir Peter advising on conservation issues, lecturing, fund-raising, establishing areas for reserves, setting up and launching the Fund in other countries. Also his travels aboard the ship *Lindblad Explorer*—a small ship that carried enthusiasts to the remotest parts of the earth. Here Peter was one of the ship's naturalists and lecturers, and not forgetting his travels as a film maker and later as presenter.

There is no doubt that Sir Peter Scott stands as the Father of Conservation, his selfless contributions with his Wildfowl & Wetlands Trust and his part as a founder of The World Wide Fund for Nature remaining as memorials.

The following bibliography was put together over a period of ten years and was first published in *Sir Peter Scott at 80*, the catalogue that was prepared for Sir Peter's retrospective exhibition in 1989 that opened in Cheltenham and then toured the country. It was further added to for the first edition of *The Art of Peter Scott* by Philippa Scott, published in 1992, then further updated for a later edition published by the Wildfowl and Wetlands Trust in 2008. And twenty-five years later items are still being added. This current listing has been updated again. The books are listed chronologically by publication date.

I came to Gloucestershire some forty-three years ago with a view to meeting my childhood hero, Peter Scott. With an abiding passion for books and art I soon started collecting his books. I found that I couldn't find a complete listing so then-education officer at Slimbridge (and friend) Joe Blossom introduced me to Sir Peter and they suggested that I might compile the bibliography. The help, support, enthusiasm and friendship I received from Sir Peter and Lady Scott to my many questions and meetings were amazing and the task would never have been completed but for their help, tolerance and patience. To spend time in their studio at Slimbridge was always a great pleasure. Creating this bibliography has been a real labour of love.

Paul Walkden, December 2015

BOOKS WRITTEN AND ILLUSTRATED OR EDITED

Morning Flight (Country Life, signed limited edition of 750 copies, October 1935. Ordinary editions: April 1936, November 1936, November 1937, October 1939, May 1941, August 1942, May 1944, August 1946, September 1947, November 1949 and November 1950.)

Wildfowl (John Player & Sons, 1936). 25 cigarette cards complete with text. (A facsimile set was re-issued with 24 cards.)

Wild Chorus (Country Life, signed limited edition of 1,250 copies, November 1938. Ordinary editions: September 1939, November 1939, April 1941, September 1942, May 1944, April 1946, April 1947, December 1948, November 1949 and June 1951.)

Battle of the Narrow Seas (Country Life, 1945. Further editions 1946. Later editions: White Lion, 1974; Purnell Book Services (book club edition), 1974; Seaforth Publishing, 2009.)

Portrait Drawings (Country Life, 1949). All copies signed by the author.

Key to the Wildfowl of the World (Severn Wildfowl Trust, 1949). First appeared in 'Second Annual Report, 1948–1949'. Reprinted as a separate booklet in 1950; revised edition published 1951.

Wild Geese and Eskimos (Country Life, 1951)

With Newman, L.H. and Fisher, J., eds., **Nature Parliament. A Book of Broadcasts** (JM Dent, 1952)

With Fisher, J., **A Thousand Geese** (Collins, 1953. Further edition 1954.)

With Hanson, H.C. and Queneau, P., **The Geography, Birds and Mammals of the Perry River Region** (The Arctic Institute of North America, 1956)

With Boyd, H., **Wildfowl of the British Isles** (Country Life, 1957)

A Coloured Key to the Wildfowl of the World (Wildfowl Trust, 1957. Further editions: Collins, 1961 (revised), 1965 (revised), 1968 (revised), 1972 (revised), 1977 (reprint), 1988 (revised), 1998 (revised); Wildfowl & Wetlands Trust, 2006 (updated and revised).)

With Scott, Philippa, **Faraway Look One** (Cassell, 1960)

With Scott, Philippa, **Faraway Look Two** (Cassell, 1960)

The Eye of the Wind (Hodder & Stoughton, 1961. 15 copies were leather-bound with each containing an original watercolour. Further editions: 1961, 1962, 1963, 1966, 1966, 1967, 1967, 1968 and 1977. Hodder paperback edition 1966 (revised), reprinted 1966, 1967.)

With Scott, Philippa, **Animals in Africa** (Cassell, 1962)

Wildlife in Danger (Brooke Bond, 1963). 50 tea cards complete with text.

Editor, illustrated by Keith Shackleton, **My Favourite Stories of Wildlife** (Lutterworth Press, 1965)

Editor, **The Launching of a New Ark** (Collins, 1965). First report of the World Wildlife Fund.

Sitwell, N., ed., **Happy the Man** (Sphere, 1967)

With Scott, Philippa, **The Wild Swans at Slimbridge** (Wildfowl Trust, 1970)

Editor, **The Living World of Animals** (Reader's Digest, 1970)

With The Wildfowl Trust, *The Swans* (Michael Joseph, 1972).
24 copies were leather-bound and signed.

Conservation of Mauritiu (Privately published, 1973). Report.

Waterfowl (Berkshire Printing Company, 1973)

Editor, *Mitchell Beazley World Atlas of Birds* (Mitchell Beazley, 1974)

Editor, *The Amazing World of Animals* (Nelson, 1975)

Wildlife in Danger (Happy House, *c*.1975). Brooke Bond tea cards:
enlarged illustrations and updated text, and new colour cover.

Observation of Wildlife (Phaidon, 1980. Signed limited edition of
200 copies c/w slipcase, 1980. Further editions: 1981 and 1987.
Wildfowl & Wetlands Trust edition, 2011.)

With Scott, Philippa, *The Swans Fly In* (Wildfowl Trust, 1983.
Further edition edited by E. Rees, 1989.)

Travel Diaries of a Naturalist,Volume 1 (Collins/Harvill, 1983).
9 presentation copies were half leather-bound, numbered and signed,
c/w slipcase.

Travel Diaries of a Naturalist, Volume 2 (Collins/Harvill, 1985).
10 presentation copies were half leather-bound, numbered and
signed, c/w slipcase.

Travel Diaries of a Naturalist, Volume 3 (Collins/Harvill, 1987).
10 presentation copies were half leather-bound, numbered and
signed, c/w slipcase.

BOOKS AND BOOKLETS ILLUSTRATED
IN WHOLE OR IN PART

Cheesman, E., *Everyday Doings of Insects* (Harrap, 1924.
Further edition 1930). 7 b/w illustrations.

Three Schoolboys, *Adventures Among Birds* (Privately published, 1926).
Limited to 25 specially bound and numbered copies and to 500 other
copies of which the first hundred are numbered 26–125 inclusive.

Roof Climber's Guide to Trinity (Privately published, 1930)

Moody, A.F., *Waterfowl and Game Birds in Captivity* (1932).
2 photographs.

Prospectus (West London Shooting Ground, 1936). 13 pencil drawings.

Kennett, Lord, *A Bird in the Bush* (Country Life, 1936). Signed limited
edition (550 copies): 3 colour plates and 24 b/w illustrations.
Ordinary edition 1 colour plate and 24 b/w illustrations.

Perry, R., *At the Turn of the Tide* (Drummond, 1938).
Colour frontispiece.

Witherby, H.F., Jourdain, F.C.R., Ticehurst, N.F., Tucker, B.W., *The Handbook of British Birds* 5-volume set (Witherby, 1938–1941). 10 colour illustrations in volume 3, 'Hawks to Ducks'.

Bratby, M., *Grey Goose* (Geoffrey Bles, 1939). Colour frontispiece with 25 b/w illustrations.

Campen Heilner, V., *A Book of Duck Shooting* (Alfred Knopf, New York, USA, 1939. Various editions). 3 mono photographs.

Bratby, M., *Through the Air* (Country Life, 1941). 25 b/w illustrations.

Parker, E., *British Sport*, Britain in Pictures (Collins, 1941). 1 colour plate.

Meynell, V., ed., *Letters of J. M. Barrie* (Peter Davies, 1942). Frontispiece painting.

Gallico, P., *The Snow Goose* (Michael Joseph, 1946. Special edition of 750 copies signed by author and illustrator. Numerous further editions.) 4 colour plates and 24 b/w illustrations.

Harman, R., *Countryside Character* (Blandford, 1946). 2 colour plates.

Laidler, G. (Pont.), *'Most of Us are Absurd'* (Collins, 1946). Frontispiece, b/w portrait of author.

Vesey-Fitzgerald, B., *British Game,* New Naturalist no. 2 (Collins, 1946). 1 colour plate.

Darwin, B., ed., *Fifty Years of 'Country Life'* (Country Life, 1947). 1 colour plate.

Pitman, I., *And Clouds Flying* (Faber, 1947). 2 colour plates, 8 mono photographs of paintings and 51 b/w illustrations.

Gregorson, R., *Lemuel* (Owl Press, signed limited edition of 250 copies, 1947. Also, ordinary edition, 1947). 31 b/w illustrations.

Pitt, F., *Frontier of a Barony* (Bellows, 1948). 1 b/w illustration.

With Dalgety, C., 'A New Race of the White-fronted Goose', *British Ornithologists Club Bulletin* Volume 68, Number 6 (British Ornithologists Club, 1948). 7 b/w illustrations.

Book of Rules (Severn Wildfowl Trust, 1948). 5 b/w illustrations.

Annual Report, 1948 (Severn Wildfowl Trust, 1948). Colour cover and 21 b/w illustrations.

Birds in London. Report by Committee on Bird Sanctuaries in the Royal Parks, 1939–1947 (Ministry of Works, 1948). Cover illustration.

Prospectus (Severn Wildfowl Trust, 1948). Colour cover and 7 b/w illustrations.

Chapman, F.S., *The Jungle is Neutral* (Chatto & Windus, 1949). B/w frontispiece, portrait of author.

Birds in London. Report by Committee on Bird Sanctuaries in the Royal Parks, 1948. (Ministry of Works, 1949). Cover illustration.

Second Annual Report, 1948–1949 (Severn Wildfowl Trust, 1949). Colour cover and 16 b/w illustrations and the 'Key to the Wildfowl of the World' with 23 b/w plates.

Kerr, J.L, and James, J., eds., *Wavy Navy,* (Harrap, 1950). 1 colour plate.

Third Annual Report, 1949–1950 (Severn Wildfowl Trust, 1950). Colour cover and 30 b/w illustrations and 4 colour plates as part one of 'The Swans, Geese and Ducks of the British Isles'.

Birds in London. Report by Committee on Bird Sanctuaries in the Royal Parks, 1949. (Ministry of Works, 1950). Cover illustration.

Birds in London. Report by Committee on Bird Sanctuaries in the Royal Parks, 1950. (Ministry of Works, 1951). Cover illustration.

Fourth Annual Report, 1950–1951 (Severn Wildfowl Trust, 1951). Colour cover and 23 b/w illustrations and 4 colour plates as part two of 'The Swans, Geese and Ducks of the British Isles'.

Prospectus (Severn Wildfowl Trust, 1951). Colour cover and back cover illustration.

Fifth Annual Report, 1951–1952 (Severn Wildfowl Trust, 1952). Colour cover and 61 b/w illustrations and 3 colour plates as part three of 'The Swans, Geese and Ducks of the British Isles'.

Savage, C., *The Mandarin Duck* (A & C Black, 1952). Colour frontispiece.

Fisher, J., *The Fulmar*, New Naturalist no. 6 (Collins, 1952). Colour frontispiece.

Hollom, P.A.D., *The Popular Handbook of British Birds* Witherby, 1952). 9 colour plates.

Tranter, N., 'Wings in the Duck Marsh', *SMT Scotland's Magazine* (December 1952). 1 colour plate.

Sixth Annual Report, 1952–1953 (Wildfowl Trust, 1954). Colour cover and 72 b/w illustrations and 3 colour plates as part four of 'The Swans, Geese and Ducks of the British Isles'.

Atkinson-Willes, G.L., *National Wildfowl Counts 1952–1954* Wildfowl Trust, 1954). 8 b/w illustrations.

Delacour, J., *Waterfowl of the World* 4 Volumes (Country Life, 1954–1964. Numerous further editions). 66 colour plates.

Atkinson-Willes, G.L., *National Wildfowl Counts 1954–1955* (Wildfowl Trust, 1955). 16 b/w illustrations.

Seventh Annual Report, 1953–1954 (Wildfowl Trust, 1955). Colour cover and 100 b/w illustrations.

Sowls, L.K., *Prairie Ducks* (University of Nebraska, USA, 1955).
B/w frontispiece.

Knight, L.A., *The Morlo* (Smith Gryphon, 1956). 2 colour plates and
30 b/w illustrations.

The Wildfowl Trust at Slimbridge (Wildfowl Trust, 1956).
2 colour illustrations.

Powell, B., *The Grey Geese Call* (Jenkins, 1956). 1 mono photograph.

Cadman, W.A., *Tales of a Wildfowler* (Collins, 1957. Tideline Books,
1983). 42 b/w illustrations.

Atkinson-Willes, G.L., *National Wildfowl Counts Fourth Report*
(Wildfowl Trust, 1957). 14 b/w illustrations.

Eighth Annual Report, 1954–1955 (Wildfowl Trust, 1957).
Colour cover and 41 b/w illustrations.

Book of Rules (Wildfowl Trust, 1958). 4 b/w illustrations.

Ninth Annual Report, 1956–1957. (Wildfowl Trust, 1958).
Colour cover and 97 b/w illustrations.

Women's Journal (February 1959). Cover illustration repeated inside.

Tenth Annual Report, 1957–1958 (Wildfowl Trust, 1959).
Colour cover and 37 b/w illustrations.

Eleventh Annual Report, 1958–1959 (Wildfowl Trust, 1960).
Colour cover and 48 b/w illustrations.

Hollom, P.A.D., *The Popular Handbook of Rarer British Birds*
(Witherby, 1960. Reprinted 1966. Second revised edition 1980).
2 colour plates.

Sedgwick, N.M., Whitaker, P. and Harrison, J., *The New Wildfowler*
(Herbert Jenkins 1961. Reprinted 1963). Colour frontispiece.

Twelfth Annual Report, 1959–1960 (Wildfowl Trust, 1961).
Colour cover and 18 b/w illustrations.

Christian, G., *Down the Long Wind* (Newnes, 1961).
Colour dust wrapper illustration.

The Story of The Wildfowl Trust (Wildfowl Trust, 1961).
Colour cover illustration.

The Wildfowler Magazine (WAGBI, 1962). B/w illustrated cover
and 1 b/w internal illustration.

Thirteenth Annual Report, 1960–1961 (Wildfowl Trust, 1962).
Colour cover and 16 b/w illustrations.

Webber, M., *Visitors' Guide to Gloucestershire* (C & D Constaple,
c.1963). 2 b/w illustrations.

Atkinson-Willes, G.L., *Wildfowl in Great Britain* (HMSO, 1963).
15 colour plates and 70 b/w illustrations.

Fourteenth Annual Report, 1961–1962 (Wildfowl Trust, 1963).
Colour cover and 18 b/w illustrations.

Atkinson-Willes. G.L., compiler, *Liquid Assets* (IUNC, 1964).
1 b/w illustration.

Fifteenth Annual Report, 1962–1963 (Wildfowl Trust, 1964).
Colour cover and 11 b/w illustrations.

Sixteenth Annual Report, 1963–1964 (Wildfowl Trust, 1965).
Colour cover and 8 b/w illustrations.

Seventeenth Annual Report, 1964–1965 (Wildfowl Trust, 1966).
Colour cover and 11 b/w illustrations.

Fisher, J., *The Shell Bird Book* (Ebury Press, 1966). 1 colour plate.

Eighteenth Annual Report, 1965–1966 (Wildfowl Trust, 1967).
Colour cover and 8 b/w illustrations.

Wildfowl 19 (Wildfowl Trust, 1968).
Colour cover and 15 b/w illustrations.

An Introduction to the Collection and Work (Wildfowl Trust, 1968).
17 b/w illustrations.

Fisher, J., Simon, N., Vincent, J., *The Red Book, Wildlife in Danger*
(Collins, 1969). 9 colour drawings and 8 b/w illustrations.

Wildfowl 20 (Wildfowl Trust, 1969).
Colour cover and 11 b/w illustrations.

Sedgwick, N.M., Whitaker, P. and Harrison, J., *The New Wildfowler
in the 1970s*. (Barrie & Jenkins, 1970. Reprinted 1970).
Colour frontispiece and colour plate.

The Wild Swans at Slimbridge (Wildfowl Trust, 1970).
Colour cover and 2 b/w illustrations.

Wildfowl 21 (Wildfowl Trust, 1970).
Colour cover and 18 b/w illustrations.

Wildfowl 22 (Wildfowl Trust, 1971).
Colour cover and 6 b/w illustrations.

HRH The Prince Philip, Duke of Edinburgh and Fisher, J.,
Wildlife Crisis (Arcadia, 1971). 7 b/w illustrations.

Chaplin, C., *The Fishwatchers' Guide to West Atlantic Coral Reefs*
(Livingston Publishing (USA), 1972). 23 colour plates.

Penny, M., *Decoys: a New Use for an Old Skill*
(The Countryman, Summer 1972). 5 b/w illustrations.

Wildfowl 23 (Wildfowl Trust, 1972).
Colour cover and 14 b/w illustrations.

Guide to Centres (Wildfowl Trust, 1973).
Colour cover and 9 b/w illustrations

Wildfowl 24 (Wildfowl Trust, 1973).
  Colour cover and 14 b/w illustrations.

Wildfowl 25 (Wildfowl Trust, 1974).
  Colour cover and 7 b/w illustrations.

Driver, P., *In Search of the Eider* (Saturn, 1974). 1 b/w plate.

Lees-Milne, J., *Ancestral Voices* (Chatto & Windus, 1975).
  Frontispiece portrait.

Exhibition Catalogue (Arthur Ackermann & Son, September/
  October 1975). Colour cover and 16 b/w plates of paintings.

Kear, J. and Duplaix-Hall, N., *Flamingos* (Poyser, 1975).
  1 colour plate and 6 b/w illustrations.

Wildfowl 26 (Wildfowl Trust, 1975).
  Colour cover and 3 b/w illustrations.

Wildfowl 27 (Wildfowl Trust, 1976).
  Colour cover and 7 b/w illustrations.

Witchell, N., *The Loch Ness Story* (Dalton, 1976. 3rd edition,
  Corgi, 1989). Cover illustrations.

Wildfowl 28 (Wildfowl Trust, 1977).
  Colour cover and 4 b/w illustrations.

Douglas-Home, H., *The Birdman, Memories of Birds*
  (Collins, 1977). 12 b/w illustrations.

Cramp, S., Simmons, K.E.L., Ferguson-Lees, I.J., Gillmor, R., Hollom,
  P.A.D., Hudson, R., Nicholson, E.M., Ogilvie, M. A., Olney, P.J.S.,
  Voous, K.H. and Wattel, J., *Handbook of the Birds of Europe,
  the Middle East and North Africa: Volume 1* (OUP, 1977).
  8 colour plates.

Wildfowl 29 (Wildfowl Trust, 1978).
  Colour cover and 3 b/w illustrations.

Wells, V. and Nicholas, M., *It's Our World Too*
  (Collins, 1978). 1 b/w cartoon.

Fitter, R.S.R., *The Penitent Butchers* (Collins, 1978).
  10 b/w illustrations and dust wrapper illustration.

Special Appeals Brochure (Wildfowl Trust, 1979).
  2 colour and 2 b/w illustrations.

Smart, M., ed., *First Technical Meeting on Western Palaearctic
  Migratory Bird Management* (International Waterfowl Research
  Bureau, 1979). 2 b/w illustrations.

Wildfowl 30 (Wildfowl Trust, 1979). Colour cover and 3 b/w illustrations.

Salmon, D., ed., *Wildfowl and Wader Counts 1979–1980*
  (Wildfowl Trust, 1980)

Wildfowl 31 (Wildfowl Trust, 1980).
Colour cover and 3 b/w illustrations.

Kear, J. and Berger, A.J., *The Hawaiian Goose* (Poyser, 1980).
17 b/w illustrations.

1980 Bird Art Exhibition catalogue (The Leigh Yawkey Woodson Art
Museum, USA, 1980). Peter Scott awarded Master Wildlife Artist.
Page of biographical notes, colour cover and four colour plates.

Mathews, G.V.T. and Smart, M., *Second International Swan
Symposium—Proceedings* (International Waterfowl Research
Bureau, 1981). 3 b/w illustrations.

Wildfowl 32 (Wildfowl Trust, 1981).
Colour cover and 3 b/w illustrations.

Stonehouse, B., *Saving the Animals* (Weidenfeld & Nicholson, 1981).
Endpaper illustrations.

McCullagh, S., *Where Wild Geese Fly* (Hart-Davis, 1981).
1 colour and 14 b/w illustrations.

Salmon, D., ed., *Wildfowl and Wader Counts 1981–1982*
(Wildfowl Trust, 1982). 5 b/w illustrations.

Ogilvie, M., *The Wildfowl of Britain and Europe*
(OUP, 1982). 7 colour plates.

Wildfowl 33 (Wildfowl Trust, 1982).
Colour cover and 6 b/w illustrations.

Kalchreuter, H., ed., *Second European Woodcock and Snipe
Workshop—proceedings* (International Waterfowl Research Bureau,
1983). 1 b/w illustration.

Hickling, R., *Enjoying Ornithology* (Poyser, 1983). 9 b/w illustrations.

Salmon, D., ed., *Wildfowl and Wader Counts 1982–1983*
(Wildfowl Trust, 1983). Cover illustration.

Wildfowl 34 (Wildfowl Trust, 1983). Colour cover and 3 b/w illustrations.

Exhibition Catalogue (Society of Wildlife Artists & Dr. Barnardo's,
December 1984). 1 b/w plate.

Wildfowl 35 (Wildfowl Trust, 1984).
Colour cover and 3 b/w illustrations.

Baker, R., *Bird Navigation, the Solution to a Mystery*
(Hodder & Stoughton, 1984). Colour cover illustration.

Inaugural Exhibition Catalogue (Society for Wildlife Art for the
Nation (SWAN), 4–12 October 1985). 'Welcome' foreword and
1 plate in b/w.

Souvenir Booklet (Wildfowl Trust, 1985).
Colour cover with b/w illustration.

Exhibition Catalogue (Wildfowl Trust, 1985). Colour cover for
wildlife art exhibition at Martin Mere.

Salmon, D. and Moser, M., eds., *Wildfowl and Wader Counts 1984–
1985* (Wildfowl Trust, 1985). Cover illustration.

Wildfowl 36 (Wildfowl Trust, 1985).
Colour cover and 3 b/w illustrations.

Ruger, A. and others, *Results of the IWRB International Waterfowl
Census 1967–1983* (International Waterfowl Research Bureau, 1986).
2 b/w cover illustrations.

Wildfowl 37 (Wildfowl Trust, 1986).
Colour cover and 3 b/w illustrations.

Viewpoint '86: Sir Peter Scott—Communicator and Conservationist
(1986). Catalogue issued to celebrate the Central Television
documentary film, 'Interest the Boy in Nature'. 21 b/w illustrations.

Shackleton, K. and Snyder, J., *Ship in the Wilderness* (Dent, 1986.
Gaia Books, 2001). 3 colour illustrations.

Owen, M., Atkinson-Willes, G.L. and Salmon, D.,
Wildfowl in Great Britain (Cambridge University Press, 1986)
70 b/w illustrations, with 2 repeated on dust wrapper.

Aickman, R., *The River Runs Uphill* (JM Pearson, 1986).
1 b/w illustration (portrait of the author).

Hammond, N., *Twentieth Century Wildlife Artists*
(Croom Helm, 1986). 4 colour and 1 b/w illustrations.

Owen, M., *Barnacle Goose Project: 1986 Report*
(Wildfowl Trust, 1987). Cover illustration.

Wildfowl 38 (Wildfowl Trust, 1987). Colour cover and 8 b/w illustrations.

Exhibition Catalogue (Society of Wildlife Artists, July/August 1987).
1 b/w plate.

Salmon, D. and others, eds., *Wildfowl and Wader Counts 1986–1987*
(Wildfowl Trust, 1987). Cover illustration.

Souvenir Booklet (Wildfowl Trust, 1987).
Colour cover with b/w illustration.

Cooke, F. and Buckley, P.A., *Avian Genetics* (Academic Press, 1988).
Cover illustration.

Wildfowl 39 (Wildfowl Trust, 1988).
Colour cover and 17 b/w illustrations.

Courtney, J., *Sir Peter Scott* (Exley, 1989).
9 colour and 2 b/w illustrations.

Exhibition Card (Arthur Ackermann & Son, 1989).
Colour cover, two b/w plates and an ink drawing.

Benington, J., *Sir Peter Scott at 80, a Retrospective* (Alan Sutton, 1989).
Colour cover, 10 colour plates and 45 painting and drawings
reproduced in b/w.

Salmon, D. and others, eds.,. *Wildfowl and Wader Counts 1988–1989*
(Wildfowl Trust, 1989). Cover illustration.

Wildfowl 40 (Wildfowl & Wetlands Trust, 1989).
Colour cover and 18 b/w illustrations.

Perring, F. and Paige, J., compilers, *Tomorrow is Too Late*
(Macmillan, 1990). 1 colour illustration.

Brynildson, I. and Hagge, W., *Birds in Art, the Masters*.
(Leigh Yawkley Woodson Art Museum, USA, 1990). 6 colour plates.

Kear, J., *Man and Wildfowl* (Poyser, 1990). 7 b/w illustrations.

Scott, Philippa, *Lucky Me* (Kenilworth, 1990). 1 b/w illustration, repeated.

Wildfowl 41 (Wildfowl & Wetlands Trust, 1990).
Colour cover and 6 b/w illustrations.

*Wildfowl Supplement Number 1. Third IWRB International Swan
Symposium* (Wildfowl & Wetlands Trust, 1991). Colour cover and
8 b/w illustrations.

Trapnell, D., *Nature in Art* (David & Charles, 1991).
1 colour illustration.

Scott, Philippa, *The Art of Peter Scott*
(Sinclair-Stevenson, 1992, reprinted 1993. Wildfowl & Wetlands
Trust, 2008). 126 colour plates and 105 b/w illustrations.

Huxley, E., *Peter Scott, Painter and Naturalist* (Faber & Faber, 1993).
8 colour and 17 b/w illustrations.

HRH The Prince Philip, Duke of Edinburgh, *Prince Philip—
a Personal Collection* (Queen's Gallery, 1994). Exhibition catalogue
for art exhibition. Colour image and page of biographical notes.

Young, L., *A Great Task of Happiness. The Life of Kathleen Scott*,
(Macmillan, 1995). 1 b/w illustration (portrait).

Bruce, E., *From Duck Pond to Deep Ocean—a Life of Adventure*
(Boldre Marine, 1997). 1 b/w illustration (portrait of author).

Hammond, N., *Modern Wildlife Painting* (Pica Press, 1998).
3 colour illustrations.

Jackson, C.E., *Dictionary of Bird Artists of the World*
(Antique Collectors Club, 1999). 2 colour illustrations.

Thomas, J., *The Rhythm of the Tide—Tales Through the Ages of
Chichester Harbour* (SMH Books, 1999). 2 b/w illustrations.

Howard, E.J., *Slipstream. A Memoir* (Macmillan, 2002).
2 b/w portraits.

Scott, Philippa, *So Many Sunlit Hours* (Wildfowl & Wetlands Trust, 2002). Colour cover and 22 b/w illustrations.

Wallace, D.I.M., *Beguiled by Birds* (Christopher Helm, 2004). 2 illustrations.

Cook, K., *Birds* (Quercus, 2007). 3 colour plates, with 1 repeated as title page spread.

Walkden, P., *The Wild Geese of the New Grounds* (The Friends of WWT Slimbridge, 2009) 8 colour plates and 37 b/w illustrations.

Kirk, G. and Phillips, J., *The Birds of Gloucestershire* (Liverpool University Press, 2013), 15 b/w illustrations.

Walkden, P., 'The Berkeley Decoys', *The Berkeley Buttress* (Friends of Berkeley Castle Newsletter, Autumn 2014. 3 b/w illustrations.

BOOKS CONTAINING CONTRIBUTIONS

Fisher, J., 'The Migration of Wild Geese', *The New Naturalist: A Journal of British Natural History* (Collins, 1948). With 3 b/w illustrations.

'B.B.', compiler, 'His Royal Highness', *The Shooting Man's Bedside Book* (Eyre and Spottiswoode, 1948)

McCulloch, Derek ('Uncle Mac of the BBC'), ed., 'The Mystery of Migration', *Uncle Mac's Children's Hour Book* (Sampson Low, Marston & Co, 1949). With 1 b/w illustration.

Prescott, D.M., ed., 'Anabel', *The Treasure Book of the World* (Blandford Press, c.1950). With a colour plate.

McCulloch, Derek, 'Summer in the Canadian Arctic', *Uncle Mac's Children's Hour Story Book*. (Collins, 1951)

Koch, L., ed., 'The Work of The Wildfowl Trust', *The Encyclopaedia of British Birds* (Waverley, 1955)

Hawkins, D., ed., 'Painting Wild Birds', *The BBC Naturalist* (Rathbone, 1957). With 2 b/w illustrations.

Peterson, Roger Tory, 'The Aura', *The Birdwatcher's Anthology* (Bonanza Books, 1957)

'Bird Spotting', *The Girls' Book of Outdoor Life* (Burke, 1957)

'Bird Spotting', *The Boys' Book of Outdoor Life*' (Burke, 1957). Slight changes to the article in *The Girls' Book of Outdoor Life*.

Taylor, R., ed., 'On Being a Naturalist', *Express Annual* (Jarrold & Sons, 1957)

'Bird Watching—Focus on Britain's Birds', *Eagle Book of Hobbies* (Hulton Press, 1958)

Hawkins, D., ed., 'Fish-Watching', *The Second BBC Naturalist* (Adprint, 1960). With 3 b/w illustrations.

Landsborough Thomson, A., ed., 'Decoy, Duck', 'Game-birds' and 'Wildfowl', *A New Dictionary of Birds* (Nelson, 1964). Also 1 colour plate and 1 b/w plate.

Vollmar, Dr. E., ed., 'Otters in Danger', *World Wildlife Fund Yearbook 1968* (WWF, 1969)

Boddey, M., ed., 'The Pond', *The Twelfth Man* (Cassell, 1971). With 3 b/w illustrations.

Jackson, P., ed., 'Tenth Anniversary Year 1971', *World Wildlife Fund Yearbook 1970–1971* (WWF, 1972)

Christion, R., ed., 'Conversion to Conservation', *The Nature-Lover's Companion* (Eyre Methuen, 1972)

Duplaix-Hall, N., ed., 'Reconciling the Irreconcilable—Wildfowl and People', *International Zoo Yearbook, Volume 13* (Zoological Society of London, 1973). With 7 b/w illustrations.

Jackson, P., ed., 'World Wildlife Tenth Birthday Address', *World Wildlife Fund Yearbook 1971–1972* (WWF, 1973)

Mallinson, J., ed., 'The Pond', *Modern Classic Animal Stories* (David & Charles, 1977)

Campbell, B. and Lack, E., eds., *A Dictionary of Birds* (Poyser, 1985). Contributor. With 1 b/w plate.

Adams, R., Chapter 7—'No Mining in Antarctica', *Antarctica—Voices from the Silent Continent* (Headway/Hodder & Stoughton, 1990)

Thatcher, K., Shelton, R., Collins, I., Leesmith, K. and Waterhouse, D., 'The Pilgrimage to Mecca' chapter from *Morning Flight*, *Wildfowling at Wells, the World of Frank Southgate* (Wells Maltings Heritage Group, 2011). Includes 2 photographs of paintings.

A SELECTION OF ARTICLES AND ILLUSTRATIONS FROM JOURNALS AND MAGAZINES

'Wild Geese', *Country Life* (24 August 1929). Article and 5 mono photographs of paintings.

'Wild Geese and Ducks', *Country Life* (30 November 1929). Article and 6 mono photographs of paintings.

Rowen, T.L., 'Those in Authority', *Granta* (21 February 1930). Portrait of Captain C.V.H.C.

'Those in Authority', *Granta* (7 March 1930). Portrait of Michael H.C. Gutteridge

'Those in Obscurity', *Granta* (13 June 1930).
    Portrait of K.C. Gandar-Dower.

'The Wariest of Fowl', *Country Life* (21 June 1930).
    Article and 5 mono photographs of paintings.

'Wildfowl in a Frost', *Country Life* (4 April 1931).
    Article and 5 mono photographs of paintings.

'The Wild Grey Geese of Norfolk', *Country Life* (19 March 1932).
    1 full page colour plate and 1 mono photograph of a painting.

'Further Attempts to Catch Wild Geese Alive',
    Country Life (27 May 1933). With 3 photographs.

Pitt, F., 'The Work of Peter Scott', *Country Life* (17 June 1933). Article
    on Ackermann's gallery exhibition. 6 mono photographs of paintings.

'Watching and Painting Wildfowl', *The Field* (24 June 1933).
    Article with 4 mono photographs of paintings.

'This Wild Goose Business: A Call That Cannot be Denied', *The Field*
    (21 October 1933). Article with 1 mono photograph of artwork.

'My Favourite Saltings and the Wildfowl That Frequent Them', *The Field*
    (18 November 1933). 1 full page colour plate and 1 mono photograph
    of artwork.

'Dinghy Racing in America', *Country Life* (25 November 1933).
    Article with 3 mono photographs of sketches.

'Pintails Travelling', *The Illustrated Sporting and Dramatic News*
    (23 December 1933). Colour centre-spread, self-portrait of Peter
    Scott, and article.

'Wildfowl in the December Frost', *Country Life* (10 February 1934).
    Article and 3 mono photographs of paintings.

Percy, Lord W., 'Mr. Peter Scott's Pictures', *Country Life* (7 April 1934).
    3 mono photographs of paintings.

'Mr. Spriggs and the Crane', *Cornhill* (October 1934). Fiction.

'Contrasts Among Wildfowl', *The Field* (17 November 1934).
    Article with 1 mono photograph of painting.

'Paintings by Peter Scott', *Country Life* (18 May 1935).
    3 mono photographs of paintings.

Pitt, F., 'The Work of Peter Scott', *Country Life* (30 November 1935).
    Book review of *Morning Flight*, featuring 4 colour plates.

'Barnacle Bill', *Country Life Annual, 'Country Fair'* (1938).
    1 colour illustration.

'Peter Scott the Goose Man', *Illustrated Magazine* (24 June 1939).
    Text and 13 photographs including 6 of paintings.

'Snow Geese', *Country Life* (1940)

'Burning Ship (an extract from a letter)', *Convoy Magazine* (Collins, 1944). Number one in a series of booklets.

'The Magic of Wild Geese', *Animal Pictorial* (Autumn 1945). 1 colour plate.

'Wild Geese of the Severn', *Country Life* (7 March 1947). Article with 4 mono photographs.

'In Search of Greater Snow Geese', *Country Life* (16 May 1947). Article with colour plate of painting and 6 mono photographs.

'Wild Geese in Winter', *The Times* (6 December 1947)

'The Severn Wildfowl Trust', *Journal of the RSPB* (Winter 1947–1948)

'The Severn Widfowl Trust', *Gloucestershire Countryside* (January–March 1948). 3 mono photographs.

'Catching Wild Geese', *Country Life* (2 April 1948). Article with 6 mono photographs.

'The Wildfowl Problem', *Country Sportsman* (April 1948). With 3 photographs.

'Wild Geese: a Severnside Sanctuary', *Bournville Works Magazine* (May 1948). Article with 3 photographs.

'Studying Wildfowl on the Severn Estuary', *Sport and Country Magazine* (7 May 1948). Article that includes 12 photographs.

'The Severn Wildfowl Trust', *The Guide Magazine* (25 June 1948). With 4 mono photographs.

'Duck Decoys and Wild Geese', *Illustrated London News* (26 June 1948)

'Wild Geese and Their Music', *Boy's Own Paper* (December 1948). 1 b/w illustration.

'More About Severn Wildfowl', *Bournville Works Magazine* (January 1949). 2 illustrations and 2 photographs.

Newman, L. Hugh, 'Where the Wild Geese Gather', *Everybody's Weekly* (5 November 1949). 9 mono photographs.

'Happy Ending to an Arctic Expedition', *News Chronicle* (14 November 1949). Reprinted as a separate booklet.

'The Mysterious Sense of Direction', *The London Mystery Magazine* (Volume 1, Number 1, 1949). 5 b/w illustrations.

'Peter Scott Tells His Own Story', *Ladies' Journal* (September 1950). Article includes 4 photographs.

'HRH Princess Margaret', *Woman's Journal* (December 1950). Portrait for front cover.

Newman, L. Hugh, 'Nature Parliament' and 'Whither Do You Wander' *Collins Magazine* (January 1951). 1 photograph and 3 photographs.

Hochbaum, A., 'Over Manitoba Marshes', *The Beaver* (September 1951). 5 mono photographs of paintings and colour cover.

'To Save the Hawaiian Goose', *The Times* (2 June 1952). Illustrated with mono photographs. Reprinted as a separate booklet.

With Fisher, J., 'Wild Goose Chase', *Lilliput* (October/November 1952). 10 b/w illustrations.

'Wild Geese in Icelandic Fells', *The Times* (26 August 1953).

Gray, E., 'Make The Boy Interested in Natural History', *TV Mirror* (20 August 1955). Interview, illustrated with 7 mono photographs.

'Catching Wild Geese with Rocket Nets', *Country Life* (29 Sept. 1955)

'Watching Birds and Animals', *Radio Times* (3 January 1958)

'Gold C Completed', *Sailplane and Gliding Magazine* (August 1958)

'Straight and Level Please', *Sailplane and Gliding Magazine* (Oct. 1958)

'Portrait Gallery—Peter Scott', *Sunday Times* (11 October 1959)

'Slimbridge, Winter Home of the Wild Goose', *Meccano Magazine* (July 1959). 5 mono photographs.

'I Live in Gloucestershire', *Homes and Gardens* (1960). Illustrated.

'Nature of Fear', *Argosy* (March 1960)

'Search for Salvadori's Duck', *Animals* (Volume 5, Number 4)

'Skin Diving: A New World', *Animals* (Volume 5, Number 5)

'Sightseeing in East Africa's Game Parks', *Animals* (Vol. 5, Number 6)

'Peter Scott in Kenya', *Animals* (Volume 5, Number 7)

'To the South Pole with Peter Scott', *Radio Times* (22 May 1966)

'South with Scott', *Radio Times* (13 June 1968). Colour feature on the very first tourist trip to the Continent of Antarctica led by Peter Scott. 4 colour photographs.

'Species Extinction in Birds', *BTO Bird Study* (Volume 20, Number 2. June 1972). Witherby Memorial Lecture delivered at the BTO Annual conference, Swanwick.

'Feathered Friends at Slimbridge', *Woman and Home* (March 1973). Article.

With Robert Rines, 'Naming the Loch Ness Monster', *Nature* (11 December 1975)

'Personality Lieutenant-Commander Peter Scott CBE, MBE, DSC', *After the Battle* (Number 12, 1976). 7pp article includes 11 photographs, 6 of which are of Peter Scott.

'Pinkfeet and Wigeon', *Country Life* (15 February 1979). Colour cover illustration.

'The Call of the Wild Geese', *Birds* (Autumn 1980), 4 illustrations.

Simms, J.R., 'Wildfowl Spectacular', *Sunday Express Magazine* (25 October 1981). Interview.

Jackman, B., 'The Argosy of the Arctic Swans', *Sunday Times Magazine* (30 June 1985)

Soper, T., 'Renaissance Man Remembers', *BBC Wildlife* (November 1986). Interview on the eve of the 40th anniversary of WWT and the 25th Anniversary of WWF. 1 photograph.

'The Love of a Lifetime', *ASDA Naturewatch* (Spring/Summer 1988). Article about the Bewick's Swans at Slimbridge plus 1 photograph. Also article on WWT.

Nadel, A., 'Sir Peter Scott's Geese', *Telegraph Weekend Magazine* (January 1989). Interview.

Llewelyn, S., 'Great Scott', *Country Living* (April 1989). 1 colour illustration and 2 colour photographs by Philippa Scott.

A SELECTION OF BOOKS CONTAINING A FOREWORD, PREFACE OR INTRODUCTION

Newman, L. Hugh., *British Moths and Their Haunts* (Edmund Ward, 1949)

Various contributors, *The Lasting Victories*, (Lutterworth Press, 1948)

Aickman, R., *Know Your Waterways* (Coram Publishers, 1950)

Carrington, N. and Cavendish, P., *Camping by Water* (Peter Davies, 1950)

Shackleton, K., *Tidelines* (Lutterworth Press, 1951)

Savage, C., *The Mandarin Duck* (A & C Black, 1952)

Powell, B., *My Wild Goose Chase* (George Allen & Unwin, 1954)

Powell, B., *The Grey Geese Call* (Herbert Jenkins, 1956)

Simms, E., *Voices of the Wild* (Putnams, 1957)

The Dinghy Yearbook 1958 (Adlard Coles, 1958)

Sage, B.L., *A History of the Birds of Hertfordshire* (Barrie & Rockliff, 1959)

Lagus, C., *Operation Noah* (William Kimber, 1959)

Bates, F.A., *Dingle Stalk* (Young & Son, 1960)

Shell Guide to East African Birds (Shell, 1960)

Sedgwick, N.M., Whitaker, P., Harrison, J., *The New Wildfowler* (Herbert Jenkins, 1961)

Austin, O.L., *Birds of the World* (Hamlyn, 1961)

Cowie, M., *Fly, Vulture* (Harrap, 1961.

Mountfort, G., *Portrait of a River* (Hutchinson, 1962)

Roedelberger, F. and Groschoff, V., *The Wonders of Wildlife in Europe* (Constable, 1963)

Rowbotham, F.W., *The Severn Bore* (David & Charles, 1964)

Huxley, Elspeth, *Brave New Victuals* (Chatto & Windus, 1965)

Fitter, R. and Leigh-Pemberton, J., *Britain's Wildlife—Rarities and Introductions* (Nicholas Kaye with Midland Bank, 1966)

Delacour, J., *The Living Air—The Memoirs of an Ornithologist* (Country Life, 1966)

Spearman, D., *The Animal Anthology* (John Baker, 1966)

Harrison, J., *A Wealth of Wildfowl* (Andre Deutsch, 1967)

Carrigher, S., *Wild Heritage* (Panther Books, 1967)

Marshall, P., *Wild Mammals of Hong Kong* (OUP, 1967)

Austin, Oliver L., *Birds of the World* (Hamlyn, 1968)

Johnsgard, P.A., *Waterfowl—Their Biology and Natural History* (University of Nebraska Press, USA, 1968)

Fitter, R. and Leigh-Pemberton, J., *Vanishing Wild Animals of the World* (Midland Bank with Kaye & Ward, 1968)

Fisher, J., Simon, N. and Vincent, J., *The Red Book — Wildlife in Danger* (Collins, 1969)

Townsend, D., *Wild Africa's Silent Call* (George Allen & Unwin, 1969)

Boswall, J., ed., *Look* (BBC, 1969)

Sedgwick, N.M., Whitaker, P., Harrison, J., *The New Wildfowler in the 1970s* (Barrie & Jenkins, 1970)

Watkins-Pitchford, D.J., *Manka the Sky Gypsy—The Story of a Wild Goose* (Methuen, 1970). New edition of book first published in 1939.

HRH The Prince Philip, Duke of Edinburgh and Fisher, J., *Wildlife Crisis* (Hamish Hamilton, 1970). Complete with 1 b/w illustration.

Forel, O., *Hidden Art in Nature* (Harper & Row, 1972)

Ratcliffe, E.J., *Through the Badger Gate* (G Bell & Son, 1974)

Bailey, M. and M., *117 Days Adrift* (Nautical Publishing Co., 1974)

Stewart, D., *Canadian Endangered Species* (Gage Publishing, 1974)

Darnton, I., *Jungle Journeys in Ceylon* (Galaxy Books, 1975)

Fernandez, J.A.. *Donana: Spain's Wildlife Wilderness* (Collins, 1975)

Measures, D.G., *Bright Wings of Summer* (Cassell, 1976)

Hill, L. and Wood, E., *Penguin Millionaire* (David & Charles, 1976)

Lever, C., *The Naturalised Animals of the British Isles* (Hutchinson, 1977)

Owen, M., *Wildfowl of Europe* (Macmillan, 1977)

Piggott, D., *Delta Papa* (Pelham Books, 1977)

Smith, I., *Dingo King* (Wren Publishing, 1977).
Paintings and drawings by Clifton Pugh.

Mountfort, G., *Back from the Brink—Successes in Wildlife Conservation* (Hutchinson, 1978)

Gray, D., *Butterflies on My Mind* (Angus & Robertson, 1978)

Twigden, B.L., *Pisces Tropicani* (Lansdowne Editions, 1978).
An artist's collection of portraits of 26 species of coral reef fishes.

Larsen, T., *The World of the Polar Bear* (Hamlyn, 1978)

Bond, C., Siegfried, R., Johnson, P., *Antarctica* (Hamlyn, 1979)

Owen, M., *Wild Geese of the World* (BT Batsford, 1980)

Gould, J., *The Birds of Great Britain* 5-volume boxed set (Eric Maylin, 1980). Limited edition of 1,100 copies.

Drummond, M. and Rodhouse, P., *The Yachtsman's Naturalist* (Angus & Robertson, 1980)

Scott, G.H., *From Guns to Binoculars* (Providence Press, 1980)

Buxton, C., *Survival in the Wild* (Collins, 1980)

Mountfort, G., *Saving the Tiger* (Michael Joseph, 1981)

Stonehouse, B., *Saving the Animals—The World Wildlife Fund Book of Conservation* (Weidenfeld & Nicolson, 1981)

The Wildlife of the Oman and its Neighbours (Stacey International, 1981)

The Wildlife of Saudi Arabia and its Neighbours (Stacey International, 1981)

Allen, R., *How to Save the World* (Corgi, 1982)

Woods, R.W., *Falkland Island Birds* (Anthony Nelson, 1982)

Whitten, T., *The Gibbons of Siberut* (JM Dent, 1982)

Scott's Last Expedition—the Journals (Methuen, 1983)

Randall, J.E., *Red Sea Reef Fishing* (Immel Publishing, 1983)

Hosking, E. and Hale, W.G., *Eric Hosking's Waders* (Croom Helm, 1983)

Fleming, Sir C., *George Edward Lodge—Unpublished Bird Paintings* (Michael Joseph, 1983)

Burton, J.A., *The National Trust Book of British Wild Animals* (Jonathan Cape, 1984)

Linton, J.M. and Moore, C.W., *The Story of Wild Goose Jack: the Life and Work of Jack Miner* (CBC Enterprises, 1984)

Cusa, N., *Tunnicliffe's Birdlife* (Clive Holloway Books, 1985)

Shackleton, K., *Ship in the Wilderness* (JM Dent, 1986)

Maclean, G.L., *Ducks of the Sub-Saharan Africa* (Acorn Books, 1986

Lever, C., *Naturalised Birds of the World*
    (Longman Scientific & Technical, 1987)

Mearns, B. and R., *Biographies for Birdwatchers* (Academic Press, 1988)

Greenpeace Book of Antarctica, A New View of the Seventh Continent
    (Dorling Kindersley, 1988)

Morrison, P., *Bird Habitats of Great Britain and Ireland*
    (Michael Joseph, 1989)

Steel, J., *Bird Quest* (Berwick Bridge Studios, 1989)

Begbie, E., *The New Wildfowler—Third Edition* (Stanley Paul, 1989)

Flower, R., *Oundle and the Public School* (Stacey International, 1989)

Bond, C. and Siegfried, R., *Antarctica: No Single Country,
    No Single Sea* (New Holland, 1990)

WORKS CONSULTED

The Field (21 October 1933)

Morning Flight (Country Life, 1935)

Wild Chorus (Country Life, 1938)

Uncle Mac's Children's Hour Book (Sampson Low, Marston & Co, 1948)

RSPB Members' Magazine (Winter 1947–1948)

Bulletin of the British Ornithologist's Club (Volume XVIII, 7 May 1948)

The New Naturalist (Collins, 1948)

Country Sportsman (April 1948)

Country Life (2 April 1948)

Booklet of Rules (Severn Wildfowl Trust, 1948)

Boy's Own Paper (December 1948)

Scott, Lady Kathleen, *Self-Portrait of an Artist: Diaries of Lady Kennet* (Hazell Watson & Viney, 1949)

The London Mystery Magazine (Volume 1, Number 1, 1949)

The Treasure Book of the World (Blandford Press, 1950)

Ladies' Journal (September 1950)

Uncle Mac's Children's Hour Story Book (Collins, 1951)

The Times (2 June 1952)

Lilliput (October-November 1952)

Country Life (29 September 1955)

The BBC Naturalist (Rathbone Books, 1957)

The Birdwatcher's Anthology (Bonanza Books, 1957)

Meccano Magazine (Volume XLIV, Number 7, July 1959)

Argosy (March 1960)

The Second BBC Naturalist (Adprint, 1960)

The Eye of the Wind (Hodder & Stoughton, 1961)

The Launching of a New Ark (Collins, 1965)

Look (BBC, 1969)

The Twelfth Man (Cassell, 1971)

World Wildlife Yearbook 1970–1971 (WWF, 1972)

World Wildlife Yearbook 1971–1972 (WWF, 1973)

International Zoo Yearbook 13 (Zoological Society of London, 1973)

Travel Diaries of a Naturalist Vols. 1, 2, 3 (Collins, 1983, 1985, 1987)

Scott, Philippa, *Lucky Me* (Kenilworth Press, 1990)

Peter Scott—Painter and Naturalist (Faber & Faber, 1993)

Scott, Philippa, *So Many Sunlit Hours* (Wildfowl & Wetlands Trust, 2002)

KEY TO ILLUSTRATIONS